Reagan at CPAC

Preface by Vice President Mike Pence
Afterword by former U.S. Attorney General Edwin Meese III

Reagan at CPAC
The Words That Continue to Inspire a Revolution

**Introduction by Matt Schlapp
Chairman of the American
Conservative Union**

REGNERY
PUBLISHING
A Division of Salem Media Group

Regnery® is a registered trademark of Salem Communications Holding Corporation

Cataloging-in-Publication data on file with the Library of Congress

ISBN 978-1-62157-954-0
ebook ISBN 978-1-62157-948-9

Published in the United States by
Regnery Publishing
A Division of Salem Media Group
300 New Jersey Ave NW
Washington, DC 20001
www.Regnery.com

Manufactured in the United States of America

10 9 8 7 6 5 4 3 2 1

Books are available in quantity for promotional or premium use. For information on discounts and terms, please visit our website: www.Regnery.com.

This book is dedicated to the thousands of CPAC activists and volunteers, speakers and staff, and the millions of attendees and viewers whose work and service have preserved our country over the years.

Contents

Preface

A Time for Choosing: The Speech That Started Our Revolution

Vice President Mike Pence

Ronald Reagan inspired millions of Americans to leave what he called the "pale pastels" of liberalism and to embrace the bold-colored banner of conservatism. Reagan had blazed that trail in his own life, and his words inspired me, along with so many others, to follow in his path. What drew us to his cause wasn't so much the crisp clarity of his words as the strength of his vision.

Reagan earned his title as the "Great Communicator" because he communicated great ideas—namely, the timeless principles that make America exceptional. No speech since the Gettysburg Address has more vividly illuminated those principles than his national address on October 27, 1964: *A Time for Choosing*.

Reagan gave the speech in the final days of Barry Goldwater's ill-fated 1964 presidential campaign. Just one week later, the Democratic incumbent, President Lyndon Johnson, would win a forty-four-state landslide. But while it was Johnson's victory that marked the high-water point of America's postwar liberalism, it was Reagan's *A Time for Choosing* speech that marked the birth of modern conservatism.

"The Speech," as it came to be known, began a stirring in the hearts and homes of blue-collar, working-class families—people like Reagan himself, who had voted Democrat all their lives but who now were drawn to a different, clearer, and more uplifting vision.

And they began to organize. Just two months after the broadcast, the American Conservative Union was founded, and throughout the 1970s, the conservative movement gained strength as the failures of big-government liberalism became more evident by the day: double-digit inflation, high unemployment, a growing disrespect for American institutions and values, and an increasingly aggressive Soviet Union.

And in 1980, the movement made history when, defying all the predictions of the Washington establishment, Ronald Reagan won a landslide victory for president.

Today, we face our own time for choosing, and Reagan's words are just as relevant now as they were when Reagan gave this speech fifty-four years ago.

Honesty is the axis on which effective leadership turns, and Reagan had the strength and confidence to know what he was prepared to fight for—and to fight against. He didn't mince words when he declared communism "the most dangerous enemy that has ever faced mankind in his long climb from the swamp to the stars." And he was clear as day when he said there was no left or right, only up or down—up to man's age-old dream, "the ultimate in individual freedom consistent with law and order, or down to the ant heap of totalitarianism."

But along with the clarity and toughness, there was something else: a boundless faith in the American people.

Reagan didn't gloss over the details of his arguments; he equipped his audience with facts and figures. He truly believed if the American people could see the whole picture, they'd make the right decision.

As he said, it was a betrayal of the American Revolution to think that "a little intellectual elite in a far-distant capital can plan our lives for us better than we can plan them ourselves." It's why Reagan later said that if he had to sum up the speech's message, it would be the first three words of the Constitution: "We the People."

Reagan roused the American people to believe again in their capacity for self-government—he took a passive "us" and turned it into an active "we."

And he was such a beloved figure to the movement that he spoke thirteen times at the American Conservative Union's flagship event—CPAC. Each of these speeches is reprinted here, and each of them contains pearls of truth that shine brightly in our own day.

For my part, I poured over Reagan's remarks time and again when I drafted my own speeches for CPAC and when I was on the campaign trail in 2016. I've spoken at CPAC over a dozen times, but I could only hope to echo the wit and wisdom of the man who first brought me into the conservative movement nearly forty years ago.

Reagan's speeches and his story call to mind another strong, plain-speaking leader who followed an unlikely path to the White House, a man I've had the great privilege to serve alongside, the forty-fifth President of the United States Donald Trump.

The similarities between the two are striking. As I said in a speech at the Ronald Reagan Presidential Library in September of 2016, "The smart set in Washington, D.C. mocked and dismissed [Reagan] in many ways. He was referred to as a simpleton by some. They said he was little more than a celebrity and an entertainer who entered politics late in life. Sound familiar?"

But the American people were tired of being told—of being dismissed by their "betters." And so folks who had never voted in a presidential election began to lean in and listen to the eloquence and common sense of these uncommonly talented men. In their voices, the American people heard the rare and unmistakable sound of men unbound by Washington niceties and pretense of power.

In short, both men stood out for the same reason: they spoke the truth to the American people.

We are fortunate that they did—because the fact is, every day in America is a time for choosing. Like Ronald Reagan in his time, President Donald Trump and this generation are choosing in their time to defend and advance the great principles on which this nation was founded. And I hope everyone who has the chance to read old Dutch's words today will be inspired to join our cause and do their part, in this time, to make America great again.

Mike Pence is the vice president of the United States and has spoken at CPAC over a dozen times.

Foreword

Dan Schneider

The following pages present a suite of speeches drawn from two-and-a-half-decades' worth of appearances by Ronald Reagan at the Conservative Action Political Conference (CPAC). Taken together, they form a fascinating portrait of the fortieth president and the century he helped shape.

A Time for Choosing; *We Will Be as a City Upon a Hill*; *The New Republican Party*; *Our Time is Now*; *America's Purpose in the World*; it's all captured here. From describing the correct vision of conservatism to the decision to stay in—and transform—the Republican Party, to the first and brilliant articulation of his foreign policy, readers can enjoy Reagan's wisdom in its brilliant totality.

But these speeches can't be pinned exclusively to the twenty-first century. The content of each speech is deeply rooted in the political philosophy defined during the English and Scottish enlightenment, finding its best expression in the Declaration of Independence and the U.S. Constitution. The important thing to note is that Reagan's words and ideas are timeless. They are for all people and for all times.

These speeches also reflect what animated his political career. Reagan believed that the American people can and ought to govern themselves.

There are many reasons why Reagan is celebrated. His eloquence, grace, and moral clarity; his economic and foreign policies; all these things are praiseworthy. But Reagan's greatest achievement was how he connected America's first generation of statesmen philosophers to the real people and real problems of his day. Ideas matter, and the philosophy that birthed conservatism is, without a doubt, the greatest set of ideas in human history.

America was founded on an audacious principle: that citizens, rather than some far-off monarch or elitist parliament, can govern themselves. The Founders insisted that they and their co-colonists should have the say-so when it came to taxation, the establishment of laws, and the future of their country. These freedoms were not granted by King George, but by a much greater power; a higher, eternal power.

What George Washington, Thomas Jefferson, James Madison, Alexander Hamilton, and their peers gave us was the only country on the planet ever established on the premise that people can govern themselves. No other nation was ever formed on such a premise or for such a purpose. Not Germany, not Canada, not England, not Japan. One who sifts through history in search of a parallel will be left ultimately emptyhanded.

This is the thing that makes America extraordinary. It is what makes America great. And it is the central and common theme in all of the speeches collected here. That's not just because Reagan not only believed it, but because it was the most revolutionary idea of his time, just as it was the most revolutionary idea two centuries before.

When Reagan entered the political arena, taxes levied from across the Atlantic on paper goods had been replaced with an even more rapacious federal government, with multiplying agencies and social programs all promising to do good but requiring the relinquishment of our liberty.

He reminded his fellow citizens—first likeminded conservatives, then the rest of America—that it was their duty to stand up to those who would take away their rights, whether they be Democrats or Republicans, and that they should refuse those in power the authority to dictate how they should run their lives, determine how best to spend their income, or educate their children without consent. The antidote to totalitarianism—both the soft, creeping domestic variety and the nuclear-armed version in the east—was freedom, and unwavering confidence in the inherent sovereignty of the person.

This is what Ronald Reagan articulated so lucidly in his CPAC speeches. As such, they are a timely reminder of what made him so exceptional, and why our nation is worth fighting for.

Introduction

It Can Be Done

Matt Schlapp

T he spirit of the American conservative revolution is more needed today than it ever was. And no leader has ever embodied the spirit of conservatism as gracefully or as powerfully as President Ronald Reagan.

Reagan was a simple American, but a most unique political leader. More than any other virtue, he was a man of courage. He taught us all to stand for our beliefs, fearlessly and without apology. Reagan's beliefs, their genesis, and their current challenges were explained in every speech he gave. Thirteen of those speeches were delivered at the Conservative Political Action Conference, or CPAC, which remains one of the most relevant political gatherings of our day.

By 1980, he had accomplished what seemed impossible: he was elected to the presidency at the most senior age in American history. How did he win? In no small part, by espousing and embodying the philosophy so clearly delineated in his national television endorsement of Senator Barry Goldwater. *A Time for Choosing*—included here and arguably Reagan's most famous speech—inspired Americans with more than an ordinary prospect of pure political victory. The speech was, as Reagan's speeches always were, a fulsome expression of the courage it takes to stand against collectivism, statism, and forces of anti-individualism—in short, a stand against socialism.

Reagan was concerned then, as we still are now, that the theories of Marx, Lenin, and Trotsky would find an insidious foothold in the next generation. He expressed prophetic concern about the Democratic Party turning so hard left that it would eventually push not only himself, but all ordinary hardworking Americans aside. More than any man of the twentieth century, Reagan made the case against communism from the public pulpit and the Situation Room. He famously said his strategy concerning the Soviets was simple: "We win; they lose."

Ronald Reagan knew his CPAC appearances made a lasting impression on young attendees. Today, over fifty percent of CPAC attendees are college aged or younger; a trend which will inevitably continue as the Left further radicalizes public education. Reagan realized that the future of the conservative revolution would only be insured if he could pass his wisdom down to the youth. He pushed CPAC management to commit to low student prices and making the conference a place where the young felt welcomed—a commitment not found in any contract, but held sacred by all of us at the ACU today.

Sadly most of us never met Ronald Reagan, and as the years pass, it will be all too easy for young Americans to miss his historical relevance. But CPAC plays an important role in teaching the philosophy Reagan lived and led by. In so doing, we offer a timely medicine to the disease of socialism infecting the hearts of young Americans. In service of that goal, the American Conservative Union has grown fourfold in the last five years. We have expanded our ratings of

Congress into every state capital and our national conference has become the largest conservative event of the calendar year. Allies across the globe partner with ACU to bring CPAC to their countries. As we teach the principles of conservative philosophy, we also continue to engage politically and in elections. Our most aggressive area of growth has been the savvy use all forms of modern communication to spread our message and engage in all the major fights of the day. Reagan never gave up; neither will we.

Like the children of the greatest generation, we worry about living up to the expectations of the founders of the ACU. When considering the proper use of our time and resources, we often find ourselves asking: "What would Reagan do?" This book intends to answer that question. His words from the '60s, '70s, and '80s are still inspiring and sobering. It's true that many of America's problems have remained, but we now know—because history has shown—how Reagan's conservativism brings greater freedom, joy, and purpose to our society than any other ideology in the world.

In the following pages, you'll discover how relevant Reagan's words are for yourself. Presented here for the first time are fourteen of his speeches, analyzed and interpreted by some of the most brilliant contemporary conservatives of our time. They are arranged in chronological order, followed by commentaries that will inspire and enlighten you to the true and lasting meaning of his words. Each speech and commentary reiterates the enduring theme of Reagan's presidency: "It can be done."

Now that's a charge to which we can all rise.

Matt Schlapp is the chairman of the American Conservative Union.

A Time for Choosing

1964

T hank you. Thank you very much. Thank you and good evening. The sponsor has been identified, but unlike most television programs, the performer hasn't been provided with a script. As a matter of fact, I have been permitted to choose my own words and discuss my own ideas regarding the choice that we face in the next few weeks.

I have spent most of my life as a Democrat. I recently have seen fit to follow another course. I believe that the issues confronting us cross party lines. Now, one side in this campaign has been telling us that the issues of this election are the maintenance of peace and prosperity. The line has been used, "We've never had it so good."

But I have an uncomfortable feeling that this prosperity isn't something on which we can base our hopes for the future. No nation in history has ever survived a tax burden that reached a third of its national income. Today, thirty-seven cents out of every dollar earned in this country is the tax collector's share, and yet our government continues to spend $17 million a day more than the government takes in. We haven't balanced our budget twenty-eight out of the last thirty-four years. We've raised our debt limit three times in the last twelve months, and now our national debt is one and a half times bigger than all the combined debts of all the nations of the world. We have $15 billion in gold in our treasury; we don't own an ounce. Foreign dollar claims are $27.3 billion. And we just had announced that the dollar of 1939 will now purchase forty-five cents in its total value.

As for the peace that we would preserve, I wonder who among us would like to approach the wife or mother whose husband or son has died in South Vietnam and ask them if they think this is a peace that should be maintained indefinitely. Do they mean peace, or do they mean we just want to be left in peace? There can be no real peace while one American is dying some place in the world for the rest of us. We're at war with the most dangerous enemy that has ever faced mankind in his long climb from the swamp to the stars, and it's been said if we lose that war, and in so doing lose this way of freedom of ours, history will record with the greatest astonishment that those who had the most to lose did the least to prevent its happening. Well, I think it's time we ask ourselves if we still know the freedoms that were intended for us by the Founding Fathers.

Not too long ago, two friends of mine were talking to a Cuban refugee, a businessman who had escaped from Castro, and in the midst of his story, one of my friends turned to the other and said, "We don't know how lucky we are." And the Cuban stopped and said, "How lucky you are? I had someplace to escape to." And in that sentence, he told us the entire story. If we lose freedom here, there's no place to escape to. This is the last stand on earth.

And this idea that government is beholden to the people, that it has no other source of power except the sovereign people, is still the newest and the most unique idea in all the long history of man's relation to man.

This is the issue of this election: whether we believe in our capacity for self-government or whether we abandon the American revolution and confess that a little intellectual elite in a far-distant capitol can plan our lives for us better than we can plan them ourselves.

You and I are told increasingly we have to choose between a left or right. Well, I'd like to suggest there is no such thing as a left or right. There's only an up or down: man's old, old-aged dream, the ultimate in individual freedom consistent with law and order, or down to the ant heap of totalitarianism. And regardless of their sincerity, their humanitarian motives, those who would trade our freedom for security have embarked on this downward course.

In this vote-harvesting time, they use terms like the "Great Society," or as we were told a few days ago by the president, we must accept a greater government activity in the affairs of the people. But they've been a little more explicit in the past and among themselves; and all of the things I now will quote have appeared in print. These are not Republican accusations. For example, they have voices that say, "The Cold War will end through our acceptance of a not undemocratic socialism." Another voice says, "The profit motive has become outmoded. It must be replaced by the incentives of the welfare state." Or, "Our traditional system of individual freedom is incapable of solving the complex problems of the twentieth century." Senator Fulbright has said at Stanford University that the Constitution is outmoded. He referred to the president as "our moral teacher and our leader," and he says he is "hobbled in his task by the restrictions of power imposed on him by this antiquated document." He must "be freed," so that he "can do for us" what he knows "is best." And Senator Clark of Pennsylvania, another articulate spokesman, defines liberalism as "meeting the material needs of the masses through the full power of centralized government."

Well, I, for one, resent it when a representative of the people refers to you and me, the free men and women of this country, as "the masses." This is a term we haven't applied to ourselves in America. But beyond that, "the full power of centralized government"—this was the very thing the Founding Fathers sought to minimize. They knew that governments don't control things. A government can't control the economy without controlling people. And they know when a government sets out to do that, it must use force and coercion to achieve its purpose. They also knew, those Founding Fathers, that outside of its legitimate functions, government does nothing as well or as economically as the private sector of the economy.

Now, we have no better example of this than government's involvement in the farm economy over the last thirty years. Since 1955, the cost of this program has nearly doubled. One-fourth of farming in America is responsible for eight-five percent of the farm surplus. Three-fourths of farming is out on the free market and has known a twenty-one percent increase in the per capita consumption of all its produce. You see, that one-fourth of farming—that's regulated and controlled by the federal government. In the last three years, we've spent forty-three dollars in the feed grain program for every dollar bushel of corn we don't grow.

Senator Humphrey last week charged that Barry Goldwater, as president, would seek to eliminate farmers. He should do his homework a little better, because he'll find out that we've had a decline of five million in the farm population under these government programs. He'll also find that the Democratic administration has sought to get from Congress [an] extension of the farm program to include that three-fourths that is now free. He'll find that they've also asked for the right to imprison farmers who wouldn't keep books as prescribed by the federal government. The secretary of agriculture asked for the right to seize farms through condemnation and resell them to other individuals. And contained in that same program was a provision that would have allowed the federal government to remove two million farmers from the soil.

At the same time, there's been an increase in the Department of Agriculture employees. There's now one for every thirty farms in the United States, and still they can't tell us how sixty-six shiploads of grain headed for Austria disappeared without a trace, and Billie Sol Estes never left shore.

Every responsible farmer and farm organization has repeatedly asked the government to free the farm economy, but how—who are farmers to know what's best for them? The wheat farmers voted against a wheat program. The government passed it anyway. Now the price of bread goes up; the price of wheat to the farmer goes down.

Meanwhile, back in the city, under urban renewal the assault on freedom carries on. Private property rights [are] so diluted that public interest is almost anything a few government planners decide it should be. In a program that takes from the needy and gives to the greedy, we see such spectacles as in Cleveland, Ohio, a million-and-a-half-dollar building completed only three years ago must be destroyed to make way for what government officials call a "more compatible use of the land." The president tells us he's now going to start building public housing units in the thousands, where heretofore, we've only built them in the hundreds. But FHA [Federal Housing Authority] and the Veterans Administration tell us they have 120,000 housing units they've taken back through mortgage foreclosure. For three decades, we've sought to solve the problems of unemployment through government planning, and the more the plans fail, the more the planners plan. The latest is the Area Redevelopment Agency.

They've just declared Rice County, Kansas a depressed area. Rice County, Kansas, has two hundred oil wells, and the 14,000 people there have over $30 million on deposit in personal savings in their banks. And when the government tells you you're depressed, lie down and be depressed.

We have so many people who can't see a fat man standing beside a thin one without coming to the conclusion the fat man got that way by taking advantage of the thin one. So, they're going to solve all the problems of human misery through government and government planning. Well, now, if government planning and welfare had the answer—and they've had almost thirty years of it—shouldn't we expect government to read the score to us once in a while? Shouldn't they be telling us about the decline each year in the number of people needing help? The reduction in the need for public housing?

But the reverse is true. Each year the need grows greater; the program grows greater. We were told four years ago that 17 million people went to bed hungry each night. Well that was probably true. They were all on a diet. But now we're told that 9.3 million families in this country are poverty-stricken on the basis of earning less than three thousand dollars a year. Welfare spending [is] ten times greater than in the dark depths of the Depression. We're spending $45 billion on welfare. Now do a little arithmetic, and you'll find that if we divided the $45 billion up equally among those nine million poor families, we'd be able to give each family 4,600 dollars a year. And this added to their present income should eliminate poverty. Direct aid to the poor, however, is only running only about six hundred dollars per family. It would seem that someplace, there must be some overhead.

Now, so now we declare "war on poverty," or "you, too, can be a Bobby Baker." Now do they honestly expect us to believe that if we add one billion dollars to the 45 billion we're spending, one more program to the thirty-odd we have—and remember, this new program doesn't replace any, it just duplicates existing programs—do they believe that poverty is suddenly going to disappear by magic? Well, in all fairness, I should explain there is one part of the new program that isn't duplicated. This is the youth feature. We're now going to solve the dropout problem, juvenile delinquency, by reinstituting something like the old CCC camps [Civilian Conservation Corps], and we're going to put our young people in these camps. But again, we do some arithmetic, and we find that we're going to spend each year just on room and board for each young person we help $4,700 a year. We can send them to Harvard for 2,700! Of course, don't get me wrong, I'm not suggesting Harvard is the answer to juvenile delinquency.

But seriously, what are we doing to those we seek to help? Not too long ago, a judge called me here in Los Angeles. He told me of a young woman who'd come before him for a divorce. She had six children, was pregnant with her seventh. Under his questioning, she revealed her husband was a laborer earning $250 a month. She wanted a divorce to get an eighty dollar raise. She's eligible for $330 a month in the Aid to Dependent Children Program. She got the idea from two women in her neighborhood who'd already done that very thing.

Yet anytime you and I question the schemes of the do-gooders, we're denounced as being against their humanitarian goals. They say we're always "against" things—we're never "for" anything.

Well, the trouble with our liberal friends is not that they're ignorant; it's just that they know so much that isn't so.

Now, we're for a provision that destitution should not follow unemployment by reason of old age, and to that end, we've accepted Social Security as a step toward meeting the problem.

But we're against those entrusted with this program when they practice deception regarding its fiscal shortcomings, when they charge that any criticism of the program means that we want to end payments to those people who depend on them for a livelihood. They've called it "insurance" to us in a hundred million pieces of literature. But then they appeared before the Supreme Court and they testified it was a welfare program. They only use the term "insurance" to sell it to the people. And they said Social Security dues are a tax for the general use of the government, and the government has used that tax. There is no fund, because Robert Byers, the actuarial head, appeared before a congressional committee and admitted that Social Security as of this moment is $298 billion in the hole. But he said there should be no cause for worry because as long as they have the power to tax, they could always take away from the people whatever they needed to bail them out of trouble. And they're doing just that.

A young man, twenty-one years of age, working at an average salary—his Social Security contribution would, in the open market, buy him an insurance policy that would guarantee $220 a month at age sixty-five. The government promises 127. He could live it up until he's thirty-one and then take out a policy that would pay more than Social Security. Now, are we so lacking in business sense that we can't put this program on a sound basis, so that people who do require those payments will find they can get them when they're due—that the cupboard isn't bare?

Barry Goldwater thinks we can.

At the same time, can't we introduce voluntary features that would permit a citizen who can do better on his own to be excused upon presentation of evidence that he had made provision for the non-earning years? Should we not allow a widow with children to work, and not lose the benefits supposedly paid for by her deceased husband? Shouldn't you and I be allowed to declare who our beneficiaries will be under this program, which we cannot do? I think we're for telling our senior citizens that no one in this country should be denied medical care because of a lack of funds. But I think we're against forcing all citizens, regardless of need, into a compulsory government program, especially when we have such examples, as was announced last week, when France admitted that their Medicare program is now bankrupt. They've come to the end of the road.

In addition, was Barry Goldwater so irresponsible when he suggested that our government give up its program of deliberate, planned inflation so that when you do get your Social Security pension, a dollar will buy a dollar's worth, and not forty-five cents worth?

I think we're for an international organization, where the nations of the world can seek peace. But I think we're against subordinating American interests to an organization that has become so structurally unsound that today you can muster a two-thirds vote on the floor of the General Assembly among nations that represent less than ten percent of the world's population. I think we're against the hypocrisy of assailing our allies because here and there they cling to a colony, while we engage in a conspiracy of silence and never open our mouths about the millions of people enslaved in the Soviet colonies in the satellite nations.

I think we're for aiding our allies by sharing of our material blessings with those nations which share in our fundamental beliefs, but we're against doling out money government to government, creating bureaucracy, if not socialism, all over the world. We set out to help nineteen countries. We're helping 107. We've spent $146 billion. With that money, we bought a two-million-dollar yacht for Haile Selassie. We bought dress suits for Greek undertakers, extra wives for Kenya[n] government officials. We bought a thousand TV sets for a place where they have no electricity. In the last six years, fifty-two nations have bought seven billion dollars' worth of our gold, and all fifty-two are receiving foreign aid from this country.

No government ever voluntarily reduces itself in size. So, governments' programs, once launched, never disappear.

Actually, a government bureau is the nearest thing to eternal life we'll ever see on this earth.

Federal employees—federal employees number two and a half million; and federal, state, and local, one out of six of the nation's work force employed by government. These proliferating bureaus, with their thousands of regulations, have cost us many of our constitutional safeguards. How many of us realize that today, federal agents can invade a man's property without a warrant? They can impose a fine without a formal hearing, let alone a trial by jury? And they can seize and sell his property at auction to enforce the payment of that fine. In Chico County, Arkansas, James Wier over-planted his rice allotment. The government obtained a $17,000 judgment. And a U.S. marshal sold his 960-acre farm at auction. The government said it was necessary as a warning to others to make the system work.

Last February 19 at the University of Minnesota, Norman Thomas, six-times candidate for president on the Socialist Party ticket, said, "If Barry Goldwater became president, he would stop the advance of socialism in the United States." I think that's exactly what he will do.

But as a former Democrat, I can tell you Norman Thomas isn't the only man who has drawn this parallel to socialism with the present administration, because back in 1936, Mr. Democrat himself, Al Smith, the great American, came before the American people and charged that the leadership of his party was taking the party of Jefferson, Jackson, and Cleveland down the road under the banners of Marx, Lenin, and Stalin. And he walked away from his party, and he never returned until the day he died—because to this day, the leadership of that party has been taking that party, that honorable party, down the road in the image of the labor Socialist Party of England.

Now, it doesn't require expropriation or confiscation of private property or business to impose socialism on a people. What does it mean whether you hold the deed or the title to your business or property if the government holds the power of life and death over that business or property? And such machinery already exists. The government can find some charge to bring against any concern it chooses to prosecute. Every businessman has his own tale of harassment. Somewhere, a perversion has taken place. Our natural, unalienable rights are now considered to be a dispensation of government, and freedom has never been so fragile, so close to slipping from our grasp as it is at this moment.

Our Democratic opponents seem unwilling to debate these issues. They want to make you and I believe that this is a contest between two men—that we're to choose just between two personalities.

Well what of this man that they would destroy—and in destroying, they would destroy that which he represents, the ideas that you and I hold dear? Is he the brash and shallow and trigger-happy man they say he is? Well I've been privileged to know him "when." I knew him long before he ever dreamed of trying for high office, and I can tell you personally I've never known a man in my life I believed so incapable of doing a dishonest or dishonorable thing.

This is a man who, in his own business before he entered politics, instituted a profit-sharing plan before unions had ever thought of it. He put in health and medical insurance for all his employees. He took fifty percent of the profits before taxes and set up a retirement program, a pension plan for all his employees. He sent monthly checks for life to an employee who was ill and couldn't work. He provides nursing care for the children of mothers who work in the stores. When Mexico was ravaged by the floods in the Rio Grande, he climbed in his airplane and flew medicine and supplies down there.

An ex-GI told me how he met him. It was the week before Christmas during the Korean War, and he was at the Los Angeles airport trying to get a ride home to Arizona for Christmas. And he said that [there were] a lot of servicemen there and no seats available on the planes. And then a voice came over the loudspeaker and said, "Any men in uniform wanting a ride to Arizona, go to runway such-and-such," and they went down there, and there was a fellow named Barry Goldwater sitting in his plane. Every day in those weeks before Christmas, all day long, he'd load up the plane, fly it to Arizona, fly them to their homes, fly back over to get another load.

During the hectic split-second timing of a campaign, this is a man who took time out to sit beside an old friend who was dying of cancer. His campaign managers were understandably impatient, but he said, "There aren't many left who care what happens to her. I'd like her to know I care." This is a man who said to his nineteen-year-old son, "There is no foundation like the rock of honesty and fairness, and when you begin to build your life on that rock, with the cement of the faith in God that you have, then you have a real start." This is not a man who could carelessly send other people's sons to war. And that is the issue of this campaign that makes all the other problems I've discussed academic, unless we realize we're in a war that must be won.

Those who would trade our freedom for the soup kitchen of the welfare state have told us they have a utopian solution of peace without victory. They call their policy "accommodation." And they say if we'll only avoid any direct confrontation with the enemy, he'll forget his evil ways and learn to love us. All who oppose them are indicted as warmongers. They say we offer simple answers to complex problems. Well, perhaps there is a simple answer—not an easy answer—but simple: if you and I have the courage to tell our elected officials that we want our national policy based on what we know in our hearts is morally right.

We cannot buy our security, our freedom from the threat of the bomb, by committing an immorality so great as saying to a billion human beings now enslaved behind the Iron Curtain, "Give up your dreams of freedom because to save our own skins, we're willing to make a deal with your slave masters." Alexander Hamilton said, "A nation which can prefer disgrace to danger is prepared for a master and deserves one." Now let's set the record straight. There's no argument over the choice between peace and war, but there's only one guaranteed way you can have peace, and you can have it in the next second: surrender.

Admittedly, there's a risk in any course we follow other than this, but every lesson of history tells us that the greater risk lies in appeasement, and this is the specter our well-meaning liberal friends refuse to face—that their policy of accommodation is appeasement, and it gives no choice between peace and war, only between fight or surrender. If we continue to accommodate, continue to back and retreat, eventually we have to face the final demand—the ultimatum. And what then—when Nikita Khrushchev has told his people he knows what our answer will be? He has told them that we're retreating under the pressure of the Cold War, and someday when the time comes to deliver the final ultimatum, our surrender will be voluntary, because by that time, we will have been weakened from within spiritually, morally, and economically. He believes this because from our side he's heard voices pleading for "peace at any price" or "better red than dead," or as one commentator put it, he'd rather "live on his knees than die on his feet." And therein lies the road to war, because those voices don't speak for the rest of us.

You and I know and do not believe that life is so dear and peace so sweet as to be purchased at the price of chains and slavery. If nothing in life is worth dying for, when did this begin—just in the face of this enemy? Or should Moses have told the children of Israel to live in slavery under the pharaohs? Should Christ have refused the cross? Should the patriots at Concord Bridge have thrown down their guns and refused to fire the shot heard 'round the world? The martyrs of history were not fools, and our honored dead who gave their lives to stop the advance of the Nazis didn't die in vain. Where, then, is the road to peace? Well, it's a simple answer after all.

You and I have the courage to say to our enemies, "There is a price we will not pay." There is a point beyond which they must not advance. And this—this is the meaning in the phrase of Barry Goldwater's "peace through strength." Winston Churchill said, "The destiny of man is not measured by material computations. When great forces are on the move in the world, we learn we're spirits—not animals." And he said, "There's something going on in time and space, and beyond time and space, which, whether we like it or not, spells duty."

You and I have a rendezvous with destiny.

We'll preserve for our children this, the last best hope of man on earth, or we'll sentence them to take the last step into a thousand years of darkness.

We will keep in mind and remember that Barry Goldwater has faith in us. He has faith that you and I have the ability and the dignity and the right to make our own decisions and determine our own destiny.

Thank you very much.

We Will Be as a City upon a Hill

1974

There are three men here tonight I am very proud to introduce. It was a year ago this coming February when this
country had its spirits lifted as they have never been lifted
in many years. This happened when planes began landing on American soil and in the Philippines, bringing back men who had lived
with honor for many miserable years in North Vietnam prisons.
Three of those men are here tonight, John McCain, Bill Lawrence
and Ed Martin. It is an honor to be here tonight. I am proud that
you asked me, and I feel more than a little humble in the presence
of this distinguished company.

There are men here tonight who, through their wisdom, their
foresight, and their courage, have earned the right to be regarded
as prophets of our philosophy. Indeed, they are prophets of our
times. In years past when others were silent or too blind to the facts,
they spoke up forcefully and fearlessly for what they believed to be
right. A decade has passed since Barry Goldwater walked a lonely
path across this land, reminding us that even a land as rich as ours

can't go on forever borrowing against the future, leaving a legacy of debt for another generation and causing a runaway inflation to erode the savings and reduce the standard of living. Voices have been raised trying to rekindle in our country all of the great ideas and principles which set this nation apart from all the others that preceded it, but louder and more strident voices utter easily sold clichés.

Cartoonists with acid-tipped pens portray some of the reminders of our heritage and our destiny as old-fashioned. They say that we are trying to retreat into a past that actually never existed. Looking to the past in an effort to keep our country from repeating the errors of history is termed by them as "taking the country back to McKinley." Of course, I never found that was so bad—under McKinley we freed Cuba. On the span of history, we are still thought of as a young upstart country celebrating soon only our second century as a nation, and yet we are the oldest continuing republic in the world.

I thought that tonight, rather than talking on the subjects you are discussing, or trying to find something new to say, it might be appropriate to reflect a bit on our heritage.

You can call it mysticism if you want to, but I have always believed that there was some divine plan that placed this great continent between two oceans to be sought out by those who were possessed of an abiding love of freedom and a special kind of courage.

This was true of those who pioneered the great wilderness in the beginning of this country, as it is also true of those later immigrants who were willing to leave the land of their birth and come to a land where even the language was unknown to them. Call it chauvinistic, but our heritage does set us apart.

Some years ago, a writer, who happened to be an avid student of history, told me a story about that day in the little hall in Philadelphia where honorable men, hard-pressed by a king who was flouting the very law they were willing to obey, debated whether they should take the fateful step of declaring their independence from that king. I was told by this man that the story could be found in the writings of Jefferson. I confess, I never researched or made an effort to verify it. Perhaps it is only legend. But story, or legend, he described the atmosphere, the strain, the debate, and that as men for the first time faced the consequences of such an irretrievable act, the walls resounded with the dread word of treason and its price—the gallows and the headman's axe. As the day wore on the issue hung in the balance, and then, according to the story, a man rose in the small gallery. He was not a young man, and was obviously calling on all the energy he could muster. Citing the grievances that had brought them to this moment, he said, "Sign that parchment. They may turn every tree into a gallows, every home into a grave, and yet the words of that parchment can never die. For the mechanic in his workshop, they will be words of hope, to the slave in the mines—freedom." And he added, "If my hands were freezing in death, I would sign that parchment with my last ounce of strength. Sign, sign if the next moment the noose is around your neck, sign even if the hall is ringing with the sound of headman's axe, for that parchment will be the textbook of freedom, the bible of the rights of man forever." And then it is said he fell back exhausted. But fifty-six delegates, swept by his eloquence, signed the Declaration of Independence, a document destined to be as immortal as any work of man can be. And according to the story, when they turned to thank him for his timely oratory, he could not be found, nor were there any who knew who he was or how he had come in or gone out through the locked and guarded doors.

Well, as I say, whether story or legend, the signing of the document that day in Independence Hall was miracle enough. Fifty-six men, a little band so unique—we have never seen their like since—pledged their lives, their fortunes, and their sacred honor. Sixteen gave their lives, most gave their fortunes, and all of them preserved their sacred honor. What manner of men were they? Certainly, they were not an unwashed, revolutionary rabble, nor were they adventurers in a heroic mood. Twenty-four were lawyers and jurists, eleven were merchants and tradesmen, nine were farmers. They were men who would achieve security but valued freedom more.

And what price did they pay? John Hart was driven from the side of his desperately ill wife. After more than a year of living almost as an animal in the forest and in caves, he returned to find his wife had died and his children had vanished. He never saw them again, his property was destroyed, and he died of a broken heart—but with no regret, only pride in the part he had played that day in Independence Hall. Carter Braxton of Virginia lost all his ships—they were sold to pay his debts. He died in rags. So, it was with Ellery, Clymer, Hall, Walton, Gwinnett, Rutledge, Morris, Livingston, and Middleton. Nelson, learning that Cornwallis was using his home for a headquarters, personally begged Washington to fire on him and destroy his home. He died bankrupt. It has never been reported that any of these men ever expressed bitterness or renounced their action as not worth the price. Fifty-six rank-and-file, ordinary citizens had founded a nation that grew from sea to shining sea, five million farms, quiet villages, cities that never sleep—all done without an area redevelopment plan, urban renewal or a rural legal assistance program.

Now we are a nation of 211 million people with a pedigree that includes bloodlines from every corner of the world. We have shed that American-melting-pot blood in every corner of the world, usually in defense of someone's freedom. Those who remained of that remarkable band we call our Founding Fathers tied up some of the loose ends about a dozen years after the Revolution. It had been the first revolution in all man's history that did not just exchange one set of rulers for another. This had been a philosophical revolution. The culmination of men's dreams for six thousand years were formalized with the

Constitution, probably the most unique document ever drawn in the long history of man's relation to man. I know there have been other constitutions, new ones are being drawn today by newly emerging nations. Most of them, even the one of the Soviet Union, contain many of the same guarantees as our own Constitution, and still there is a difference. The difference is so subtle that we often overlook it, but it is so great that it tells the whole story. Those other constitutions say, "Government grants you these rights," and ours says, "You are born with these rights, they are yours by the grace of God, and no government on earth can take them from you."

Lord Acton of England, who once said, "Power corrupts, and absolute power corrupts absolutely," would say of that document, "They had solved with astonishing ease and unduplicated success two problems which had heretofore baffled the capacity of the most enlightened nations. They had contrived a system of federal government which prodigiously increased national power and yet respected local liberties and authorities, and they had founded it on a principle of equality without surrendering the securities of property or freedom." Never in any society has the preeminence of the individual been so firmly established and given such a priority.

In less than twenty years we would go to war because the God-given rights of the American sailors, as defined in the Constitution, were being violated by a foreign power. We served notice then on the world that all of us together would act collectively to safeguard the rights of even the least among us. But still, in an older, cynical world, they were not convinced. The great powers of Europe still had the idea that one day this great continent would be open again to colonizing and they would come over and divide us up.

In the meantime, men who yearned to breathe free were making their way to our shores. Among them was a young refugee from the Austro-Hungarian Empire. He had been a leader in an attempt to free Hungary from Austrian rule. The attempt had failed, and he fled to escape execution. In America, this young Hungarian, Koscha by name, became an importer by trade and took out his first citizenship papers. One day, business took him to a Mediterranean port. There was a large Austrian warship under the command of an admiral in the harbor. He had a manservant with him. He had described to this manservant what the flag of his new country looked like. Word was passed to the Austrian warship that this revolutionary was there, and in the night, he was kidnapped and taken aboard that large ship. This man's servant, desperate, walking up and down the harbor, suddenly spied a flag that resembled the description he had heard. It was a small American war sloop. He went aboard and told Captain Ingraham, of that war sloop, his story. Captain Ingraham went to the American Consul. When the American Consul learned that Koscha had only taken out his first citizenship papers, the consul washed his hands of the incident. Captain Ingraham said, "I am the senior officer in this port and I believe, under my oath of my office, that I owe this man the protection of our flag."

He went aboard the Austrian warship and demanded to see their prisoner, our citizen. The admiral was amused, but they brought the man on deck. He was in chains and had been badly beaten. Captain Ingraham said, "I can hear him better without those chains," and the chains were removed. He walked over and said to Koscha, "I will ask you one question; consider your answer carefully. Do you ask the protection of the American flag?" Koscha nodded dumbly, "Yes," and the captain said, "You shall have it." He went back and told the frightened consul what he had done. Later in the day, three more Austrian ships sailed into harbor. It looked as though the four were getting ready to leave. Captain Ingraham sent a junior officer over to the Austrian flag ship to tell the admiral that any attempt to leave that harbor with our citizen aboard would be resisted with appropriate force. He said that he would expect a satisfactory answer by four o'clock that afternoon. As the hour neared, they looked at each other through the glasses. As it struck four, he had them roll the cannons into the ports and had them light the tapers with which they would set off the cannons—one little sloop. Suddenly the lookout tower called out and said, "They are lowering a boat," and they rowed Koscha over to the little American ship.

Captain Ingraham then went below and wrote his letter of resignation to the United States Navy. In it he said, "I did what I thought my oath of office required, but if I have embarrassed my country in any way, I resign." His resignation was refused in the United States Senate with these words: "This battle that was never fought may turn out to be the most important battle in our nation's history." Incidentally, there is to this day, and I hope there always will be, a USS *Ingraham* in the United States Navy.

I did not tell that story out of any desire to be narrowly chauvinistic or to glorify aggressive militarism, but it is an example of government meeting its highest responsibility.

In recent years, we have been treated to a rash of noble-sounding phrases. Some of them sound good, but they don't hold up under close analysis. Take for instance the slogan so frequently uttered by the young senator from Massachusetts, "The greatest good for the greatest number." Certainly, under that slogan, no modern-day Captain Ingraham would risk even the smallest craft and crew for a single citizen. Every dictator who ever lived has justified the enslavement of his people on the theory of what was good for the majority.

We are not a warlike people. Nor is our history filled with tales of aggressive adventures and imperialism, which might come as a shock to some of the placard painters in our modern demonstrations. The lesson of Vietnam, I think, should be that never again will young Americans be asked to fight and possibly die for a cause unless that cause is so meaningful that we, as a nation, pledge our full resources to achieve victory as quickly as possible.

I realize that such a pronouncement, of course, would possibly be laying one open to the charge of warmongering—but that would also be ridiculous. My generation has paid a higher price and has fought harder for freedom than any generation that had ever lived. We have known four wars in a single lifetime. All were horrible, all could have been avoided if at a particular moment in time we had made it plain that we subscribed to the words of John Stuart Mill when he said that "war is an ugly thing, but not the ugliest of things."

The decayed and degraded state of moral and patriotic feeling which thinks nothing is worth a war is worse. The man who has nothing which he cares about more than his personal safety is a miserable creature and has no chance of being free unless made and kept so by the exertions of better men than himself.

The widespread disaffection with things military is only a part of the philosophical division in our land today. I must say to you who have recently, or presently are still receiving an education, I am awed by your powers of resistance. I have some knowledge of the attempts that have been made in many classrooms and lecture halls to persuade you that there is little to admire in America. For the second time in this century, capitalism and the free enterprise are under assault. Privately owned business is blamed for spoiling the environment, exploiting the worker, and seducing, if not outright raping, the customer. Those who make the charge have the solution, of course—government regulation and control. We may never get around to explaining how citizens who are so gullible that they can be suckered into buying cereal or soap that they don't need and would not be good for them, can at the same time be astute enough to choose representatives in government to which they would entrust the running of their lives.

Not too long ago, a poll was taken on 2,500 college campuses in this country. Thousands and thousands of responses were obtained. Overwhelmingly, sixty-five, seventy, and seventy-five percent of the students found business responsible, as I have said before, for the things that were wrong in this country. That same number said that government was the solution and should take over the management and the control of private business. Eighty percent of the respondents said they wanted government to keep its paws out of their private lives.

We are told every day that the assembly-line worker is becoming a dull-witted robot and that mass production results in standardization. Well, there isn't a socialist country in the world that would not give its copy of Karl Marx for our standardization.

Standardization means production for the masses and the assembly line means more leisure for the worker—freedom from back-breaking and mind-dulling drudgery that man had known for centuries past. Karl Marx did not abolish child labor or free the women from working in the coal mines in England—the steam engine and modern machinery did that.

Unfortunately, the disciples of the new order have had a hand in determining too much policy in recent decades. Government has grown in size and power and cost through the New Deal, the Fair Deal, the New Frontier, and the Great Society. It costs more for government today than a family pays for food, shelter, and clothing combined. Not even the Office of Management and Budget knows how many boards, commissions, bureaus, and agencies there are in the federal government, but the federal registry, listing their regulations, is just a few pages short of being as big as the Encyclopedia Britannica.

During the Great Society, we saw the greatest growth of this government. There were eight cabinet departments and twelve independent agencies to administer the federal health program. There were thirty-five housing programs and twenty transportation projects. Public utilities had to cope with twenty-seven different agencies on just routine business. There were 192 installations and nine departments, with one thousand projects having to do with the field of pollution.

One congressman found the federal government was spending four billion dollars on research in its own laboratories, but did not know where they were, how many people were working in them, or what they were doing. One of the research projects was the "Demography of Happiness," and for 249,000 dollars we found that "people who make more money are happier than people who make less, young people are happier than old people, and people who are healthier are happier than people who are sick." For fifteen cents, they could have bought an Almanac and read the old bromide, "It's better to be rich, young and healthy, than poor, old, and sick."

The course that you have chosen is far more in tune with the hopes and aspirations of our people than are those who would sacrifice freedom for some fancied security.

Standing on the tiny deck of the *Arabella* in 1630 off the Massachusetts coast, John Winthrop said, "We will be as a city upon a hill. The eyes of all people are upon us, so that if we deal falsely with our God in this work we have undertaken and so cause Him to withdraw His present help from us, we shall be made a story and a byword throughout the world." Well, we have not dealt falsely with our God, even if He is temporarily suspended from the classroom.

When I was born, my life expectancy was ten years less than I have already lived. That's a cause of regret for some people in California, I know. Ninety percent of Americans at that time lived beneath what is considered the poverty line today, three-quarters lived in what is considered substandard housing. Today, each of those figures is less than ten percent. We have increased our life expectancy by wiping out, almost totally, diseases that still ravage mankind in other parts of the world. I doubt if the young people here tonight know the names of some of the diseases that were commonplace when we were growing up. We have more doctors per thousand people than any nation in the world. We have more hospitals than any nation in the world.

When I was your age, believe it or not, none of us knew that we even had a racial problem. When I graduated from college and became a radio sport announcer broadcasting major league baseball, I didn't have a Hank Aaron or a Willie Mays to talk about. The Spalding Guide said baseball was a game for Caucasian gentlemen. Some of us then began editorializing and campaigning against this. Gradually we campaigned against all those other areas where the constitutional rights of a large segment of our citizenry were being denied. We have not finished the job. We still have a long way to go, but we have made more progress in a few years than we have made in more than a century.

One-third of all the students in the world who are pursuing higher education are doing so in the United States. The percentage of our young Negro community that is going to college is greater than the percentage of whites in any other country in the world.

One-half of all the economic activity in the entire history of man has taken place in this republic. We have distributed our wealth more widely among our people than any society known to man. Americans work less hours for a higher standard of living than any other people. Ninety-five percent of all our families have an adequate daily intake of nutrients—and a part of the five percent that don't are trying to lose weight. Ninety-nine percent have gas or electric refrigeration, ninety-two percent have televisions, and an equal number have telephones. There are 120 million cars on our streets and highways—and all of them are on the street at once when you are trying to get home at night. But isn't this just proof of our materialism—the very thing that we are charged with? Well, we also have more churches, more libraries, we support voluntarily more symphony orchestras and opera companies, non-profit theaters, and publish more books than all the other nations of the world put together.

Somehow America has bred a kindliness into our people unmatched anywhere, as has been pointed out in that best-selling record by a Canadian journalist. We are not a sick society. A sick society could not produce the men that set foot on the moon, or who are now circling the earth above us in the Skylab. A sick society bereft of morality and courage did not produce the men who went through those years of torture and captivity in Vietnam. Where did we find such men? They are typical of this land as the Founding Fathers were typical. We found them in our streets, in the offices, the shops, and the working places of our country and on the farms.

We cannot escape our destiny, nor should we try to do so. The leadership of the free world was thrust upon us two centuries ago in that little hall of Philadelphia. In the days following World War II, when the economic strength and power of America was all that stood between the world and the return to the dark ages, Pope Pius XII said, "The American people have a great genius for splendid and unselfish actions. Into the hands of America God has placed the destinies of an afflicted mankind."

We are indeed, and we are today, the last best hope of man on earth.

Assuring America's Future by Depending on Her Past

Katie Pavlich

COMMENTARY ON

We Will Be as a City upon a Hill

President Reagan's speech at the inaugural Conservative Political Action Conference came in 1974, just six years before officially declaring his run for the White House. It would be his first of thirteen addresses to the conference that has become a driving force behind conservative policy and principle for nearly a half-century.

At the time, Reagan was viewed by the American Conservative Union as the leader who could rally conservatives and restore our country after decades of liberalism had led us astray. Eventually, that support in the wake of Goldwater's failed presidential run paid off for Reagan. He was elected governor of California and managed it back from ruin, was proudly pro-life, believed that free markets create prosperity, warned against government spendthrifts who "borrow against the future," and most importantly, vowed to fight for America and the freedoms we still stand for today.

At the first gathering of conservatives at CPAC, Reagan chose to forgo remarks debating current political topics and instead made the decision to focus on America's heritage and journey into the future.

Reagan said that this country belongs to everyone who is "possessed of an abiding love of freedom and a special kind of courage. This was true of those who pioneered the great wilderness in the beginning of this country, as it is also true of those later immigrants who were willing to leave the land of their birth and come to a land where even the language was unknown to them. Call it chauvinistic, but our heritage does set us apart."

This concept is hardly chauvinistic, but instead expresses reverence for those first Americans whose sacrifices made our unique democracy possible.

Reagan never shied away from the fact that America was the best and most free country on the face of the planet. He regularly promoted American exceptionalism throughout his life. He did so early on in his political career as governor of California, throughout his presidency— which freed nations around the globe—and continued to promote our American values throughout the world after his presidency.

But Reagan knew American exceptionalism came at a price, paid in the past by bold men who rejected the rule of a faraway king. He understood the painful and risky decisions that were made before July 4, 1776 in order to establish a free nation based on the liberty of the individual. Death was the consequence for failure, but because the Founding Fathers cared so deeply about America, they moved forward anyway. Putting everything on the line—their lives, fortune, and sacred honor—was worth it.

The signing of the Declaration of Independence, a document that created a new nation and declared war on the most powerful military in the world, was a miracle. Reagan knew this and often reminded the audience of its importance. He did this to ensure that future generations never took America's history for granted.

In addition to his promotion of freedom, Reagan stressed America's crucial adherence to the United States Constitution as another example of what sets America apart from the rest of the globe, calling it "the culmination of man's dreams." He noted that other nations had chartered their own constitutions, and that "[t]he difference [between the U.S. Constitution and the others] is so subtle that we often overlook it, but it is so great that it tells the whole story. Those other constitutions say, 'Government grants you these rights,' and ours says, 'You are born with these rights, they are yours by the grace of God, and no government on earth can take them from you.'"

Reagan repeatedly warned that in order to preserve this founding principle of the sovereign individual, limits on the size of government are essential. After all, the larger the government becomes, the more it squeezes and limits personal liberty.

"Now we are a nation of 211 million people with a pedigree that includes blood lines from every corner of the world. We have shed that American-melting-pot blood in every corner of the world, usually in defense of someone's freedom," he said.

America today remains the same as Reagan praised it to be in 1974. His words have echoed through the generations to encourage and inspire the most incredible and blessed country on earth while reminding us that we must work each day to protect that which makes America so special.

"We cannot escape our destiny, nor should we try to do so. The leadership of the free world was thrust upon us two centuries ago in that little hall of Philadelphia," Reagan concluded. "We are indeed, and we are today, the last best hope of man on earth."

So long as America stays true to our founding and destiny, we will forever be a shining city on a hill for the entire world to see.

Katie Pavlich is the editor of Townhall.com and a Fox News contributor.

Let Them Go
Their Way

1975

S ince our last meeting, we have been through a disastrous
election. It is easy for us to be discouraged, as pundits hail
that election as a repudiation of our philosophy and even as
a mandate of some kind or other. But the significance of the election
was not registered by those who voted, but by those who stayed
home. If there was anything like a mandate, it will be found among
almost two-thirds of the citizens who refused to participate.

Bitter as it is to accept the results of the November election, we
should have reason for some optimism. For many years now, we
have preached the "gospel," in opposition to the philosophy of so-
called liberalism which was, in truth, a call to collectivism.

Now, it is possible we have been persuasive to a greater degree
than we had ever realized. Few, if any, Democratic party candidates
in the last election ran as liberals. Listening to them, I had the eerie
feeling we were hearing reruns of Goldwater speeches. I even
thought I heard a few of my own.

31

Bureaucracy was assailed, and fiscal responsibility hailed. Even George McGovern donned sackcloth and ashes and did penance for the good people of South Dakota.

But let's not be so naive as to think we are witnessing a mass conversion to the principles of conservatism. Once sworn into office, the victors reverted to type. In their view, apparently, the ends justified the means.

The "Young Turks" had campaigned against "evil politicians." They turned against committee chairmen of their own party, displaying a taste and talent as cutthroat power politicians quite in contrast to their campaign rhetoric and idealism. Still, we must not forget that they molded their campaigning to fit what even they recognized was the mood of the majority. And we must see to it that the people are reminded of this as they now pursue their ideological goals—and pursue them they will.

I know you are aware of the national polls which show that a greater, and increasing, number of Americans—Republicans, Democrats and independents—classify themselves as "conservatives" than ever before. And a poll of rank-and-file union members reveals dissatisfaction with the amount of power their own leaders have assumed, and a resentment of their use of that power for partisan politics. Would it shock you to know that in that poll, sixty-eight percent of rank-and-file union members of this country came out endorsing right-to-work legislation?

These polls give cause for some optimism, but at the same time, reveal a confusion that exists and the need for a continued effort to "spread the word."

In another recent survey, of 35,000 college and university students polled, three-fourths blame American business and industry for all of our economic and social ills. The same three-fourths think the answer is more, and virtually complete, regimentation and

government control of all phases of business—including the imposi-
tion of wage and price controls. Yet, eighty percent in the same poll
want less government interference in their own lives.

In 1972, the people of this country had a clear-cut choice, based
on the issues, to a greater extent than any election in half a century.
In overwhelming numbers, they ignored party labels, not so much to
vote for a man, or even a policy, as to repudiate a philosophy. In doing
so, they repudiated that final step into the welfare state—that call for
the confiscation and redistribution of their earnings on a scale far
greater than what we now have. They repudiated the abandonment
of national honor and a weakening of this nation's ability to protect
itself.

A study has been made that is so revealing that I'm not surprised
it has been ignored by a certain number of political commentators
and columnists. The political science department of Georgetown
University researched the mandate of the 1972 election and recently
presented its findings at a seminar.

Taking several major issues which, incidentally, are still the issues
of the day, they polled rank-and-file members of the Democratic party
on their approach to these problems. Then they polled the delegates
to the two major national conventions—the leaders of the parties.

They found the delegates to the Republican convention almost
identical in their responses to those of the rank-and-file Republicans.
Yet, the delegates to the Democratic convention were miles apart from
the thinking of their own party members.

The mandate of 1972 still exists. The people of America have
been confused and disturbed by events since that election, but they
hold an unchanged philosophy.

Our task is to make them see that what we represent is identical to
their own hopes and dreams of what America can and should be. If
there are questions as to whether the principles of conservatism hold

up in practice, we have the answers to them. Where conservative principles have been tried, they have worked. Governor Meldrim Thomson is making them work in New Hampshire; so is Arch Moore in West Virginia and Mills Godwin in Virginia. Jack Williams made them work in Arizona and I'm sure Jim Edwards will in South Carolina.

If you will permit me, I can recount my own experience in California.

When I went to Sacramento eight years ago, I had the belief that government was no deep, dark mystery; that it could be operated efficiently by using the same common sense practiced in our everyday life, in our homes, in business, and private affairs.

The "lab test" of my theory—California—was pretty messed up after eight years of a roadshow version of the Great Society. Our first and only briefing came from the outgoing director of finance, who said: "We're spending one million dollars more a day than we're taking in. I have a golf date. Good luck!" That was the most cheerful news we were to hear for quite some time.

California state government was increasing by about five thousand new employees a year. We were the welfare capital of the world with sixteen percent of the nation's caseload. Soon, California's caseload was increasing by 40,000 a month.

We turned to the people themselves for help. Two hundred and fifty experts in the various fields volunteered to serve on task forces at no cost to the taxpayers. They went into every department of state government and came back with 1,800 recommendations on how modern business practices could be used to make government more efficient. We adopted 1,600 of them.

We instituted a policy of "cut, squeeze, and trim" and froze the hiring of employees as replacements for retiring employees or others leaving state service.

After a few years of struggling with the professional welfarists, we again turned to the people. First, we obtained another task force

and, when the legislature refused to help implement its recommendations, we presented the recommendations to the electorate.

It still took some doing. The legislature insisted our reforms would
not work; that the needy would starve in the streets; that the workload
would be dumped on the counties; that property taxes would go up
and that we'd run up a deficit the first year of $750 million.

That was four years ago. Today, the needy have had an average
increase of forty-three percent in welfare grants in California, but the
taxpayers have saved two billion dollars by the caseload not increasing that 40,000 a month. Instead, there are some 400,000 fewer on
welfare today than then.

Forty of the state's fifty-eight counties have reduced property
taxes for two years in a row—some for three. That 750-million-
dollar deficit turned into an 850-million-dollar surplus, which we
returned to the people in a one-time tax rebate. That wasn't easy. One
state senator described that rebate as "an unnecessary expenditure
of public funds."

For more than two decades, governments—federal, state, local—
have been increasing in size two-and-a-half times faster than the
population increase. In the last ten years, they have increased the cost
in payroll seven times as fast as the increase in numbers.

We have just turned over to a new administration in Sacramento
a government virtually the same size it was eight years ago. With the
state's growth rate, this means that government absorbed a workload
increase, in some departments as much as sixty-six percent.

We also turned over—for the first time in almost a quarter of a
century—a balanced budget and a surplus of $500 million. In these
eight years just passed, we returned to the people in rebates, tax
reductions, and bridge toll reductions $5.7 billion. All of this is con-
trary to the will of those who deplore conservatism and profess to be
liberals, yet all of it is pleasing to its citizenry.

Make no mistake, the leadership of the Democratic party is still out of step with the majority of Americans.

Speaker Carl Albert recently was quoted as saying that our problem is "sixty percent recession, thirty percent inflation, and ten percent energy." That makes as much sense as saying two and two make twenty-two.

Without inflation, there would be no recession. And unless we curb inflation, we can see the end of our society and economic system. The painful fact is we can only halt inflation by undergoing a period of economic dislocation—a recession, if you will.

We can take steps to ease the suffering of some who will be hurt more than others, but if we turn from fighting inflation and adopt a program only to fight recession, we are on the road to disaster.

In his first address to Congress, the president asked Congress to join him in an all-out effort to balance the budget. I think all of us wish that he had reissued that speech instead of this year's budget message.

What side can be taken in a debate over whether the deficit should be $52 billion or $70 billion or $80 billion preferred by the profligate Congress?

Inflation has one cause, and one cause only: government spending more than government takes in. And the cure to inflation is a balanced budget. We know, of course, that after forty years of social tinkering and Keynesian experimentation, that we can't do this all at once, but it can be achieved. Balancing the budget is like protecting your virtue: you have to learn to say "no."

This is no time to repeat the shopworn panaceas of the New Deal, the Fair Deal, and the Great Society. John Kenneth Galbraith, who, in my opinion, is living proof that economics is an inexact science, has written a new book. It is called *Economics and the Public Purpose*. In it, he asserts that market arrangements in our economy have given us inadequate housing, terrible mass transit, poor health care, and a host of other miseries. And then, for the first time to my knowledge, he advances socialism as the answer to our problems.

Shorn of all side issues and extraneous matter, the problem underlying all others is the worldwide contest for the hearts and minds of mankind. Do we find the answers to human misery in freedom as it is known, or do we sink into the deadly dullness of the socialist ant heap?

Those who suggest that the latter is some kind of solution are, I think, open to challenge. Let's have no more theorizing when actual comparison is possible. There is in the world a great nation, larger than ours in territory and populated with 250 million capable people. It is rich in resources and has had more than fifty uninterrupted years to practice socialism without opposition.

We could match them, but it would take a little doing on our part. We'd have to cut our paychecks back by seventy-five percent; move sixty million workers back to the farm; abandon two-thirds of our steel-making capacity; destroy forty million television sets; tear up fourteen of every fifteen miles of highway; junk nineteen of every twenty automobiles; tear up two-thirds of our railroad track; knock down seventy percent of our houses; and rip out nine out of every ten telephones. Then, all we have to do is find a capitalist country to sell us wheat on credit to keep us from starving.

Our people are in a time of discontent. Our vital energy supplies are threatened by possibly the most powerful cartel in human history. Our traditional allies in Western Europe are experiencing political and economic instability bordering on chaos.

We seem to be increasingly alone in a world grown more hostile, but we let our defenses shrink to pre-Pearl Harbor levels. And we are conscious that in Moscow, the crash build-up of arms continues. The SALT II agreement in Vladivostok, if not renegotiated, guarantees the Soviets a clear missile superiority sufficient to make a "first strike" possible with little fear of reprisal. Yet, too many congressmen demand further cuts in our own defenses, including delay, if not cancellation, of the B-1 bomber.

I realize that millions of Americans are sick of hearing about Indochina, and perhaps it is politically unwise to talk of our obligation to Cambodia and South Vietnam. But we pledged—in an agreement that brought our men home and freed our prisoners—to give our allies arms and ammunition to replace on a one-for-one basis what they expend in resisting the aggression of the communists who are violating the ceasefire and are fully aided by their Soviet and Red Chinese allies. Congress has already reduced the appropriation to half of what they need and threatens to reduce it even more.

Can we live with ourselves if we, as a nation, betray our friends and ignore our pledged word? And, if we do, who would ever trust us again? To consider committing such an act so contrary to our deepest ideals is symptomatic of the erosion of standards and values. And this adds to our discontent.

We did not seek world leadership; it was thrust upon us. It has been our destiny almost from the first moment this land was settled. If we fail to keep our rendezvous with destiny or, as John Winthrop said in 1630, "Deal falsely with our God," we shall be made "a story and byword throughout the world."

Americans are hungry to feel once again a sense of mission and greatness.

I don't know about you, but I am impatient with those Republicans who after the last election rushed into print saying, "We must broaden the base of our party," when what they meant was to fuzz up and blur even more the differences between ourselves and our opponents.

It was a feeling that there was not a sufficient difference now between the parties that kept a majority of the voters away from the polls. When have we ever advocated a closed-door policy? Who has ever been barred from participating?

Our people look for a cause to believe in. Is it a third party we need, or is it a new and revitalized second party, raising a banner of no pale pastels, but bold colors which make it unmistakably clear where we stand on all of the issues troubling the people?

Let us show that we stand for fiscal integrity and sound money, and above all, for an end to deficit spending with ultimate retirement of the national debt.

Let us also include a permanent limit on the percentage of the people's earnings government can take without their consent.

Let our banner proclaim a genuine tax reform that will begin by simplifying the income tax so that workers can compute their obligation without having to employ legal help.

And let it provide indexing—adjusting the brackets to the cost of living—so that an increase in salary merely to keep pace with inflation does not move the taxpayer into a surtax bracket. Failure to provide this means an increase in government's share and would make the worker worse off than he was before he got the raise.

Let our banner proclaim our belief in a free market as the greatest provider for the people. Let us also call for an end to the nitpicking, the harassment, and over-regulation of business and industry which restricts expansion and our ability to compete in world markets.

Let us explore ways to ward off socialism, not by increasing government's coercive power, but by increasing participation by the people in the ownership of our industrial machine.

Our banner must recognize the responsibility of government to protect the law-abiding, holding those who commit misdeeds personally accountable.

And we must make it plain to international adventurers that our love of peace stops short of "peace at any price."

We will maintain whatever level of strength is necessary to preserve our free way of life.

A political party cannot be all things to all people. It must represent certain fundamental beliefs which must not be compromised to political expediency, or simply to swell its numbers.

I do not believe I have proposed anything that is contrary to what has been considered Republican principle. It is at the same time the very basis of conservatism. It is time to reassert that principle and raise it to full view. And if there are those who cannot subscribe to these principles, then let them go their way.

Conservatism Goes Mainstream

Morton C. Blackwell

Let Them Go Their Way

Two disastrous election defeats, ten years apart in 1964 and 1974, caused many conservative activists to wonder whether the Republican Party was a viable political vehicle for our principles. Each time, powerful speeches by Ronald Reagan persuaded millions of principled conservatives to stick with Republicans.

The 1964 speech, *A Time for Choosing*, was given in support of Republican presidential nominee Barry Goldwater. It was prerecorded by Reagan and broadcasted on national television on October 27, 1964, a few days before Senator Goldwater's crushing defeat on November 3.

By October 27, most conservatives working our hearts out for Goldwater were sure he would lose badly. But Reagan's powerful speech for Goldwater nevertheless thrilled us. The speech raised more than a million dollars from thousands of Americans who sent last minute contributions to the Goldwater campaign.

It's fair to say that the speech launched Reagan's political career. It generated a groundswell of support that led to his running for governor of California in 1966.

Reagan's election for governor followed by two successful four-year terms began to persuade many movement conservatives that he should be elected president of the United States.

Some of us came to that conclusion earlier than others.

As executive director of the College Republican National Committee, I joined M. Stanton Evans and others for a meeting in the office of businessman John L. Ryan in Indianapolis in February of 1968. Later, the longtime chairman of the American Conservative Union, Stan, was then-editor of the *Indianapolis News*. The purpose of the meeting was to discuss what might be done to nominate Ronald Reagan for President in 1968.

In 1964, I served as a delegate from Louisiana to the Republican National Convention in San Francisco, where I turned out to be Barry Goldwater's youngest elected national delegate. In 1968, "Reagan for President" support was strong in the Louisiana Republican Party. I was then elected as a Louisiana alternate delegate for Reagan to the 1968 Republican National Convention in Miami Beach.

Reagan did eventually run for the 1968 Republican presidential nomination, but he started campaigning just before the convention. Many conservatives, including South Carolina Senator Strom Thurmond, had already committed to support Richard Nixon.

On the first and only ballot, with a majority of 667 delegate votes required, Nixon narrowly won the 1968 presidential nomination with 692 delegates. Nelson Rockefeller ran second and Reagan ran third. Had Nixon not won a majority on the first ballot, he would have lost votes on the next ballot. Many Nixon delegates, especially in the South (including several from Louisiana), would have voted for Reagan on the second ballot.

Nixon won the 1968 general election easily against Democrat Hubert Humphrey, and won the 1972 election by a landslide against Democrat George McGovern.

Vice President Spiro Agnew's tough criticism of leftists in government and the news media made him a hero to conservatives, but on October 10, 1973, he pled guilty to a charge of felony tax evasion and resigned as vice president.

Two days later, on October 12, President Nixon made the terrible mistake of nominating U.S. House Minority Leader and Congressman Gerald Ford for vice president. The Senate confirmed Ford as vice president by a vote of ninety-two to three. The U.S. House confirmed Ford by a vote of 387 to 35.

Nixon could have nominated and won confirmation for almost any prominent Republican to replace Agnew. He could have named any respected conservative Republican leader. He could have picked, for instance, recently re-elected Governor Ronald Reagan of California. Instead, Nixon picked Ford, a non-controversial moderate.

By then, Nixon had to know the Democrats were determined to oust him as president if they could.

If Nixon had nominated Ronald Reagan, Congress surely would have confirmed him. If Nixon had chosen a principled and charismatic vice president like Reagan, the Democrats probably would not have gone all the way to remove Nixon from office. Instead, Nixon nominated Ford, a man who almost all Democrats certainly preferred to Nixon in the Oval Office.

With his selection of Ford as vice president, Nixon incentivized the Democrats to do him in.

The Watergate break-in during his reelection campaign hadn't prevented Nixon's overwhelming victory in November of 1972, but the scandal of the attempted cover-up grew larger and larger until

Nixon was thoroughly disgraced. Facing inevitable impeachment, he was forced to resign on August 9, 1974.

When he was confirmed by Congress, President Ford promptly nominated, and Congress confirmed, conservatives' worst Republican enemy for vice president: Nelson Rockefeller of New York.

The November 1974 midterm elections were an unmitigated disaster for Republicans. Under Nixon, they had not held a majority in either house of Congress. In these midterms, Republicans lost forty-eight U.S. House seats and suffered a net loss of three U.S. Senate seats. Now Democrats had sixty Senate seats and two-thirds of the House.

Conservatives who had worked through the Republican Party for decades, struggling against content-free Republican Party leadership all the while, were furious.

Some conservatives began to consider the possibility that the badly weakened Republican Party could no longer serve as a political vehicle for conservative principles. Could conservatives start from scratch and build a new major party?

The thought tempted some people, but it was a bad idea. American history has repeatedly demonstrated that it's a lot easier to take over an existing major party than to create a new major party.

Four months after the awful November 1974 elections and two months after he completed his second successful term as governor of California in January of 1975, former Governor Reagan was scheduled to address what was already the most important national gathering of movement conservatives in Washington, D.C.: the annual Conservative Political Action Conference.

I attended all of Ronald Reagan's annual speeches at CPAC. His March 1, 1975 speech, *Let Them Go Their Way*, is one of his most important. He filled the address with ringing affirmations of conservative principles, touches of humor, interesting stories, polite modesty, and well-deserved outrage for leftist behavior.

One sentence stands out as most powerful. It certainly had the greatest effect on the future of the Republican Party. Reagan asked: "Is it a third party we need, or is it a new and revitalized second party, raising a banner of no pale pastels, but bold colors which make it unmistakably clear where we stand on all of the issues troubling the people?"

In June of 1975, American Conservative Union National Chairman M. Stanton Evans publicly called for Governor Reagan to challenge President Ford for the 1976 Republican presidential nomination.

The rest, as they say, is history. But conservatives recall it as a rendezvous with destiny.

Morton C. Blackwell is the president of the Leadership Institute and has served for decades on the Board of the American Conservative Union. For the first three years of the Reagan administration, he was a special assistant to the president on the White House staff. Since 1988, he has served as the national committeeman of the Republican Party of Virginia.

The New
Republican Party

1977

I'm happy to be back with you in this annual event after missing
last year's meeting. I had some business in New Hampshire that
wouldn't wait.

Three weeks ago, here in our nation's capital, I told a group of
conservative scholars that we are currently in the midst of a reordering of the political realities that have shaped our time. We
know today that the principles and values that lie at the heart of
conservatism are shared by the majority.

Despite what some in the press may say, we who are proud to
call ourselves "conservative" are not a minority of a minority party;
we are part of the great majority of Americans of both major parties
and of most of the independents as well.

A Harris poll released September 7, 1975 showed eighteen
percent identifying themselves as liberal and thirty-one percent as
conservative, with forty-one percent as middle of the road. A few
months later, on January 5, 1976, by a forty-three to nineteen

plurality, those polled by Harris said they would "prefer to see the country move in a more conservative direction than a liberal one."

Last October 24, the Gallup organization released the result of a poll taken right in the midst of the presidential campaign.

Respondents were asked to state where they would place themselves on a scale ranging from "right-of-center," which was defined as "conservative," to "left-of-center," which was defined as "liberal."

Thirty-seven percent viewed themselves as left-of-center or liberal; twelve percent placed themselves in the middle; fifty-one percent said they were right-of-center, that is, conservative.

What I find interesting about this particular poll is that it offered those polled a range of choices on a left-right continuum. This seems to me to be a more realistic approach than dividing the world into strict left and rights. Most of us, I guess, like to think of ourselves as avoiding both extremes, and the fact that a majority of Americans chose one or the other position on the right end of the spectrum is really impressive.

Those polls confirm that most Americans are basically conservative in their outlook. But once we have said this, we conservatives have not solved our problems, we have merely stated them clearly. Yes, conservatism can and does mean different things to those who call themselves conservatives.

You know, as I do, that most commentators make a distinction between [what] they call "social" conservatism and "economic" conservatism. The so-called social issues—law and order, abortion, busing, quota systems—are usually associated with blue-collar, ethnic, and religious groups themselves traditionally associated with the Democratic Party. The economic issues—inflation, deficit spending, and big government—are usually associated with Republican Party members and independents who concentrate their attention on economic matters.

Now, I am willing to accept this view of two major kinds of conservatism—or, better still, two different conservative constituencies. But at the same time, let me say that the old lines that once clearly divided these two kinds of conservatism are disappearing.

In fact, the time has come to see if it is possible to present a program of action based on political principle that can attract those interested in the so-called "social" issues and those interested in "economic" issues. In short, isn't it possible to combine the two major segments of contemporary American conservatism into one politically effective whole?

I believe the answer is: yes, it is possible to create a political entity that will reflect the views of the great, hitherto [unacknowledged], conservative majority. We went a long way toward doing it in California. We can do it in America. This is not a dream, a wistful hope. It is and has been a reality. I have seen the conservative future and it works.

Let me say again what I said to our conservative friends from the academic world: what I envision is not simply a melding together of the two branches of American conservatism into a temporary uneasy alliance, but the creation of a new, lasting majority.

This will mean compromise. But not a compromise of basic principle. What will emerge will be something new, something open and vital and dynamic, something the great conservative majority will recognize as its own, because at the heart of this undertaking is principled politics.

I have always been puzzled by the inability of some political and media types to understand exactly what is meant by adherence to political principle. All too often in the press and the television evening news it is treated as a call for "ideological purity." Whatever ideology may mean—and it seems to mean a variety of things, depending upon who is using it—it always conjures up in my mind a picture of a rigid, irrational clinging to abstract theory in the face of reality. We have to recognize that in this country, "ideology" is a scare word. And for good reason. Marxist-Leninism is, to give but one example, an ideology. All the facts of the real world have to be fitted to the Procrustean bed of Marx and Lenin. If the facts don't happen to fit the ideology, the facts are chopped off and discarded.

I consider this to be the complete opposite to principled conservatism. If there is any political viewpoint in this world which is free from slavish adherence to abstraction, it is American conservatism.

When a conservative states that the free market is the best mechanism ever devised by the mind of man to meet material needs, he is merely stating what a careful examination of the real world has told him is the truth.

When a conservative says that totalitarian communism is an absolute enemy of human freedom, he is not theorizing—he is reporting the ugly reality captured so unforgettably in the writings of Alexander Solzhenitsyn.

When a conservative says it is bad for the government to spend more than it takes in, he is simply showing the same common sense that tells him to come in out of the rain.

When a conservative says that busing does not work, he is not appealing to some theory of education—he is merely reporting what he has seen down at the local school.

When a conservative quotes Jefferson that government that is closest to the people is best, it is because he knows that Jefferson risked his life, his fortune, and his sacred honor to make certain that what he and his fellow patriots learned from experience was not crushed by an ideology of empire.

Conservatism is the antithesis of the kind of ideological fanaticism that has brought so much horror and destruction to the world. The common sense and common decency of ordinary men and women, working out their own lives in their own way—this is the heart of American conservatism today. Conservative wisdom and principles are derived from willingness to learn, not just from what is going on now, but from what has happened before.

The principles of conservatism are sound because they are based on what men and women have discovered through experience in not just one generation or a dozen, but in all the combined experience of mankind. When we conservatives say that we know something about political affairs, and that we know can be stated as principles, we are saying that the principles we hold dear are those that have been found, through experience, to be ultimately beneficial for individuals, for families, for communities, and for nations—found through the often-bitter testing of pain, or sacrifice and sorrow.

One thing that must be made clear in post-Watergate is this: the American new conservative majority we represent is not based on abstract theorizing of the kind that turns off the American people, but on common sense, intelligence, reason, hard work, faith in God, and the guts to say, "Yes, there are things we do strongly believe in, that we are willing to live for, and yes, if necessary, to die for." That is not "ideological purity." It is simply what built this country and kept it great.

Let us lay to rest, once and for all, the myth of a small group of ideological purists trying to capture a majority. Replace it with the reality of a majority trying to assert its rights against the tyranny of powerful academics, fashionable left-revolutionaries, some economic illiterates who happen to hold elective office, and the social engineers who dominate the dialogue and set the format in political and social affairs. If there is any ideological fanaticism in American political life, it is to be found among the enemies of freedom on the left or right—those who would sacrifice principle to theory, those who worship only the god of political, social, and economic abstractions, ignoring the realities of everyday life. They are not conservatives.

Our first job is to get this message across to those who share most
of our principles. If we allow ourselves to be portrayed as ideological
shock troops without correcting this error, we are doing ourselves and
our cause a disservice. Wherever and whenever we can, we should
gently but firmly correct our political and media friends who have
been perpetuating the myth of conservatism as a narrow ideology.
Whatever the word may have meant in the past, today conservatism
means principles evolving from experience and a belief in change
when necessary, but not just for the sake of change.

Once we have established this, the next question is: what will be
the political vehicle by which the majority can assert its rights?

I have to say, I cannot agree with some of my friends—perhaps
including some of you here tonight—who have answered that question
by saying this nation needs a new political party.

I respect that view and I know that those who have reached it have
done so after long hours of study. But I believe that political success
of the principles we believe in can best be achieved in the Republican
Party. I believe the Republican Party can hold and should provide the
political mechanism through which the goals of the majority of Americans can be achieved. For one thing, the biggest single grouping of
conservatives is to be found in that party. It makes more sense to build
on that grouping than to break it up and start over. Rather than a
third party, we can have a new first party made up of people who
share our principles. I have said before that if a formal change in name
proves desirable, then so be it. But tonight, for purpose of discussion,
I'm going to refer to it simply as the New Republican Party.

And let me say so there can be no mistakes as to what I mean: the
New Republican Party I envision will not be, and cannot, be one
limited to the country club-big business image that, for reasons both
fair and unfair, it is burdened with today. The New Republican Party
I am speaking about is going to have room for the man and the

woman in the factories, for the farmer, for the cop on the beat and
the millions of Americans who may never have thought of joining
our party before, but whose interests coincide with those represented
by principled Republicanism. If we are to attract more working men
and women of this country, we will do so not by simply "making
room" for them, but by making certain they have a say in what goes
on in the party. The Democratic Party turned its back on the majority of social conservatives during the 1960s. The New Republican
Party of the late '70s and '80s must welcome them, seek them out,
enlist them, not only as rank-and-file members, but as leaders and as
candidates.

The time has come for Republicans to say to black voters:
"Look, we offer principles that black Americans can, and do, support." We believe in jobs, real jobs; we believe in education that is
really education; we believe in treating all Americans as individuals
and not as stereotypes or voting blocs—and we believe that the
long-range interest of black Americans lies in looking at what each
major party has to offer, and then deciding on the merits. The
Democratic Party takes the black vote for granted. Well, it's time
black America and the New Republican Party move toward each
other and create a situation in which no black vote can be taken for
granted.

The New Republican Party I envision is one that will energetically
seek out the best candidates for every elective office, candidates who
not only agree with, but understand, and are willing to fight for a
sound, honest economy for the interests of American families and
neighborhoods and communities and a strong national defense. And
these candidates must be able to communicate those principles to the
American people in language they understand. Inflation isn't a textbook problem. Unemployment isn't a textbook problem. They should
be discussed in human terms.

Our candidates must be willing to communicate with every level of society, because the principles we espouse are universal and cut across traditional lines. In every congressional district, there should be a search made for young men and women who share these principles and they should be brought into positions of leadership in the local Republican Party groups. We can find attractive, articulate candidates if we look, and when we find them, we will begin to change the sorry state of affairs that has led to a Democratic-controlled Congress for more than forty years. I need not remind you that you can have the soundest principles in the world, but if you don't have candidates who can communicate those principles, candidates who are articulate as well as principled, you are going to lose election after election. I refuse to believe that the good Lord divided this world into Republicans who defend basic values and Democrats who win elections. We have to find tough, bright young men and women who are sick and tired of clichés and the pomposity and the mind-numbing economic idiocy of the liberals in Washington.

It is at this point, however, that we come across a question that is really the essential one: what will be the basis of this new Republican Party? To what set of values and principles can our candidates appeal? Where can Americans who want to know where we stand look for guidance?

Fortunately, we have an answer to that question. That answer was provided last summer by the men and women of the Republican Party—not just the leadership, but the ones who have built the party on local levels all across the country.

The answer was provided in the 1976 platform of the Republican Party.

This was not a document handed down from on high. It was hammered out in free and open debate among all those who care about our party and the principles it stands for.

The Republican platform is unique. Unlike any other party platform I have ever seen, it answers not only programmatic questions for the immediate future of the party, but also provides a clear outline of the underlying principles upon which those programs are based.

The New Republican Party can and should use the Republican platform of 1976 as the major source from which a Declaration of Principles can be created and offered to the American people.

Tonight, I want to offer to you my own version of what such a declaration might look like. I make no claim to originality. This declaration I propose is relatively short, taken, for most part, word for word from the Republican platform. It concerns itself with basic principles, not with specific solutions.

We, the members of the New Republican Party, believe that the preservation and enhancement of the values that strengthen and protect individual freedom, family life, communities and neighborhoods, and the liberty of our beloved nation should be at the heart of any legislative or political program presented to the American people. Toward that end, we therefore commit ourselves to the following propositions and offer them to each American believing that the New Republican Party, based on such principles, will serve the interest of all the American people.

We believe that liberty can be measured by how much freedom Americans have to make their own decisions, even their own mistakes. Government must step in when one's liberties impinge on one's neighbors. Government must protect constitutional rights, deal with other governments, protect citizens from aggressors, assure equal opportunity, and be compassionate in caring for those citizens who are unable to care for themselves.

Our federal system of local-state-national government is designed to sort out on what level these actions should be taken. Those concerns of a national character—such as air and water pollution that do not respect state boundaries, or the national transportation system, or efforts to safeguard your civil liberties—must, of course, be handled on the national level.

As a general rule, however, we believe that government action should be taken first by the government that resides as close to you as possible.

We also believe that Americans, often acting through voluntary organizations, should have the opportunity to solve many of the social problems of their communities. This spirit of freely helping others is uniquely American and should be encouraged in every way by government.

Families must continue to be the foundation of our nation.

Families—not government programs—are the best way to make sure our children are properly nurtured, our elderly are cared for, our cultural and spiritual heritages are perpetuated, our laws are observed, and our values are preserved.

Thus, it is imperative that our government's programs, actions, officials, and social welfare institutions never be allowed to jeopardize the family. We fear the government may be powerful enough to destroy our families; we know that it is not powerful enough to replace them. The New Republican Party must be committed to working always in the interest of the American family.

Every dollar spent by government is a dollar earned by individuals. Government must always ask: are your dollars being wisely spent? Can we afford it? Is it not better for the country to leave your dollars in your pocket?

Elected officials, their appointees, and government workers are expected to perform their public acts with honesty, openness, diligence, and special integrity.

Government must work for the goal of justice and the elimination of unfair practices, but no government has yet designed a more productive economic system or one which benefits as many people as the American market system.

The beauty of our land is our legacy to our children. It must be protected by us so that they can pass it on intact to their children.

The United States must always stand for peace and liberty in the world and the rights of the individual. We must form sturdy partnerships with our allies for the preservation of freedom. We must be ever willing to negotiate differences, but equally mindful that there are American ideals that cannot be compromised. Given that there are other nations with potentially hostile design, we recognize that we can reach our goals only while maintaining a superior national defense, second to none.

In his inaugural speech, President Carter said that he saw the world "dominated by a new spirit." He said, and I quote: "The passion for freedom is on the rise."

Well, I don't know how he knows this, but if it is true, then it is the most unrequited passion in human history. The world is being dominated by a new spirit, all right, but it isn't the spirit of freedom.

It isn't very often you see a familiar object that shocks and frightens you. But the other day, I came across a map of the world created by Freedom House, an organization monitoring the state of freedom in the world for the past twenty-five years. It is an ordinary map, with one exception: it shows the world's nations in white for free, shaded for partly free, and black for not free.

Almost all of the great Eurasian land mass is completely colored black, from the western border of East Germany, through middle and eastern Europe, through the awesome spaces of the Soviet Union, on to the Bering Strait in the north, down past the immensity of China, still further down to Vietnam and the South China Sea—in all that huge, sprawling, inconceivably immense area, not a single political or personal or religious freedom exists. The entire continent of Africa, from the Mediterranean to the Cape of Good Hope, from the Atlantic to the Indian Ocean, all that vastness is almost totally unfree. In the tiny nation of Tanzania alone, according to a report in the New York Times, there are three thousand people in detention for political crimes—that is more than the total being held in South Africa. The Mideast has only one free state: Israel. If a visitor from another planet were to approach earth, and if this planet showed free nations in light and unfree nations in darkness, the pitifully small beacons of light would make him wonder what was hidden in that terrifying, enormous blackness.

We know what is hidden: Gulag. Torture. Families—and human beings—broken apart. No free press, no freedom of religion. The ancient forms of tyranny revived and made even more hideous and strong through what Winston Churchill once called "a perverted science." Men rotting for years in solitary confinement because they have different political and economic beliefs—solitary confinement that drives the fortunate ones insane and makes the survivors wish for death.

Only now and then do we in the West hear a voice from out of that darkness. Then there is silence—the silence of human slavery. There is no more terrifying sound in human experience, with one possible exception. Look at that map again. The very heart of the darkness is the Soviet Union, and from that heart comes a different sound. It is the whirring sound of machinery and the whisper of the computer technology we ourselves have sold them. It is the sound of building; building of the strongest military machine ever devised by man. Our military strategy is designed to hopefully prevent a war. Theirs is designed to win one. A group of eminent scientists, scholars, and intelligence experts offer a survey showing that the Soviet Union is driving for military superiority and are derided as hysterically making, quote, "a worst case," unquote, concerning Soviet intentions and capabilities.

But is it not precisely the duty of the national government to be prepared for the worst case? Two senators, after studying the North Atlantic Treaty Organization, have reported to the Armed Forces Committee that Soviet forces in Eastern Europe have the capability to launch, with little warning, a "potentially devastating" attack in Central Europe from what is termed a "standing alert."

Reading their report, one can almost see the enormous weight of the parts of the earth that are under tyranny shifting in an irresistible tilt toward that tiny portion of land in freedom's light. Even now in Western Europe, we have communists in the government of Italy, France appeasing terrorists, and England—for centuries the model or the sword of freedom in Western Europe—weak, dispirited, turning inward.

A "worst case?" How could you make a good case out of the facts as they are known? The Soviet Union, poised on the edge of free Europe, capable of striking from a standing start, has modern tanks in far greater numbers than the outmoded vehicles of NATO. We have taken comfort from NATO's superiority in the air, but now the Soviet Union has made a dramatic swing away from its historic defensive air posture to one capable of supporting offensive action. NATO's southern flank is described in the Senate report with a single word: shambles.

The report is simply reality as it was, with different names and faces, in Europe in the late 1930s when so many refused to believe and thought, if we don't look, the threat will go away.

We don't want hysteria. We don't want distortion of Soviet power. We want truth. And above all, we want peace. And to have [recognition] that the United States has to immediately re-examine its entire view of the world and develop a strategy of freedom. We cannot be the second-best superpower for the simple reason that he who is second is last. In this deadly game, there are no silver medals for second.

President Carter, as a candidate, said he would cut five to seven billion dollars from the defense budget. We must let him know that while we agree, there must be no fat in our armed forces. Those armed forces must be capable of coping with the new reality presented to us by the Russians, and cutting seven billion dollars out of our defense budget is not the way to accomplish this. Some years ago, a young president said, we will make any sacrifice, bear any burden, and we will, to preserve our freedom.

Our relationship with mainland China is clouded. The so-called "Gang of Four" are up one day and down the next, and we are seeing the pitfalls of making deals with charismatic personalities and living legends. The charisma fades as the living legends die, and those who take their place are interested not in our best wishes, but in power. The keyword for China today is turmoil. We should watch and observe and analyze as closely and rationally as we can.

But in our relationships with the mainland of China, we should always remember that the conditions and possibilities for and the realities of freedom exist to an infinitely greater degree with our Chinese friends in Taiwan. We can never go wrong if we do what is morally right, and the moral way—the honorable way—is to keep our commitment, our solemn promise to the people of Taiwan. Our liberal friends have made much of the lack of freedom in some Latin American countries. Senator Edward Kennedy and his colleagues here in Washington let no opportunity pass to let us know about horrors in Chile.

Well, I think when the United States of America is considering a deal with a country that hasn't had an election in almost eight years, where the press is under the thumb of a dictatorship, where ordinary citizens are abducted in the night by secret police, where military domination of the country is known to be harsh on dissenters, and when these things are documented, we should reject overtures from those who rule such a country.

But the country I'm describing is not Chile—it is Panama.

We are negotiating with a dictatorship that comes within the portion of that map colored black for no freedom. No civil rights. One-man rule. No free press.

Candidate Carter said he would never relinquish "actual control" of the Panama Canal. President Carter is negotiating with a dictatorship whose record on civil and human rights is as I have just described, and the negotiations concern the rights guaranteed to us by treaty which we will give up under a threat of violence. In only a few weeks we will mark the second anniversary of the death of freedom for the Vietnamese. An estimated 300,000 of them are being "re-educated" in concentration camps to forget about freedom.

There is only one major question on the agenda of national priorities and that is the state of our national security. I refer, of course, to the state of our armed forces—but also to our state of mind, to the way we perceive the world. We cannot maintain the strength we need to survive, no matter how many missiles we have, no matter how many tanks we build, unless we are willing to reverse the trend of deteriorating faith in and continuing abuse of our national intelligence agencies. Let's stop the sniping and the propaganda and the historical revisionism and let the CIA and the other intelligence agencies do their job.

Let us reverse the trend of public indifference to problems of national security. In every congressional district, citizens should join together, enlist and educate neighbors, and make certain that congressmen know we care. The front pages of major newspapers on the East Coast recently headlined and told in great detail of a takeover— the takeover of a magazine published in New York—not a nation losing its freedom. You would think, from the attention it received in the media, that it was a matter of blazing national interest whether the magazine lived or died. The tendency of much of the media to ignore the state of our national security is too well-documented for me to go on.

My friends, the time has come to start acting to bring about the great conservative majority party we know is waiting to be created.

And just to set the record straight, let me say this about our friends who are now Republicans but who do not identify themselves as conservatives: I want the record to show that I do not view the new revitalized Republican Party as one based on a principle of exclusion. After all, you do not get to be a majority party by searching for groups you won't associate or work with. If we truly believe in our principles, we should sit down and talk. Talk with anyone, anywhere, at any time if it means talking about the principles for the Republican Party. Conservatism is not a narrow ideology, nor is it the exclusive property of conservative activists.

We've succeeded better than we know. Little more than a decade ago, more than two-thirds of Americans believed the federal government could solve all our problems and do so without restricting our freedom or bankrupting the nation.

We warned of things to come, of the danger inherent in unwarranted government involvement in things not its proper province. What we warned against has come to pass. And today, more than two-thirds of our citizens are telling us, and each other, that social engineering by the federal government has failed. The Great Society is great only in power, in size, and in cost. And so are the problems it set out to solve. Freedom has been diminished and we stand on the brink of economic ruin.

Our task now is not to sell a philosophy, but to make the majority of Americans, who already share that philosophy, see that modern conservatism offers them a political home. We are not a cult, we are members of a majority. Let's act and talk like it.

The job is ours and the job must be done. If not by us, who? If not now, when?

Our party must be the party of the individual. It must not sell out the individual to cater to the group. No greater challenge faces our society today than ensuring that each one of us can maintain his dignity and his identity in an increasingly complex, centralized society.

Extreme taxation, excessive controls, oppressive government, competition with business, galloping inflation, frustrated minorities, and forgotten Americans are not the products of free enterprise. They are the residue of centralized bureaucracy, of government by a self-anointed elite.

Our party must be based on the kind of leadership that grows and takes its strength from the people. Any organization is in actuality only the lengthened shadow of its members. A political party is a mechanical structure created to further a cause. The cause, not the mechanism, brings and holds the members together. And our cause must be to rediscover, reassert, and reapply America's spiritual heritage to our national affairs.

Then, with God's help, we shall indeed be as a city upon a hill with the eyes of all people upon us.

America's Purpose
in the World

1978

A s a part-time journalist faced with producing a syndicated daily radio broadcast and twice-a-week newspaper column, I find being on the mailing lists of an almost endless array of organizations most helpful. Now, some of the flood of materials crosses my desk very swiftly. But not all of it. One thick handout I got late last year was especially fascinating, not only because of content but just because it was mailed to me at all.

It was from the White House Press Office. Under the title "Domestic and Foreign Policy Accomplishments" it told me, in twenty-one single-spaced pages, of the wonders of the Carter administration's first year.

Beginning with the modest statement that "the president tackled directly and comprehensively major domestic problems that had been almost completely ignored in previous years," it then recited an impressive list of major accomplishments. True, the White House hadn't claimed to find a way to control the weather or to eliminate crab grass on the White House lawn, but it did think it had solved—or nearly solved—our energy problems, Social Security's $17-trillion deficit, the size of a big government (we added 52,000 new employees in the first ten months of 1977), the welfare mess, and a host of other problems that have been center stage in American life for quite some time.

Tonight, perhaps we should discuss some of those White House claims and see if they have stood the test of even the three months that have passed since they were made. I know that's a little cruel— like checking up on someone's New Year's resolutions. After all, the administration has scarcely gotten a single domestic program worth noting through Congress. I'll tell you what. Let us concentrate on the administration's handling of foreign affairs, national security, and its sense of priorities.

On priorities, there is the matter of issuing the former budget director a diplomatic passport; the taking of depositions from bartenders and issuing a thirty-three-page denial that the president's chief aide expectorated at, or in the direction of, a young woman. It boggles the mind to think what they would have done if he'd spit on the sidewalk. Then there was the solemn oath to appoint and retain a U.S. attorney who goes investigating suspected wrongdoing on the part of congressmen who belong to the president's own party.

Moving on to the Carter administration's record in foreign affairs, let me say a few words about Panama and our canal there. And I do mean a few words.

With yesterday's vote on the so-called Neutrality Treaty, you might say that round one is over. Now, there has been confusion in some news reports which called this the "first treaty," saying that the Senate would next take up the "second treaty." Actually, the Senate decided to reverse the procedure. The Neutrality Treaty is the second treaty. They just voted on it first. Next, they will deal with the basic treaty, the one called the Panama Canal Treaty. It is the basic treaty because it is the one which would relinquish our rights and would actually eliminate the canal zone as soon as it goes into effect—if it does.

I hope the Senate will devote as much detailed attention to this basic treaty as it did to the Neutrality Treaty. Meanwhile, I can't get a question out of my head. It is this: even though the Neutrality Treaty supposedly guarantees our right to go back in to defend the Canal after 1999, if there is no canal zone, wouldn't any such move on our part be branded as interference in the internal affairs of Panama?

On the other hand, if the basic treaty is not ratified, the Neutrality Treaty itself won't have much meaning because our rights and our presence in the canal zone would continue. And, when all is said and done, it is always easier to defend something you have than to get back something you gave away.

My fundamental concern has always been primarily with this basic treaty which would eliminate our rights there. I think there are alternatives to it which would be better for all concerned.

You are all activists, and I know you will make your views known to your elected representatives on this next treaty debate.

My purpose tonight, however, is not to repeat my views on this question. Panama is an important issue. The final outcome is not yet certain, and certainly the matter won't end with the final vote in the Senate. In a way, that will only begin it.

But, whatever the outcome on Capitol Hill, the smug assumptions of many of the treaties' proponents have been successfully and vigorously challenged.

Few Americans accept the belief of some of those now in positions of importance in guiding our foreign policy that America's purpose in the world is to appease the mighty out of a sense of fear or to appease the weak out of a sense of guilt.

But a question remains. Is the faulty thinking that has led us to these particular treaties an isolated particle, or is it part of a much larger whole?

In reviewing the foreign policy of this administration, one can only come to the conclusion that the mistaken assumptions that led to its course on the Panama Canal treaties are being duplicated around the world.

Its policy is rooted in well-meaning intentions, but it shows a woeful uncertainty as to America's purpose in the world.

The administration means to do good by espousing a human rights doctrine it cannot define, much less implement. In the process, this policy has met with scorn from our enemies and alarm from our friends. That self-graded, twenty-one-page White House report card said, with regard to human rights, "The president has strengthened our human rights policy and we are letting it be known clearly that the United States stands with the victims of repression." Is that why our representatives at the Belgrade Conference remained silent in the face of a final report that contained not one word about Russian violations of the human rights provisions in the Helsinki Agreement?

If the Carter administration "stands with the victims of repression," the people of Cuba, Panama, Vietnam, Cambodia, and the mainland of China have yet to hear about it. The fact is, the Carter human rights policy is whatever his appointees who guide it want it to be. In practice, they have ceaselessly scolded authoritarian governments of countries that are friendly and ignored authoritarian and totalitarian countries that are not.

Mr. Carter might find a reading of the historian Charles Beard informative. Nearly forty years ago, Beard concluded that the defect of a foreign policy based on what he called "the selfish sacrifice required by an absolute morality" was the inability to understand "the limited nature of American powers to relieve, restore, and maintain life beyond its own sphere of interest and control—a recognition of the hard fact that the United States...did not possess the power...to assure the establishment of democratic and pacific government."

But, by using a combination of heavy-handed moves against allied countries, on the one hand, and making "preemptive concessions" toward unfriendly or potentially unfriendly countries on the other, the Carter administration has managed to convey the view that it desperately wants the whole world to have democratic institutions that would be the envy of the most ardent ACLU lawyer, and that wishing will make it so.

That view of the world ranks along with belief in the Tooth Fairy. But confusion of purpose and a false sense of guilt are not the only elements in this administration's foreign policy.

Too often, the president is advised by men and women who are forever trapped in the tragic but still fresh memory of a lost war. And from Vietnam they have drawn all the wrong lessons. When they say "never again," they mean the United States should never again resist communist aggression.

In saying "never again," implying that the war should have been lost—that it is all right for the victors to conduct a brutal campaign against their own people, violating even minimal human rights.

That it is alright to ignore these massive violations and alright for us to seek better relations with the governments responsible. That White House document lists as an "accomplishment" as the fact that "the administration has started the process of normalizing relations" with the communist conquerors of South Vietnam. The lesson we should have learned from Vietnam is that never again will Americans be asked to fight and die unless they are permitted to win. We need a foreign policy stripped of platitudes, can't and mere moral earnestness—an earnestness fatally compromised by the massive crimes of some of the communist world's newer members.

This pattern of communist violations of human rights should come as no surprise to us. Over and over again, newly established Marxist regimes have committed them. In the 1920s and '30s, it was the Soviet Union, in the late '40s, the new Iron Curtain countries, in the '50s and through the Cultural Revolution of the '60s, it was Communist China and Cuba, and now it is Vietnam and Cambodia.

The problem with much of the Carter team is that they know too little, not too much, of history. And, they have lost faith in their own country's past and traditions.

Too often, that team has operated under the assumption that the United States must prove and reprove and prove again its goodness to the world. Proving that we are civilized in a world that is often uncivilized—and unapologetically so—is hardly necessary.

The themes of a sound foreign policy should be no mystery, nor the result of endless agonizing reappraisals. They are rooted in our past—in our very beginning as a nation.

The Founding Fathers established a system which meant a radical break from that which preceded it. A written constitution would provide a permanent form of government, limited in scope, but effective in providing both liberty and order. Government was not to be a matter of self-appointed rulers, governing by whim or harsh ideology. It was not to be government by the strongest or for the few. Our principles were revolutionary. We began as a small, weak republic. But we survived. Our example inspired others, imperfectly at times, but it inspired them nevertheless. This constitutional republic, conceived in liberty and dedicated to the proposition that all men are created equal, prospered and grew strong. To this day, America is still the abiding alternative to tyranny. That is our purpose in the world—nothing more and nothing less.

To carry out that purpose, our fundamental aim in foreign policy must be to ensure our own survival and to protect those others who share our values. Under no circumstances should we have any illusions about the intentions of those who are enemies of freedom. Our communist adversaries have little regard for human rights because they have little interest in human freedom. The ruling elites of those countries wish only one thing: to preserve their privileges and to eliminate the nagging reminder that others have done and are doing better under freedom.

Every American president since World War II has known or quickly learned that the Soviet Union, for example, is not benign in its intentions.

The Soviet Union has no interest in maintaining the status quo. It does not accept our soft definition of "detente." To the Soviet Union, "detente" is an opportunity to expand its sphere of influence around the world.

The Soviet Union has steadily increased its capacity for such expansion. That capability has grown enormously since 1945 and, above all, since 1962 when the Cold War was first declared "over" by the hopeful and naive.

Today, the USSR continues its drive to dominate the world in military capability: on land, on water, and in the air. Meanwhile, the Carter administration seems confused and torn, partly believing the realities and partly listening to those who believe that preemptive concession by the Soviets. But they don't bargain that way. They understand strength; they exploit weakness and take advantage of inexperience. And, possibly, it was inexperience that led the president to placate the most dovish members of his party by scuttling the B-1 bomber—one of his bargaining chips—even before the SALT II negotiations began.

One of the reasons given for cancellation of the B-1 was economy, and even here there was a lack of accuracy. First of all, the price given for the aircraft was what the price will be in 1986 if inflation continues—which incidentally suggests a lack of resolve in the administration's anti-inflation fight. Second, we were told the B-52 or the F-111 could be modified to do the job the B-1 was supposed to do. Here, the cost differential shrinks sizably when we look at the facts. The modification itself is quite costly, and we can double that cost. It will take two planes to substitute for every B-1 because the B-1 carries twice the payload the others will. It will carry that load twice as fast in a plane only half the size of a B-52, and it is far less vulnerable to the Soviet defense system.

While confusion and conflicting advice seem to tug and pull at the White House, the Soviet Union continues to build up its capability for world domination. It has even gone so far as to put entire factories underground and to disperse much of its industrial capacity—the most sophisticated civil defense program ever developed. The knowledge that our strategic missiles, if they ever had to be used, would inflict minimal damage on the Soviets, compared to the havoc theirs would produce on our continent, should, in itself, be sufficient to spur the administration to making certain that we be number one in the world in terms of national defense capabilities. So far, though, this does not seem to be a White House priority.

Today, we can see the brunt of the Soviet Union's capabilities at work in the Horn of Africa.

To most Americans, that part of the world seems remote, as Korea and Vietnam seemed remote, along with those other places where the Soviets have sought advantage.

In Ethiopia, formerly a close friend of the United States, the Soviets with their Cuban foreign legion have turned that country into a free-fire zone in order to subdue Ethiopia's two principal enemies, Somalia and the Eritrean rebels.

The Soviet goal is obvious: to secure a permanent foothold for itself on the Red Sea. If the Soviets are successful—and it looks more and more as if they will be—then the entire Horn of Africa will be under their influence, if not their control. From there, they can threaten the sea lanes carrying oil to western Europe and the United States, if and when they choose.

More immediately, control of the Horn of Africa would give Moscow the ability to destabilize those governments on the Arabian Peninsula which have proven themselves strongly anti-communist. Among them are some of the world's principal oil exporters.

Moscow can also turn its full attention south if it can ensure its position in the Horn of Africa. It takes no great stretch of the imagination to see that Rhodesia is a tempting target. Cuban leaders now boast that it is.

What are we doing about it? Apparently, our response to the Rhodesian settlement proposed by the moderate black leaders and Prime Minister Ian Smith is not to tell the Soviets—behind the scenes—to get lost or risk pressures elsewhere that they won't like. No, our response seems to be best summed up by our ambassador to the United Nations, who is unhappy with the moderate, democratic solution in Rhodesia because he's afraid, he says, it will bring on a massive Soviet arms buildup. What does he think we're having now? He seems to believe that the only Rhodesian plan we can afford to support is one to the liking of the two terrorist guerrilla leaders. But if they have their way, one or the other of them will become the sole power in Rhodesia, fronting of course for the Soviet Union. Unless we want to make the world safe for terrorist guerrillas, the only sensible course is for us to support the moderate solution in Rhodesia and quietly tell Moscow to keep its hands off—unless, of course, we are too weak to do that. Is that what Mr. Young is trying to tell us? I hope not, for a Marxist Rhodesia would lead to even more tempting targets for Moscow in Africa. Perhaps Djibouti, Sudan, Chad, the old Spanish Sahara (where guerrillas are already in operation).

And one other which will cost us dearly. Whatever we may think of South Africa's internal policies, control of its mineral riches and its strategic position are the Soviet Union's ultimate goal in Africa.

Unless the White House can bring itself to understand these realities, it is not too much to say that in a few years we may be faced with the prospect of a Soviet empire of proteges and dependencies stretching from Addis Ababa to Capetown. Those who now reject that possibility out of hand—and they seem to have the ear of the man in the Oval Office—have yet to explain Angola, Mozambique, the situation in the Horn of Africa, or the terrorists in Rhodesia. One thing is certain: Soviet successes will not breed caution in the Kremlin. Rather, the reverse.

Those in the Carter administration who are not even inclined to protest the recent Soviet moves assure us that, sooner or later, the Soviets will make serious mistakes and our doing nothing will hasten that day.

But to say, as they do, that all is well because the Soviets are creating their own Vietnam is nonsense. These Carter advisers seem to forget that the Soviets won in Vietnam and they intend to win again—this time in Africa. They learned the true lesson of the Vietnam war: certainty of purpose and ruthlessness of execution wins wars. Vietnam held no terror for the Soviets as it did for so many Americans. And adventures in Africa hold no terror for them either.

To say, as some in the administration do, that African nationalism will stop the Soviets is the weakest reed of all. The reason is simple: African nationalism, as such, does not exist. No African government has yet condemned the Russians, nor do the halls of the Organization of African Unity ring with anti-Soviet slogans—perhaps because those halls happen to be in Addis Ababa, the capital of Ethiopia.

The criticism by African states of the Soviets that the administration seems to be so desperately hoping for will not materialize. After all, there is in Africa, as around the world, a healthy respect for power and the determined use of power.

One veteran West European diplomat put the African situation in perspective recently. He was quoted as saying: "This situation is going to make the leaders of a lot of these small, weak nations stop and think. And what do they see on the American side? Apparent indecision attempts to talk, a reluctance to give weapons to friends"— and, he might have added, a "belief that there are nasty, immoral wars of imperialist aggression and nice clean wars of national liberation."

The administration's uncertainty of purpose isn't confined to the world's current hot spots. It is apparent even in our own hemisphere.

That White House tally sheet I mentioned listed its "accomplishments" in Latin America. It said, "The administration has developed a new global approach to Latin America...."

Well, what it has done from the beginning was to accept the notions fashionable in the most liberal circles that surrender of the Panama Canal and rapprochement with Cuba were the keys to successful relations with Latin America.

Nothing could have been further from the truth. Of Panama, I have already had a good deal to say. But let me say again, we have earned no respect or lasting affection in Latin America with these treaties.

Unfortunately, our policy toward Latin America has not only entailed friendship for one dictator who is a sworn enemy and for another who routinely suppresses human rights and may be involved in the worst sort of corruption—that policy has also entailed hostility toward our friends.

Let me cite just one example, Brazil. An ally in World War II (contributing a division which saw hard action in Europe), a friend through most of the '60s and now a great hope for contributing to the future industrial strength of the West, Brazil now finds itself turned on by us—with a vengeance. Whatever the motives, human rights or worries over nuclear proliferation, the ends did not justify the means. The result is that we have nearly lost a friend without achieving any of the administration's professed objectives.

It is time to try another approach—an approach based on reality and not the slogans and romantic notions of ideologues who just happen to have access to the Oval Office.

First, let us end this cycle of American indifference, followed by frenzied activity in Latin America (as it has been elsewhere). It leaves our southern neighbors bewildered and cynical. Instead, I propose a steadier course in which Latin America's growing importance is recognized not as an act of charity, but in our own self-interest. Latin America, with all its resources and vitality, should be encouraged to join not the Third World, much less the communists' Second World, but the First World—that community of stable, prosperous, and free nations of Western Europe, North America, and Japan.

Today, there is hope that much of Latin America might do so. First, many nations have learned the cost of socialist experimentation: Argentina under the Perons, Chile under Allende, Peru under Velasco, Mexico under Echeverria. All suffered economic catastrophe. Their successors learned the bitter truth that defying the laws of economics benefits no one and, in fact, hurts most the poor whose cause those earlier leaders so demagogically espoused.

Today, as a result of those experiments which went so badly out of control, more and more of our neighbors are turning to the free market as a model of development. Their acceptance of economic rationality should be neither ignored nor penalized, but actively encouraged.

At the same time, we must recognize that Latin America is once again leaving a period of strictly military rule and entering a more democratic phase. But in this case, the United States is doing too much pushing, rather than too little.

Unhappily, the change from military to civilian rule is not an easy one. Nor can it be rushed. If it is, we will only succeed in creating weak and vulnerable democratic governments that will soon be swept out of power by just another generation of military strongmen even more convinced of the defects of democracy.

Above all, we want a free and prosperous Latin America. And, to obtain that, we cannot continue to reward our self-declared enemies and then turn around and punish our friends.

That leads me again to Panama. The treaties that have occupied so much of our attention in recent months represent both the good instincts and the bad impulses of American diplomacy.

The bad, for reasons I have repeated on many occasions: the feeling that we are guilty of some sin for which we must now atone and our inability to say "no," not out of truculence, but because it was the proper thing to say to secure our interests and to reaffirm our greater responsibility, which is leadership of all that remains of the free world.

Yes, the treaties represent the good instincts of American diplomacy, too—a spirit of generosity and willingness to change with times. A good foreign policy must have both elements: the need to say "no" and the willingness to change, in just the right proportions. Unfortunately, accepting change because it seems fashionable to do so, with little real regard for the consequences, seems to dominate our foreign policy today.

Too many in positions of importance believe that through generosity and self-effacement we can avoid trouble, whether it's with Panama and the canal or the Soviet Union and SALT.

But, like it or not, trouble will not be avoided. The American people and their elected leaders will continue to be faced with hard choices and difficult moments, for resolve is continually being tested by those who envy us our prosperity and begrudge us our freedom.

America will remain great and act responsibly so long as it exercises power—wisely, and not in the bullying sense—but exercises it, nonetheless.

Leadership is a great burden. We grow weary of it at times. And the Carter administration, despite its own cheerful propaganda about accomplishments, reflects that weariness.

But if we are not to shoulder the burdens of leadership in the free world, then who will?

The alternatives are neither pleasant nor acceptable. Great nations which fail to meet their responsibilities are consigned to the dust bin of history. We grew from that small, weak republic which had as its assets spirit, optimism, faith in God, and an unshakeable belief that free men and women could govern themselves wisely. We became the leader of the free world, an example for all those who cherish freedom.

If we are to continue to be that example—if we are to preserve our own freedom—we must understand those who would dominate us and deal with them with determination.

We must shoulder our burden with our eyes fixed on the future, but recognizing the realities of today, not counting on mere hope or wishes. We must be willing to carry out our responsibility as the custodian of individual freedom. Then we will achieve our destiny to be as a shining city on a hill for all mankind to see.

Reagan Doctrine: From Principles to Polices

KT McFarland

America's Purpose in the World

When Governor Ronald Reagan spoke at CPAC in 1978, laying out his vision of America's purpose in the world, he was dismissed by critics as a genial old man whose season had passed. They overlooked his successful governorship of California, preferring instead to focus on his two failed presidential campaigns and stubborn ideological conservatism. The smart set snickered that he was a man out of tune with his times, better suited to the World War II movies he starred in than a man capable of leading America into the future.

Indeed, the late 1970s were perilous times in the United States. The American economy was still reeling from high oil prices and gasoline rationing. We had fought and lost a long and divisive war in Vietnam. We were in retreat all around the world and hunkered down at home. Meanwhile, the Soviet Union was in the midst of a massive military buildup and expanding its reach throughout Africa, the Middle East, and Latin America. Their economy was riding high with its energy exports. Prominent economists hailed

Soviet communism as superior to American capitalism. The Cold War was raging, and we were losing. We had lost faith in ourselves and doubted our destiny. It seemed that America was a nation in decline and that our star was fading. We were in a period of malaise which even President Jimmy Carter called our "crisis in confidence."

In spite of all that, Reagan's address to American conservatives in 1978 defied the popular despondency and offered a message of confidence and purpose. He chided President Carter, the Democrats, and even some Republicans for pursuing a foreign policy which sought to "appease the mighty out of a sense of fear" and "appease the weak out of a sense of guilt." He said they were "forever trapped in the tragic, but still fresh, memory of a lost war," claiming they had put America in a defensive crouch abroad, cowering before our powerful adversaries.

Reagan chided American leaders for foolishly believing we could avoid trouble with our adversaries "through generosity and self-effacement" and "preemptive concessions." His criticisms of President Carter and the apologists around him were blunt and to the point: the Soviet Union did not have benign intentions. They understood strength and they exploited weakness and indecision. We should have no "illusions about the intentions of those who are enemies of freedom," Reagan said.

He addressed the failures of the Vietnam War head-on but warned that many had drawn the wrong lessons from it. They said, "Never again," and urged that America should withdraw from the world, abdicating the mantle of leadership. For Reagan, "never again" meant something different—that we should never again ask Americans to fight and die in a war unless they are permitted to win.

When Reagan stood before the men and women at CPAC in 1978, he boldly rejected the conventional wisdom of the day that claimed America was in retreat. Instead he reminded us of our history, unique Constitution, and belief in liberty and freedom. He said, "Our fundamental aim in foreign policy must be to ensure our own survival and to protect those others who share our values." Our purpose in the world is to provide it with the living proof that we are "still the abiding alternative to tyranny." He said it was America's "destiny to be as a shining city on a hill for all mankind to see."

Ten years and two presidential terms later, Reagan had accomplished the seemingly impossible. He had turned the American economy around, rebuilt America's defenses, negotiated arms reduction agreements with the Soviet Union, and restored America's leadership role in the world. A few years later, the Iron Curtain came down, communism was discredited, the Soviet Union collapsed, and the United States won the Cold War without firing a shot. That genial old man so many dismissed and discounted a decade before launched one of the most prosperous and peaceful periods in American history.

When he left office in 1989, Reagan gave a farewell address that remains one of the most beautiful tributes to America's purpose in the world:

> I've spoken of the shining city all my political life, but I don't know if I ever quite communicated what I saw when I said it. But in my mind, it was a tall, proud city built on rocks stronger than oceans, wind-swept, God blessed, and teeming with people of all kinds living in harmony and peace—a city with free ports that hummed with commerce and creativity, and if there had to be city walls, the walls had doors, and the doors were open to anyone with the will and the heart to get here.
>
> That's how I saw it and see it still.

Reagan's speech to CPAC that year wasn't nearly so eloquent, inspirational, or memorable. Its significance lies elsewhere, in the lesson it teaches us all: that a leader of principle, conviction, and vision can, against all odds, change not just his nation, but the world.

KT McFarland is the former deputy national security advisor to President Donald Trump and served in the Nixon and Ford administrations.

Excerpts from CPAC

1979

If we do not now reaffirm our commitment to Taiwan's safety and security in an unmistakable declaration of intent, then what is to stop this administration from unilaterally dissolving all our security treaties, including even the NATO treaty? In the light of Mr. Carter's apparent claim that he has the power to unilaterally abrogate treaties, the wisdom of testing in the courts his attempt to break our Taiwan mutual defense treaty is very clear. We await the outcome of that court test.

Bear in mind that the issue here is not friendship with the people of the mainland of China, and it is not one of attempting to wrest from the office of the presidency what by law is its prerogative.

The issue is our policy toward Taiwan and the methods by which we discharge our responsibilities and keep our word. This is what troubles the American people and troubles our friends abroad. Have we become totally unreliable and capricious? Are we so completely disorganized, so bereft of strategic vision and the qualities of leadership, so lacking in common decency and morality, so motivated by the dictates of the moment that we can, in an instant and by the stroke of a pen, put 17 million people over the side and escape the consequences?

Along with millions of Americans—Republicans, Democrats, independents; liberals, moderates, conservatives; working men and women, small businessman and big businessmen; hawks, doves, and neutralists—I again call upon this administration to face up to the responsibilities which are America's to shoulder. I call for a detailed program of specific guarantees to our friends and allies on Taiwan; a long-range program with clear and unmistakable language; one which will earn and retain the support of the American people and which will help to restore the trust and confidence of the world in an America which once again conducts itself in accordance with its own high ideals.

Since this administration seems to have such difficulty in formulating specific programs, perhaps we can be of assistance by pointing to three principles which, at minimum, must be incorporated in a specific program.

First, a basis must be found for the continuation of government-to-government relations between the United States and Taiwan; unspecified "private" contacts are not adequate.

Second, legislation must be enacted which specifically provides for the future sale of defensive arms and material to Taiwan. For this reason alone, it is essential to maintain government-to-government relations. Weapons sales cannot be left to "private" arrangements.

Third, Congress must take legislative steps which provide a sound basis for the continuation of the fifty-nine other treaties and agreements which regulate our day-to-day business with Taiwan.

As for the 900 million people of the Chinese mainland—said to make up a quarter of the population of this globe—we can say to them we seek friendship, commerce, and other mutually acceptable goals with you. We hope that the bonds of common interest will grow, and we will continue to hope that your system of government will evolve to provide you with the means of making political choices which will result in your determining your own destiny.

We wish to live in peace with you, and we shall not interfere in your affairs if you do not intervene in ours. We can help you to modernize and update your economy, and we will do so, consistent with our national security objectives.

But, when it comes to those 17 million people on Taiwan, we emphatically state that so long as they wish to retain their independence in the world; so long as they declare their unwillingness to be either "liberated" by you or unilaterally "reunited" with you—then, so long will they also have the specific and clear support of the United States of America.

Reagan's Proposed Alliances in Asia

Gordon G. Chang

America as a Faithful Ally

R onald Reagan called for "a detail program of specific guarantees to our friends and allies on Taiwan" at the Conservative Political Action Conference in 1979. America, he
argued, should have "a long-range program with clear and unmistakable language; one which will earn and retain the support of the
American people and which will help to restore the trust and confidence of the world in an America which once again conducts itself
in accordance with its own high ideals."

Reagan was moved to speak about the island republic as he
sought to stop a dangerous drift in Washington policy. In the beginning of the 1970s, Richard Nixon had turned his back on Taiwan,
gone to Beijing, sat down with Mao, and began a long-term American embrace of Chinese communism. Jimmy Carter, at the end of
that decade, had switched diplomatic recognition from the Republic of China, the state with its capital in Taipei, to the People's
Republic of China, ruled from Beijing. Carter resisted a continuing
relationship with the island republic, then called "Free China."

Henry Kissinger, who helped craft Nixon's approach to Communist China, saw Taiwan as an obstacle. When Chinese Premier Zhou Enlai demanded the U.S. recognize Taiwan as "an inalienable part of Chinese territory" in July of 1971, Kissinger, then in Beijing, was obliging to his insistent host. "As a student of history, one's prediction would have to be that the political evolution is likely to be in the direction which Prime Minster Chou En-lai indicated to me," he said. "We will not stand in the way of basic evolution."[1]

Reagan was not going to allow "political evolution," or the circumlocutions that Kissinger was resorting to, to permit communism to gobble up a small society on the path to democratization. And as Arthur Waldron of the University of Pennsylvania told me, Reagan, unlike others around him, understood that Kissinger had announced "a blueprint for a house that could not be built."[2] Simply stated, Nixon's advisor could not build an enduring relationship with Beijing and at the same time maintain American credibility in the world and honor American values.

"Reagan's mind and sense of history were both so acute that he could see far ahead the serious problems the 'experts' were unreflexively creating, as well as do what he could to avert them," Waldron wrote. "Only now do we begin to grasp his statesmen's prescience that all around him lacked."[3]

President Reagan certainly did not lack for ideas as to what to do for Taiwan. On July 14, 1982, James Lilley, then chief of the American Institute in Taiwan, gave oral promises, later to become known as the Six Assurances, to Taiwan President Chiang Ching-kuo. Twelve

---

1   Kissinger and Zhou, memcon, 4:35-11:20 PM, July 9, 1971, Box 1033: China, Henry A. Kissinger Memcons July 1971, National Security Council Files, Nixon Materials (National Security Archives), https://nsarchive2.gwu.edu/NSAEBB/NSAEBB66/ch-34.pdf

2   Arthur Waldron, telephone interview by author, October 7, 2018.

3   Arthur Waldron, e-mail message to author, October 7, 2018.

days later, Lilley, America's representative to Taipei, met Chiang again and delivered a "non-paper" repeating the substance of the Six Assurances. Weeks later, the assurances were made public.

In the Six Assurances, the Reagan administration promised the United States would not recognize Beijing's sovereignty over Taiwan and would not establish a date for the end of arms sales to the island. Moreover, Washington pledged not to consult with China before deciding what weapons to sell to Taiwan.

During the spring, Alexander Haig—once Kissinger's deputy and then secretary of state—and Vice President George H. W. Bush had urged the administration to try and placate Chinese leaders by issuing promises on arms sales that had been in discussion for several months. The White House, even after Haig was let go, acceded and issued on August 17, 1982 what is now known as the Third Communique.

At the same time, Reagan, distrustful of Chinese assurances of peaceful intent, had a secret National Security Council memorandum issued. "The U.S. willingness to reduce its arms sales to Taiwan is conditioned absolutely upon the continued commitment of China to the peaceful solution of the Taiwan-PRC differences," the memo stated. "Both in quantitative and qualitative terms, Taiwan's defense capability relative to that of the PRC will be maintained."[4]

Subsequent American presidents have allowed the military balance across the Taiwan Strait to shift decisively toward Beijing, but the Six Assurances remain a bedrock of Washington's policy. Gerrit van der Wees, a leading Taiwan proponent in America, wrote to me recently: "President Reagan's Six Assurances of 1982—together with the Taiwan Relations Act of 1979—are still the two cornerstones of America's relations with Taiwan, as they provide for continued arms

---

4   Shirley A. Kan, "China/Taiwan: Evolution of the 'One China' Policy—Key Statements from Washington, Beijing, and Taipei," Congressional Research Service Report for Congress, September 7, https://fas.org/sgp/crs/row/RL30341.pdf

sales, so Taiwan can maintain its freedom, democracy, and sovereignty."[5]

Today, Taiwan's freedom, democracy, and sovereignty are under all-out assault by China's ambitious ruler, Xi Jinping, who, in October of 2013, said Beijing could not wait indefinitely to take over Taiwan.[6] As Reagan instinctively knew, the United States had to prevent that from occurring without the consent of Taiwan's people, who did not see themselves as "Chinese" or part of the People's Republic then, and feel the same way now.

There are two primary reasons for America to come to the assistance of Taiwan at this time. First, the island occupies the junction of the South China Sea and East China Sea. Taiwan, as Admiral Ernest King said, is "the cork in the bottle," keeping China's navy and air force confined to the country's peripheral areas. At a time of increasing Chinese territorial aggression, Taiwan's role in anchoring America's western defense perimeter is critical.

Second—and more importantly—the U.S. cannot allow a militant hardline state that has been attacking the concept of representative governance to actually swallow up a democracy, especially one as important as Taiwan. What was true in Reagan's time is also true now: defending Taiwan is, in a real sense, defending America.

Reagan, the defender of freedom, knew that. Reagan said, addressing China's belligerent leaders, "When it comes to those 17 million people on Taiwan, we emphatically state that so long as they wish to retain their independence in the world—so long as they declare their unwillingness to be either 'liberated' by you or unilaterally 'reunited' with you—then, so long will they also have the specific and clear support of the United States of America."

---

5   Gerrit van der Wees, e-mail message to author, October 3, 2018.

6   See "Xi Meets Taiwan Politician Ahead of APEC Gathering," Global Times (Beijing), October 6, 2013, http://www.globaltimes.cn/content/815725.shtml#.UlJ0GW0titU

"He should be living at this hour," Waldron told me, referring to Reagan. "His country has need of him."[7]

Gordon G. Chang is a columnist, member of the Board of the American Conservative Union Foundation, and the author of The Coming Collapse of China.

---

7   Arthur Waldron, e-mail message to author, October 2, 2018.

"Our Time is Now.
Our Moment Has
Arrived."

1981

Mr. Chairman and Congressman Mickey Edwards, thank you very much. My goodness, I can't realize how much time has gone by, because I remember when I first knew Mickey, he was just a clean-shaven boy. [Laughter] But thank you for inviting me here once again. And as Mickey told you, with the exception of those two years, it is true about how often I've been here. So, let me say now that I hope we'll be able to keep this tradition going forward and that you'll invite me again next year.

And in the rough days ahead—and I know there will be such days—I hope that you'll be like the mother of the young lad in camp when the camp director told her that he was going to have to discipline her son. And she said, "Well, don't be too hard on him. He's very sensitive. Slap the boy next to him, and that will scare Irving." [Laughter] But let us also, tonight, salute those with vision who labored to found this group—the American Conservative Union, the Young Americans for Freedom, *National Review*, and Human Events.

It's been said that anyone who seeks success or greatness should first forget about both and seek only the truth, and the rest will follow. Well, fellow truth-seekers, none of us here tonight—contemplating the seal on this podium and a balanced budget in 1984—can argue with that kind of logic. For whatever history does finally say about our cause, it must say: the conservative movement in twentieth-century America held fast through hard and difficult years to its vision of the truth. And history must also say that our victory, when it was achieved, was not so much a victory of politics as it was a victory of ideas; not so much a victory for any one man or party as it was a victory for a set of principles—principles that were protected and nourished by a few unselfish Americans through many grim and heartbreaking defeats.

Now, you are those Americans that I'm talking about. I wanted to be here not just to acknowledge your efforts on my behalf, not just to remark that last November's victory was singularly your victory, not just to mention that the new administration in Washington is a testimony to your perseverance and devotion to principle, but to say, simply, "Thank you," and to say those words not as a president, or even as a conservative; thank you, as an American. I say this knowing that there are many in this room whose talents might have entitled them to a life of affluence but who chose another career out of a higher sense of duty to country. And I know, too, that the story of their selflessness will never be written up in *Time* or *Newsweek* or go down in the history books.

You know, on an occasion like this it's a little hard not to reminisce, not to think back and just realize how far we've come. The Portuguese have a word for such recollection—"saudade"—a poetic term rich with the dreams of yesterday. And surely in our past there was many a dream that went a glimmering and many a field littered with broken lances.

Who can forget that July night in San Francisco when Barry Goldwater told us that we must set the tides running again in the cause of freedom, and he said, "Until our cause has won the day, inspired the world, and shown the way to a tomorrow worthy of all our yesteryears"? And had there not been a Barry Goldwater willing to take that lonely walk, we wouldn't be here talking of a celebration tonight.

But our memories are not just political ones. I like to think back about a small, artfully written magazine named *National Review,* founded in 1955 and ridiculed by the intellectual establishment because it published an editorial that said it would stand athwart the course of history yelling, "Stop!" And then there was a spritely written newsweekly coming out of Washington named *Human Events* that many said would never be taken seriously, but it would become later "must reading" not only for Capitol Hill insiders, but for all of those in public life.

How many of us were there who used to go home from meetings like this with no thought of giving up, but still find ourselves wondering in the dark of night whether this much-loved land might go the way of other great nations that lost a sense of mission and a passion for freedom?

There are so many people and institutions who come to mind for their role in the success we celebrate tonight. Intellectual leaders like Russell Kirk, Friedrich Hayek, Henry Hazlitt, Milton Friedman, James Burnham, Ludwig von Mises—they shaped so much of our thoughts.

It's especially hard to believe that it was only a decade ago, on a cold April day on a small hill in upstate New York, that another of these great thinkers, Frank Meyer, was buried. He'd made the awful journey that so many others had: he pulled himself from the clutches of the "God That Failed," and then in his writing fashioned a vigorous new synthesis of traditional and libertarian thought—a synthesis that is today recognized by many as modern conservatism.

It was Frank Meyer who reminded us that the robust individualism of the American experience was part of the deeper current of Western learning and culture. He pointed out that a respect for law, an appreciation for tradition, and regard for the social consensus that gives stability to our public and private institutions, these civilized ideas must still motivate us even as we seek a new economic prosperity based on reducing government interference in the marketplace.

Our goals complement each other. We're not cutting the budget simply for the sake of sounder financial management. This is only a first step toward returning power to the states and communities, only a first step toward reordering the relationship between citizen and government. We can make government again responsive to people not only by cutting its size and scope and thereby ensuring that its legitimate functions are performed efficiently and justly.

Because ours is a consistent philosophy of government, we can be very clear: we do not have a social agenda, separate economic agenda, and a separate foreign agenda. We have one agenda. Just as surely as we seek to put our financial house in order and rebuild our nation's defenses, so too we seek to protect the unborn, to end the manipulation of schoolchildren by utopian planners, and permit the acknowledgement of a Supreme Being in our classrooms just as we allow such acknowledgements in other public institutions.

Now, obviously we're not going to be able to accomplish all this at once. The American people are patient. I think they realize that the wrongs done over several decades cannot be corrected instantly. You know, I had the pleasure in appearing before a Senate committee once while I was still governor, and I was challenged because there was a

Republican president in the White House who'd been there for several months—why we hadn't then corrected everything that had been done. And the only way I could think to answer him is I told him about a ranch many years ago that Nancy and I acquired. It had a barn with eight stalls in it in which they had kept cattle, and we wanted to keep horses. And I was in there day after day with a pick and a shovel, lowering the level of those stalls, which had accumulated over the years. [Laughter] And I told this senator who'd asked that question that I discovered that you did not undo in weeks or months what it had taken some fifteen years to accumulate.

I also believe that we conservatives, if we mean to continue governing, must realize that it will not always be so easy to place the blame on the past for our national difficulties. You know, one day the great baseball manager Frankie Frisch sent a rookie out to play center field. The rookie promptly dropped the first fly ball that was hit to him. On the next play, he let a grounder go between his feet and then threw the ball to the wrong base. Frankie stormed out of the dugout, took his glove away from him and said, "I'll show you how to play this position." And the next batter slammed a line drive right over second base. Frankie came in on it, missed it completely, fell down when he tried to chase it, threw down his glove, and yelled at the rookie, "You've got center field so screwed up, nobody can play it." [Laughter]

The point is we must lead a nation, and that means more than criticizing the past. Indeed, as T. S. Eliot once said, "Only by acceptance of the past will you alter its meaning."

Now, during our political efforts, we were the subject of much indifference and often times intolerance, and that's why I hope our political victory will be remembered as a generous one and our time in power will be recalled for the tolerance we showed for those with whom we disagree.

But beyond this, beyond this we have to offer America and the world a larger vision. We must remove government's smothering hand from where it does harm; we must seek to revitalize the proper functions of government. But we do these things to set loose again the energy and the ingenuity of the American people. We do these things to reinvigorate those social and economic institutions which serve as a buffer and a bridge between the individual and the state—and which remain the real source of our progress as a people.

And we must hold out this exciting prospect of an orderly, compassionate, pluralistic society—an archipelago of prospering communities and divergent institutions—a place where a free and energetic people can work out their own destiny under God.

I know that some will think about the perilous world we live in and the dangerous decade before us and ask what practical effect this conservative vision can have today. When Prime Minister Thatcher was here recently, we both remarked on the sudden, overwhelming changes that had come recently to politics in both our countries.

At our last official function, I told the prime minister that everywhere we look in the world, the cult of the state is dying. And I held out hope that it wouldn't be long before those of our adversaries who preach the supremacy of the state were remembered only for their role in a sad, rather bizarre chapter in human history. The largest planned economy in the world has to buy food elsewhere or its people would starve.

We've heard in our century far too much of the sounds of anguish from those who live under totalitarian rule. We've seen too many monuments made not out of marble or stone, but out of barbed wire and terror. But from these terrible places have come survivors, witnesses to the triumph of the human spirit over the mystique of state power, prisoners whose spiritual values made them the rulers of their guards. With their survival, they brought us "the secret of the camps," a lesson for our time and for any age: evil is powerless if the good are unafraid.

That's why the Marxist vision of man without God must eventually be seen as an empty and a false faith—the second oldest in the world—first proclaimed in the Garden of Eden with whispered words of temptation: "Ye shall be as gods." The crisis of the Western world, Whittaker Chambers reminded us, exists to the degree in which it is indifferent to God. "The Western world does not know it," he said about our struggle, "but it already possesses the answer to this problem—but only provided that its faith in God and the freedom He enjoins is as great as communism's faith in man."

This is the real task before us: to reassert our commitment as a nation to a law higher than our own, to renew our spiritual strength. Only by building a wall of such spiritual resolve can we, as a free people, hope to protect our own heritage and make it someday the birthright of all men.

There is, in America, a greatness and a tremendous heritage of idealism which is a reservoir of strength and goodness. It is ours if we will but tap it. And, because of this—because that greatness is there—there is need in America today for a reaffirmation of that goodness and a reformation of our greatness.

The dialog and the deeds of the past few decades are not sufficient to the day in which we live. They cannot keep the promise of tomorrow. The encrusted bureaucracies and the engrained procedures which have developed of late respond neither to the minority or the majority. We've come to a turning point. We have a decision to make. Will we continue with yesterday's agenda and yesterday's failures, or will we reassert our ideals and our standards, will we reaffirm our faith, and renew our purpose? This is a time for choosing.

I made a speech by that title in 1964. I said, "We've been told increasingly that we must choose between left or right." But we're still using those terms—left or right. And I'll repeat what I said then in '64. "There is no left or right. There's only an up or down," up to the ultimate in individual freedom, man's age-old dream, the ultimate in individual freedom consistent with an orderly society—or down to the totalitarianism of the ant heap. And those today who, however good their intentions, tell us that we should trade freedom for security are on that downward path.

Those of us who call ourselves conservative have pointed out what's wrong with government policy for more than a quarter of a century. Now, we have an opportunity to make policy and to change our national direction. All of us in government—in the House, in the Senate, in the executive branch—and in private life can now stand together. We can stop the drain on the economy by the public sector. We can restore our national prosperity. We can replace the overregulated society with the creative society. We can appoint to the bench distinguished judges who understand the first responsibility of any legal system is to punish the guilty and protect the innocent. We can restore to their rightful place in our national consciousness the values of family, work, neighborhood, and religion. And, finally, we can see to it that the nations of the world clearly understand America's intentions and respect for resolve.

Now we have the opportunity—yes, and the necessity—to prove that the American promise is equal to the task of redressing our grievances and equal to the challenge of inventing a great tomorrow.

This reformation, this renaissance will not be achieved, or will it be served, by those who engage in political claptrap or false promises. It will not be achieved by those who set people against people, class against class, or institution against institution. So, while we celebrate our recent political victory, we must understand there's much work before us: to gain control again of government, to reward personal initiative and risk-taking in the marketplace, to revitalize our system of federalism, to strengthen the private institutions that make up the independent sector of our society, and to make our own spiritual affirmation in the face of those who would deny man has a place before God. Not easy tasks perhaps. But I would remind you as I did on January 20, they're not impossible, because, after all, we're Americans.

This year, we will celebrate a victory won two centuries ago at Yorktown, the victory of a small, fledgling nation over a mighty world power. How many people are aware—I've been told that a British band played the music at that surrender ceremony because we didn't have a band. [Laughter] And they played a tune that was very popular in England at the time. Its title was "The World Turned Upside Down." I'm sure it was far more appropriate than they realized at that moment. The heritage from that long difficult struggle is before our eyes today in this city, in the great halls of our government and in the monuments to the memory of our great men.

It is this heritage that evokes the images of a much-loved land, a land of struggling settlers and lonely immigrants, of giant cities and great frontiers, images of all that our country is and all that we want her to be. That's the America entrusted to us, to stand by, to protect, and yes, to lead her wisely.

Fellow citizens, fellow conservatives, our time is now. Our moment has arrived. We stand together shoulder to shoulder in the thickest of the fight. If we carry the day and turn the tide, we can hope that as long as men speak of freedom and those who have protected it, they will remember us, and they will say, "Here were the brave and here their place of honor."

Thank you.

The Eight-Year Agenda of the Reagan Administration

Michael Reagan

COMMENTARY ON

Our Time Is Now

My father was born over a century ago in a small second-floor apartment on the main thoroughfare of Tampico, Illinois. The town's population in 1911 was little more than eight hundred and my grandfather worked at the variety store across the street.

These were humble beginnings for a man who so profoundly altered the course of human history. What made such a rise possible were firm beliefs that he spent his life championing. The view that each human is an individual; a respect for law; the vigilant defense of traditions; an understanding that man's rights are not a gift from government, but from God; and that the state serves the citizen, never the other way around.

Societies guided and governed by these ideals flourish. The men and women living in them can fulfill their destinies as they please and climb as high as their efforts allow. We call this philosophy conservatism. When my father first addressed CPAC as president of the United States in the winter of 1981, it was the underpinning of a revolutionary political movement.

But what was radical in 1964 and 1980 is today widely accepted. To be sure, the indifference and intolerance toward the proponents of limited government my father mentioned at CPAC endures. But today it is found in cultural outposts far from where the vast majority of Americans work, pray, and raise their families.

When my father addressed CPAC in 1981, it was as a newly minted president; the great experiment of whether conservatism was a viable governing philosophy was just beginning. In the decades since, conservatives have regularly held majorities in the federal and state legislatures, they have repeatedly sat in governors' offices, and three of the five men who followed my father into the White House were conservatives. The two who were not paid only lip service to limited government. One even feigned admiration for my father.

Over time, the lonely walk begun by Barry Goldwater, the editors of *National Review*, and most definitely the American Conservative Union, became a march of millions.

Conservatism's victories were not limited to America's elections. When he spoke to CPAC in 1981, my father took aim at international adversaries; those "who preach the supremacy of the state," the evil empire propped up on the "Marxist vision of man without God." That night, he predicted it would be viewed by history as a "false faith," and history has proven him right. The Soviet Union is dead. Though far too many still suffer under it, communism has largely vanished from the earth.

Now, though, is not the time for a conservative valedictory.

Improbably, there are those in our country today who want to revive the very things that failed so spectacularly in the Eastern Bloc and elsewhere. They are not our enemies, as the Soviets were, but rather countrymen who have forgotten or ignored what my father described at CPAC as "the secret of the camps," the lessons passed on by those who escaped communism's clutches.

In the early twenty-first century, too many have once again been seduced by a Faustian bargain: if a people will only cede their power to a set of bright minds gathered in a far-off capital, life's challenges and hardships will dissipate. Of course, my father would have reminded us that this is a lopsided bargain; one that greatly favors the governors at the expense of the governed.

And yet, a political party is wondering, bizarrely, why what didn't work in Russia can't work in America. And make no mistake, these voices are growing louder and their pathways to power are becoming clearer. The men and women who demand government do evermore have even taken to proudly calling themselves socialists once again.

Our charge in the coming years will be to counter this burgeoning program through debate and at the ballot box. To do this, we must again rally around the principles that were at the heart of my father's labors that he laid out so eloquently during his first presidential address at CPAC: the dignity of the citizen, the danger of the state, and fidelity to laws higher than our own. The alternative, a population pitted against itself based on race and class, is a road to serfdom, despotism, destitution, and disaster.

This nation, as my father said that night, was "entrusted to us, to stand by, to protect, and yes, to lead her wisely." This trust continues. And so too must our defense of the very things it was built upon.

My father was an optimist. Naturally, so too am I. If we heed his wisdom and remember the things that make our movement, America's potential will remain limitless.

Michael Reagan is the president of the Reagan Legacy Foundation, a Newsmax Media contributor and President Ronald Reagan's eldest son.

The Agenda
Is Victory

1982

M r. Toastmaster, [Representative] Mickey Edwards, thank you very much for those generous words. Rverend clergy, ladies and gentlemen, we're delighted to be here at the ninth annual Conservative Political Action Conference.

Anyone looking at the exciting program you've scheduled over these four days, and the size of this gathering here tonight, can't help but be impressed with the energy and vitality of the conservative movement in America. We owe a special debt of gratitude to the staffs of American Conservative Union, Young Americans for Freedom, Human Events, and *National Review* for making this year's conference the most successful in the brief but impressive history of this event.

Now, you may remember that when I spoke to you last year, I said the election victory we enjoyed in November of 1980 was not a victory of politics so much as it was a victory of ideas; not a victory for any one man or party, but a victory for a set of principles, principles that had been protected and nourished during the years of grim and heartbreaking defeats by a few dedicated Americans. Well, you are those Americans, and I salute you.

I've also come here tonight to remind you of how much remains to be done, and to ask your help in turning into reality even more of our hopes for America and the world. The agenda for this conference is victory—victory in this year's crucial congressional, state, and local elections.

The media coverage that you've received this week, the attention paid to you by so many distinguished Americans in and out of government—conservative and not so conservative—are testimony to the sea change that you've already brought about in American politics. But, despite the glitter of nights like this and the excitement we all still feel at the thought of enacting reforms we were only able to talk about a few years ago, we should always remember that our strength still lies in our faith in the good sense of the American people. And that the climate in Washington is still opposed to those enduring values, those "permanent things" that we've always believed in.

But Washington's fascination with passing trends and one-day headlines can sometimes cause serious problems over in the West Wing of the White House—they cause them. There's the problem of leaks. Before we even announced the giveaway of surplus cheese, the warehouse mice had hired a lobbyist. [Laughter] And then a few weeks ago, those stories broke about the Kennedy tapes. And that caused something of a stir. Al Haig came in to brief me on his trip to Europe. I uncapped my pen, and he stopped talking. [Laughter] Up on the Hill, I understand they were saying, "You need eloquence in the State Dining Room, wit in the East Room, and sign language in the Oval Office." [Laughter] It got so bad that I found myself telling every visitor there were absolutely no tape recordings being made. And if they wanted a transcript of that remark, just mention it to the potted plant on their way out. [Laughter]

But Washington is a place of fads and one-week stories. It's also a company town, and the company's name is government—big government. Now, I have a sneaking suspicion that a few of you might have agreed when we decided not to ask Congress for higher taxes. And I hope you realize it's going to take more than 402 days to completely change what's been going on for forty years. I realized that the other day when I read a story about a private citizen in Louisiana who asked the government for help in developing his property, and he got back a letter that said, "We have observed that you have not traced the title prior to 1803. Before the final approval, it will be necessary that the title be traced previous to that year." Well, the citizen's answer was eloquent.

"Gentlemen," he wrote, "I am unaware that any educated man failed to know that Louisiana was purchased from France in 1803. The title of the land was acquired by France by the right of conquest from Spain. The land came in the possession of Spain in 1492 by the discovery by an Italian sailor, Christopher Columbus. The good Queen Isabella took the precaution of receiving the blessing of the Pope. ... The Pope is emissary of the Son of God, who made the world. Therefore, I believe that it is safe to assume that He also made that part of the United States called Louisiana. And I hope to hell you're satisfied." [Laughter]

Now, changing the habits of four decades is, as I say, going to take more than 402 days. But change will come if we conservatives are in this for the long haul—if we owe our first loyalty to the ideas and principles we discussed, debated, developed, and popularized over the years. Last year, I pointed to these principles as the real source of our strength as a political movement and mentioned some of the intellectual giants who fostered and developed them—men like Frank Meyer, who reminded us that the robust individualism of America was part of deeper currents in Western civilization, currents that dictated respect for the law and the careful preservation of our political traditions.

Only a short time ago, conservatives filled this very room for a testimonial dinner to a great conservative intellect and scholar, author of *The Conservative Mind*, Russell Kirk. In a recent speech, Dr. Kirk has offered some political advice for the upcoming elections. He said now, more than ever, we must seek out the "gift of audacity." We must not become too comfortable with our new-found status in Washington. "When the walls of order are breached, the vigorous conservative must exclaim: 'Arm me, audacity, from head to foot.'" It was Napoleon, master of the huge battalions, who once said: "It is imagination that rules the human races," and Disraeli who mentioned that "success is the child of audacity."

We must approach the upcoming elections with a forthright and direct message for the American people. We must remind them of the economic catastrophe that we faced on January 20, 1981: millions out of work, inflation in double digits for two years in a row, interest rates hovering at twenty-one and a half percent, productivity and the rate of growth in the gross national product down for the third year in a row, the money supply increasing by twelve percent—and all this due to one overriding cause: government was too big and had spent too much money.

Federal spending, in the last decade, went up more than three hundred percent. In 1980 alone, it increased by seventeen percent. Almost three-quarters of the federal budget was routinely referred to as "uncontrollable," largely due to increases in programs like food stamps, which in fifteen years had increased by 16,000 percent, or Medicare and Medicaid—up by more than five hundred percent in just ten years. Our national debt was approaching one trillion dollars, and we were paying nearly $100 billion a year in interest on that debt—more than enough money to run the federal government only twenty years ago.

In an effort to keep pace, taxes had increased by 220 percent in just ten years, and we were looking at a tax increase from 1980 to 1984, already passed before we got here, of more than three hundred billion dollars. Unless we stop the spending juggernaut and reverse the trend toward even higher taxes, government by 1984 would be taking nearly one-quarter of the gross national product. Inflation and interest rates, according to several studies, would be heading toward twenty-five percent—levels that would stifle enterprise and initiative and plunge the nation into even deeper economic crisis.

At this point last year, much of the smart money in Washington was betting, as it is today, on the failure of our proposals for restoring the economy, that we could never assemble the votes we needed to get our program for economic recovery through the Congress. But assemble the votes we did. For the first time in nearly twenty-five years, we slowed the spending juggernaut and got the taxpayers out from under the federal steamroller. We cut the rate of growth in federal spending almost in half. We lowered inflation to a single-digit rate, and it's still going down. It was 8.9 percent for all of 1981, but our January figure, at an annualized rate, is only three and a half percent.

When they talk of what should be done for the poor, well, one thing alone, by reducing inflation, we increased the purchasing power of poor families by more than $250. We cut taxes for business and individuals and indexed to inflation. This last step ended once and for all that hidden profit on inflation that had made the federal bureaucracy America's largest growth industry.

We've moved against waste and fraud with a task force including our inspectors general, who have already found thousands of people who've been dead for as long as seven years still receiving benefit checks from the government. We've concentrated on criminal prosecutions and we've cut back in other areas like the multitude of films, pamphlets, and public relations experts, or, as we sometimes call them, the federal flood of flicks and flacks and foldouts.

We're cutting the size of the federal payroll by 75,000 over the next few years and are fighting to dismantle the Department of Energy and the Department of Education—agencies whose policies have frequently been exactly the opposite of what we need for real energy growth and sound education for our children.

Even now, less than five months after our program took full effect, we've seen the first signs of recovery. In January, leading economic indicators like housing permits showed an upturn. By 1983, we will begin bringing down the percentage of the gross national product consumed by both the federal deficit and by federal spending and taxes.

Our situation now is in some ways similar to that which confronted the United States and other Western nations shortly after World War II. Many economists then were predicting a return to depression once the stimulus of wartime spending was ended. But people were weary of wartime government controls, and here and in other nations like West Germany, those controls were eliminated against the advice of some experts. At first, there was a period of hardship—higher unemployment and declining growth. In fact, in 1946, our gross national product dropped fifteen percent, but by 1947, the next year, it was holding steady and in 1948, increased by four percent. Unemployment began a steady decline. And in 1949, consumer prices were decreasing. A lot of the experts underestimated the economic growth that occurs once government stops meddling and the people take over. Well, they were wrong then, and they're wrong now.

The job of this administration and of the Congress is to move forward with additional cuts in the growth of federal spending and thereby ensure America's economic recovery. We have proposed budget cuts for 1983, and our proposals have met with cries of anguish.

And those who utter the cries are equally anguished because there will be a budget deficit. They're a little like a dog sitting on a sharp rock howling with pain, when all he has to do is get up and move.

On the spending cuts now before the Congress and those tax reductions we've already passed for the American people, let me state, we're standing by our program. We will not turn back or sound retreat.

You know, if I could just interject here, some of those people who say we must change direction when we've only been on this new direction for five months—and it's only the first limited phase of the whole program—it was described pretty well by Mickey Edwards, sitting right here, while we were having dinner. He said, "If you were sliding downhill on a snowy hill, and you know there's a cliff down there ahead of you at the bottom and suddenly there's a road that turns off to the right," he said, "you don't know where that road to the right goes, but," he says, "you take it." We know where that other one goes.

In the discussion of federal spending, the time has come to put to rest the sob sister attempts to portray our desire to get government spending under control as a hard-hearted attack on the poor people of America. In the first place, even with the economies that we've proposed, spending for entitlements—benefits paid directly to individuals—will actually increase by one-third over the next five years. And in 1983, non-defense items will amount to more than seventy percent of total spending.

As Dave Stockman pointed out the other day, we're still subsidizing 95 million meals a day, providing $70 billion in health care to the elderly and poor—some 47 million people. Some 10 million or more are living in subsidized housing. And we're still providing scholarships for a million and a half students. Only here in this city of Oz would a budget this big and this generous be characterized as a miserly attack on the poor.

Now, where do some of these attacks originate? They're coming from the very people whose past policies, all done in the name of compassion, brought us the current recession. Their policies drove up inflation and interest rates, and their policies stifled incentive, creativity, and halted the movement of the poor up the economic ladder. Some of their criticism is perfectly sincere. But let's also understand that some of their criticism comes from those who have a vested interest in a permanent welfare constituency and in government programs that reinforce the dependency of our people.

Well, I would suggest that no one should have a vested interest in poverty or dependency; that these tragedies must never be looked at as a source of votes for politicians or paychecks for bureaucrats. They are blights on our society that we must work to eliminate, not institutionalize.

Now, there are those who will always require help from the rest of us on a permanent basis, and we'll provide that help. To those with temporary need, we should have programs that are aimed at making them self-sufficient as soon as possible. How can limited government and fiscal restraint be equated with lack of compassion for the poor? How can a tax break that puts a little more money in the weekly paychecks of working people be seen as an attack on the needy?

Since when do we in America believe that our society is made up of two diametrically opposed classes—one rich, one poor—both in a permanent state of conflict and neither able to get ahead except at the expense of the other? Since when do we in America accept this alien and discredited theory of social and class warfare? Since when do we in America endorse the politics of envy and division?

When we reformed the welfare system in California and got the cheaters and the undeserving off the welfare rolls, instead of hurting the poor, we were able to increase their benefits by more than forty percent. By reducing the cost of government, we can continue bringing down inflation, the cruelest of all economic exploitations of the poor and the elderly. And by getting the economy moving again, we can create a vastly expanded job market that will offer the poor a way out of permanent dependency.

One man who held this office, a president vastly underrated by history, Calvin Coolidge, pointed out that a nation that is united in its belief in the work ethic and its desire for commercial success and economic progress is usually a healthy nation—a nation where it is easier to pursue the higher things in life like the development of science, the cultivation of the arts, the exploration of the great truths of religion, and higher learning.

In arguing for economy in government, President Coolidge spoke of the burden of excessive government. He said: "I favor a policy of economy, not because I wish to save money, but because I wish to save people. The men and women of this country who toil are the ones who bear the cost of the government. Every dollar that we save means that their life will be so much the more abundant. Economy is idealism in its most practical form." And this is the message we conservatives can bring to the American people about our economic program. Higher productivity, a larger gross national product, a healthy Dow Jones average—they are our goals and are worthy ones.

But our real concerns are not statistical goals or material gain. We want to expand personal freedom, to renew the American dream for every American. We seek to restore opportunity and reward, to value again personal achievement and individual excellence. We seek to rely on the ingenuity and energy of the American people to better their own lives and those of millions of others around the world.

We can be proud of the fact that a conservative administration has pursued these goals by confronting the nation's economic problems head-on. At the same time, we dealt with one other less publicized but equally grave problem: the serious state of disrepair in our national defenses.

The last Democratic administration had increased real defense spending at a rate of 3.3 percent a year. You know how much inflation was, so they were actually losing ground. By 1980, we had fighter planes that couldn't fly, navy ships that couldn't leave port, a rapid deployment force that was neither rapid nor deployable and not much of a force.

The protection of this nation's security is the most solemn duty of any president, and that's why I've asked for substantial increases in our defense budget—substantial, but not excessive.

In 1962, President Kennedy's defense budget amounted to forty-four percent of the entire budget. Ours is only twenty-nine percent. In 1962, President Kennedy's request for military spending was 8.6 percent of the gross national product. Ours is only 6.3 percent. The Soviet Union outspends us on defense by fifty percent, an amount equal to fifteen percent of their gross national product. During the campaign, I was asked any number of times: if I were faced with a choice of balancing the budget or restoring our national defenses, what would I do? Every time I said, "Restore our defenses." And every time I was applauded.

So, let me be very clear. We will press for further cuts in federal spending. We will protect the tax reductions already passed. We will spend on defense what is necessary for our national security. I have no intention of leading the Republican Party into next fall's election on a platform of higher taxes and cut-rate defense. If our opponents want to go to the American people next fall and say, "We're the party that tried to cut spending, we're the party that tried to take away your tax cuts, we're the party that wanted a bargain-basement military and held a fire sale on national security," let's give them all the running room they want.

There are other matters on the political agenda for this coming year, matters I know that you've been discussing during the course of this conference. I hope one of them will be our attempt to give government back to the people. One hundred and thirty-two federal grants-in-aid in 1960 have grown to over five hundred in 1981. Our federalism proposal would return the bulk of these programs to state and local governments, where they can be made more responsive to the people.

We're deeply committed to this program, because it has its roots in deep conservative principles. We've talked a long time about revitalizing our system of federalism. Now, with a single, bold stroke, we can restore the vigor and health of our state and local governments. This proposal lies at the heart of our legislative agenda for the next year, and we'll need your active support in getting it passed.

There are other issues before us. This administration is unalterably opposed to the forced busing of school children, just as we also support constitutional protection for the right of prayer in our schools. And there is the matter of abortion. We must with calmness and resolve help the vast majority of our fellow Americans understand that the more than one and a half a million abortions performed in America in 1980 amount to a great moral evil, an assault on the sacredness of human life.

And, finally, there's the problem of crime—a problem whose gravity cannot be underestimated. This administration has moved in its appointments to the federal bench and in its legislative proposals for bail and parole reform to assist in the battle against the lawless. But we must always remember that our legal system does not need reform so much as it needs transformation. And this cannot occur at just the federal level. It can really occur only when a society as a whole acknowledges principles that lie at the heart of modern conservatism. Right and wrong matters, individuals are responsible for their actions. Society has a right to be protected from those who prey on the innocent.

This, then, is the political agenda before us. Perhaps more than any group, your grassroots leadership, your candidate recruitment and training programs, your long years of hard work and dedication have brought us to this point and made this agenda possible.

We live today in a time of climactic struggle for the human spirit, a time that will tell whether the great civilized ideas of individual liberty, representative government, and the rule of law under God will perish or endure.

Whittaker Chambers, who sought idealism in communism and found only disillusionment, wrote very movingly of his moment of awakening. It was at breakfast, and he was looking at the delicate ear of his tiny baby daughter, and he said that, suddenly, looking at that, he knew that couldn't just be an accident of nature. He said, while he didn't realize it at the time, he knows now that in that moment, God had touched his forehead with His finger.

And later he wrote: "For in this century, within the next decades, will be decided for generations whether all mankind is to become communist, whether the whole world is to become free, or whether in the struggle, civilization as we know it is to be completely destroyed or completely changed. It is our fate to live upon that turning point in history." We've already come a long way together. Thank you for all that you've done for me, for the common values we cherish. Join me in a new effort, a new crusade.

Nostalgia has its time and place. Coming here tonight has been a sentimental journey for me, as I'm sure it has been for many of you. But nostalgia isn't enough. The challenge is now. It's time we stopped looking backward at how we got here.

We must ask ourselves tonight how we can forge and wield a popular majority from one end of this country to the other, a majority united on basic, positive goals with a platform broad enough and deep enough to endure long into the future, far beyond the lifespan of any single issue or personality.

We must reach out and appeal to the patriotic and fundamental ideals of average Americans who do not consider themselves "movement" people, but who respond to the same American ideals that we do. I'm not talking about some vague notion of an abstract, amorphous American mainstream. I'm talking about "Main Street" Americans in their millions. They come in all sizes, shapes, and colors—blue-collar workers, blacks, Hispanics, shopkeepers, scholars, service people, housewives, and professional men and women. They are the backbone of America, and we can't move America without moving their hearts and minds as well.

Fellow Americans, our duty is before us tonight. Let us go forward, determined to serve selflessly a vision of man with God, government for people, and humanity at peace. For it is now our task to tend and preserve, through the darkest and coldest nights, that "sacred fire of liberty" that President Washington spoke of two centuries ago, a fire that tonight remains a beacon to all the oppressed of the world, shining forth from this kindly, pleasant, greening land we call America.

God bless you and thank you.

Conservatives Press Forward

Wayne LaPierre

The Agenda Is Victory

H e wasn't called the "Great Communicator" for nothing. Yet for all his skillful oratory, the masterfulness of President Ronald Reagan came from the personal nature of the man himself and his natural connection to the hearts of the American public.

Many people may have forgotten (if they are old enough to remember at all) the historic breakthrough of hope, optimism, and national pride that President Reagan rekindled. His 1982 speech at the Conservative Political Action Conference was one in a long line of examples of the case he made for an optimistic future for the American people. So often, President Reagan expressed his hope for the country to the good hearts of Americans; hope to protect their values and freedoms that so many political and media elites had seemed to abandon.

That was always Reagan. He loved Americans and the freedoms and principles that have always made our nation the greatest in the world, and was never shy about cutting through the bureaucratic fog of the elites in Washington, D.C. to stand and fight for those values.

His love of our constitutional freedom led the National Rifle Association (NRA), for the first time in its history, to issue a Presidential campaign endorsement and mobilize to help get him elected. As an NRA Honorary Life Member, the president addressed the NRA convention in 1983, saying, "It does my spirit good to be with people who never lose faith in America, who never stop believing in her future, and who never back down one inch from defending the constitutional freedoms that are every American's birthright."

That was Ronald Reagan. Optimistic, hopeful, and always believing in the American spirit.

In 1982, the president slammed Washington, D.C. as a big government "company town" of one-week news stories and political fads. He challenged the CPAC audience to "always remember that our strength still lies in our faith in the good sense of the American people."

Throughout the speech—whether discussing his economic plan, federal spending, criminal justice reform, or national defense—Reagan addressed the issues from the clear prism of expanding individual freedom and renewing the American dream of opportunity for every citizen.

The president, even back in 1982, spoke to the cultural divisions promoted by the political and media elites. "Since when do we in America endorse the politics of envy and division," he asked, while reminding us that we are all Americans.

"I'm talking about 'Main Street' Americans in their millions," he said. "They come in all sizes, shapes, and colors—blue-collar workers, blacks, Hispanics, shopkeepers, scholars, servicepeople, housewives, and professional men and women. They are the backbone of America, and we can't move America without moving their hearts and minds as well."

In his speech, President Reagan captured this truth: that all our freedoms and values are interconnected whole cloth, as a fabric of the spirit and character of America. This vibrant tapestry of values we share is too often at risk in today's divisive and troubling times.

The president strikes at the glorious vein of the American spirit of individualism; the one that led our Founders to break from the tyranny of King George to forge a new nation—the first country in the world founded not on a race, religion, or royalty, but on a set of God-given principles we call "inalienable rights."

Those principles remain as relevant today as they were when America was founded and as critical as when Ronald Reagan led our nation. Through his soaring and inspirational words, President Reagan captured our imagination of America as a "greening land" of hope for the freedom that still yearns in the hearts and souls of us all.

Ronald Reagan was one of America's good guys. That is why he connected so well to men and women all over this country, and why, for so many Americans, he continues to stand as a personal beacon of shining freedom.

The president also reminds us that sentimentality and fond reflections on the past do not suffice to defend our democracy. "Nostalgia isn't enough," Reagan said. "The challenge is now."

His challenge now rests on our shoulders, for in his own words, "We live today in a time of climactic struggle for the human spirit, a time that will tell whether the great civilized ideas of individual liberty, representative government, and the rule of law under God will perish or endure."

His words could not be more prescient today, and the hopeful freedoms he fought for then could not be in more dire need of our defense than now.

Wayne LaPierre is CEO and executive vice president of the National Rifle Association.

We Will Not Be
Turned Back

1983

L adies and gentlemen, Mr. Chairman, [Representative Mickey
Edwards, ACU Chairman], reverend clergy, I thank you very
much for those very kind words, and I thank you all for
certainly a most hearty and warm welcome.

I'm grateful to the American Conservative Union, Young Americans for Freedom, *National Review*, and Human Events for organizing this third annual memorial service for the Democratic
platform of 1980. Someone asked me why I wanted to make it three
in a row. Well, you know how the Irish love wakes. [Laughter]

But I'm delighted to be back here with you, at your tenth annual
conference. In my last two addresses, I've talked about our common
perceptions and goals, and I thought I might report to you here
tonight on where we stand in achieving those goals—a sort of
"State of the Reagan Report," if you will.

Now, I'm the first to acknowledge that there's a good deal left
unfinished on the conservative agenda. Our cleanup crew will need
more than two years to deal with the mess left by others for over half

a century. But I'm not disheartened. In fact, my attitude about that unfinished agenda isn't very different from that expressed in an anecdote about one of my favorite presidents, Calvin Coolidge. [Laughter]

Some of you may know that after Cal Coolidge was introduced to the sport of fishing by his Secret Service detail, it got to be quite a passion with him, if you can use that word about "Silent Cal." Anyway, he was once asked by reporters how many fish were in one of his favorite angling places, the River Brule. And Coolidge said the waters were estimated to carry 45,000 trout. And then he said: "I haven't caught them all yet, but I sure have intimidated them."

Well, it's true we haven't brought about every change important to the conscience of a conservative, but we conservatives can take a great deal of honest pride in what we have achieved. In a few minutes, I want to talk about just how far we've come and what we need to do to win further victories. But right now, I think a word or two on strategy is in order. You may remember that in the past, I mentioned that it was not our task as conservatives to just point out the mistakes made over all the decades of liberal government, not just to form an able opposition, but to govern, to lead a nation. And I noted this would make new demands upon our movement, upon all of us.

For the first time in half a century, we've developed a whole new cadre of young conservatives in government. We've shown that conservatives can do more than criticize; we've shown that we can govern and move our legislation through the Congress.

Now, I know there's concern over attempts to roll back some of the gains that we've made. And it seems to me that here we ought to give some thought to strategy—to making sure that we stop and think before we act. For example, some of our critics have been saying recently that they want to take back the people's third-year tax cut and abolish tax indexing. And some others, including members of my staff, wanted immediately to open up a verbal barrage against them.

Well, I hope you know that sometimes it's better if a president doesn't say exactly what's on his mind. There's an old story about a farmer and a lawyer that illustrates my point.

It seems that these two got into a pretty bad collision, a traffic accident. They both got out of their cars. The farmer took one look at the lawyer, and walked back to his car, got a package, brought it back. There was a bottle inside, and he said, "Here, you look pretty shook up. I think you ought to take a nip of this, it'll steady your nerves." Well, the lawyer did. And the farmer said, "You still look a bit pale. How about another?" And the lawyer took another swallow. And under the urging of the farmer, he took another and another and another. And then, finally, he said he was feeling pretty good and asked the farmer if he didn't think that he ought to have a little nip, too. And the farmer said, "Not me, I'm waiting for the state trooper."

I wonder if we can't learn something from that farmer. If our liberal friends really want to head into the next election under the banner of taking away from the American people their first real tax cut in nearly twenty years; if, after peering into their heart of hearts, they feel they must tell the American people that over the next six years they want to reduce the income of the average family by three thousand dollars; and if they want to voice these deeply held convictions in an election year—well, fellow conservatives, who are we to stifle the voices of conscience?

Now, in talking about our legislative agenda, I know that some of you have been disturbed by the notion of standby tax increases in the so-called "out years." Well, I wasn't wild about the idea myself. But the economy is getting better, and I believe these improvements are only the beginning. And with some luck, and if the American people respond with the kind of energy and initiative they've always shown in the past, well, maybe it's time we started thinking about some standby tax cuts, too.

But you know, with regard to the economy, I wonder if our political adversaries haven't once again proved that they're our best allies. They spent the last sixteen months or so placing all the responsibility for the state of the economy on our shoulders. And with some help from the media, it's been a pretty impressive campaign. They've created quite an image—we're responsible for the economy.

Well, I assume that we're responsible then for inflation which, after back-to-back years in double digits before we got here, has now been reduced to 3.9 percent in 1982. And for the last three months of the year, it ran at only 1.1 percent. In 1982, real wages increased for the first time in three years. Interest rates, as you've already been told, have dropped dramatically, with the prime rate shrinking by nearly fifty percent. And in December, the index of leading indicators was a full 6.3 percent above last March's low point and has risen in eight of the last nine months. Last month, housing starts were up ninety-five percent and building permits eighty-eight percent over the last year at this time. New home sales are up to by fifty-four percent since April, and inventories of unsold homes are at the lowest levels in more than a decade. Auto production this quarter is scheduled to increase by twenty-two percent, and General Motors alone is putting 21,400 of their workers back on the jobs. Last month's sharp decline in the unemployment rate was the most heartening sign of all. It would have taken a five billion dollar jobs bill to reduce unemployment by the same amount—and it didn't cost us anything.

It's time to admit our guilt, time we admitted that our liberal critics have been right all the time. And they should go right on telling the American people that the state of economy is precisely the fault of that wicked creature, Kemp-Roth and its havoc-wreaking twin, Reaganomics.

Let's confess, let's admit that we've turned the corner on the economy. And we're especially proud of one thing: when we hit heavy weather, we didn't panic, we didn't go for fast bromides and quick fixes, the huge tax increases or wage and price controls recommended by so many. And our stubbornness, if you want to call it that, will quite literally pay off for every American in the years ahead.

So, let me pledge to you tonight: carefully, we have set out on the road to recovery. We will not be deterred. We will not be turned back. I reject the policies of the past, the policies of tax and tax, spend and spend, elect and elect. The lesson of these failed policies is clear; I've said this before: you can't drink yourself sober or spend yourself rich, and you can't prime the pump without pumping the prime—as somebody did, like to twenty-one and a half percent in 1980.

And a word is in order here on the most historic of all the legislative reforms we've achieved in the last two years—that of tax indexing. You can understand the terror that strikes in the heart of those whose principal constituency is big government. Bracket creep is government's hidden incentive to inflate the currency and bring on inflation, and indexing will end that. It will end those huge, hidden subsidies for bigger and bigger government. In the future, if we get indexing planted firmly as a law of the land, the advocates of big government who want money, more money for their social spending, their social engineering schemes, will have to go to the people and say right out loud, "We want more money from your weekly paycheck, so we're raising your taxes." Do that instead of sneaking it out by way of inflation, which they have helped bring on.

So, all the professional Washingtonians, from bureaucrats to lobbyists to the special interest groups, are frightened—plain scared—and they're working overtime to take this one back. Well, I think I speak for all conservatives when I say tax indexing is non-negotiable. It's a fight we'll take to the people, and we'll win.

But I think you can see how even this debate shows things are changing for the better. It highlights the essential differences between two philosophies now contending for power in American political life. One is the philosophy of the past—a philosophy that has as its constituents an ill-assorted mix of elitists and special interest groups who see government as the principal vehicle of social change, who believe that the only thing we have to fear is the people, who must be watched and regulated and superintended from Washington.

On the other hand, our philosophy is at the heart of the new political consensus that emerged in America at the beginning of this decade, one that I believe all—well, I believe it will dominate American politics for many decades. The economic disasters brought about by too much government were the catalysts for this consensus. During the '70s, the American people began to see misdirected, overgrown government as the source of many of our social problems—not the solution.

This new consensus has a view of government that's essentially that of our Founding Fathers—that government is the servant, not the master; that it was meant to maintain order, to protect our nation's safety, but otherwise, in the words of that noted political philosopher, schnozzle Jimmy Durante: "Don't put no constrictions on da people. Leave 'em da heck alone."

The overriding goal during the past two years has been to give the government back to the American people, to make it responsive again to their wishes and desires, to do more than bring about a healthy economy or a growing gross national product. We've truly brought about a quiet revolution in American government.

For too many years, bureaucratic self-interest and political maneuvering held sway over efficiency and honesty in government. Federal dollars were treated as the property of bureaucrats, not taxpayers. Those in the federal establishment who pointed to the misuse of those dollars were looked upon as malcontents or troublemakers.

Well, this administration has broken with what was a kind of a buddy system. There have been dramatic turnabouts in some of the more scandal-ridden and wasteful federal agencies and programs. Only a few years ago, the General Service Administration was racked by indictments and report after report of inefficiency and waste. Today at GSA, Jerry Carmen has not only put the whistleblowers back in charge, he's promoted them and given them new responsibilities. Just listen to this little set of figures. Today, General Service Administration work-in-progress time is down from thirty days to seven, even while the agency has sustained budget cuts of twenty percent, office space reductions of twenty percent, and the attrition of seven thousand employees.

At the Government Printing Office, under Dan Sawyer, losses of millions of dollars have suddenly been ended as the workforce was cut through attrition and a hiring freeze, and overtime pay was cut by six million dollars in one year alone. The government publication program, which ran a cumulative loss of $20 million over a three-year period, registered a $3.9 million profit, and the GPO as a whole has experienced a profit of $4.1 million last year.

It is said by some that this administration has turned a blind eye to waste and fraud at the Pentagon while overzealously concentrating on the social programs. Well, at the Pentagon, under Cap Weinberger's leadership and our superb service secretaries, Jack Marsh, John Lehman, and Verne Orr, we have identified more than a billion dollars in savings on waste and fraud, and, over the next seven years, multiyear procurement and other acquisition initiatives will save us almost $30 billion.

Now, these are only three examples of what we're attempting to do to make government more efficient. The list goes on. We have wielded our inspectors general as a strike force accounting for nearly $17 billion in savings in eighteen months. With Peter Grace's help, we've called on top management executives and experts from the private sector to suggest modern management techniques for every aspect of government operations. And with an exciting new project called Reform 88, we're going to streamline and reorganize the processes that control the money, information, personnel, and property of the federal bureaucracy—the maze through which nearly two trillion dollars passes each year and which includes 350 different payroll systems and 1,750 personnel offices.

There is more, much more—from cutting down wasteful travel practices to reducing paperwork, from aggressively pursuing the $40 billion in bad debts owed the federal government to reducing publication of more than seventy million copies of wasteful or unnecessary government publications.

But, you know, making government responsive again to the people involves more than eliminating waste and fraud and inefficiency. During the decades when government was intruding into areas where it's neither competent nor needed, it was also ignoring its legitimate and constitutional duties such as preserving the domestic peace and providing for the common defense.

I'll talk about that in a moment. I know you've already heard about that today, some of you. But on the matter of domestic order, a few things need to be said. First of all, it is abundantly clear that much of our crime problem was provoked by a social philosophy that saw man as primarily a creature of his material environment. The same liberal philosophy that saw an era of prosperity and virtue ushered in by changing man's environment through massive federal spending programs also viewed criminals as the unfortunate products of poor socioeconomic conditions or an underprivileged upbringing. Society, not the individual, they said, was at fault for criminal wrongdoing. We are to blame. Now, we conservatives have been warning about the crime problem for many years, about that permissive social philosophy that did so much to foster it, about a legal system that seemed to specialize in letting hardened criminals go free. And now, we have the means and the power to do something. Let's get to work.

Drug pusher after drug pusher, mobster after mobster has escaped justice by taking advantage of our flawed bail and parole system. Criminals who have committed atrocious acts have cynically utilized the technicalities of the exclusionary rule, a miscarriage of justice unique to our legal system. Indeed, one National Institute of Justice study showed that of those arrested for drug felonies in Los Angeles County in 1981, thirty-two percent were back out on the streets because of perceived problems with the exclusionary rule.

Now, the exclusionary rule—that isn't a law that was passed by Congress or a state legislature, it's what is called case law, the result of judicial decisions. If a law enforcement officer obtains evidence as the result of a violation of the laws regarding search and seizure, that evidence cannot be introduced in a trial even if it proves the guilt of the accused. Now, this is hardly punishment of the officer for his violation of legal procedures, and its only effect, in many cases, is to free someone patently guilty of a crime.

I don't know, maybe I've told you this before, but I have to give you a glaring example of what I've taken too much time to explain here. [In] San Bernardino, California, several years ago, two narcotics agents, based on the evidence they had, obtained a legal warrant to search the home of a man and woman suspected of peddling heroin. They searched the home. They didn't find anything. But as they were leaving, just on a hunch, they turned back to the baby in the crib and took down the diapers, and there was the stash of heroin. The evidence was thrown out of court and the couple went free because the baby hadn't given permission for the violation of its constitutional rights.

Well, this administration has proposed vital reforms of our bail and parole systems and criminal forfeiture and sentencing statutes.

These reforms were passed by the Senate ninety-five to one last year. Our anti-crime package never got out of committee in the House of Representatives. Do you see a target there? The American people want these reforms, and they want them now. I'm asking tonight that you mobilize all the powerful resources of this political movement to get these measures passed by the Congress.

On another front, all of you know how vitally important it is for us to reverse the decline in American education, to take responsibility for the education of our children out of the hands of the bureaucrats and put it back in the hands of parents and teachers. That's why the Congress must stop dithering. We need those tuition tax credits. We need a voucher system for the parents of disadvantaged children. We need education savings accounts, a sort of IRA for college. And finally—and don't think for a moment I've given up—we need to eliminate that unnecessary and politically engendered Department of Education.

There are other steps we're taking to restore government to its rightful duties, to restore the political consensus upon which this nation was founded. Our Founding Fathers prohibited a federal establishment of religion, but there is no evidence that they intended to set up a wall of separation between the state and religious belief itself.

The evidence of this is all around us. In the Declaration of Independence, alone, there are no fewer than four mentions of a Supreme Being. "In God We Trust" is engraved on our coinage. The Supreme Court opens its proceedings with a religious invocation. And the Congress opens each day with prayer from its chaplains. The schoolchildren of the United States are entitled to the same privileges as Supreme Court justices and congressmen. Join me in persuading the Congress to accede to the overwhelming desire of the American people for a constitutional amendment permitting prayer in our schools.

And finally, on our domestic agenda, there is a subject that weighs heavily on all of us—the tragedy of abortion on demand. This is a grave moral evil and one that requires the fullest discussion on the floors of the House and Senate. As we saw in the last century with the issue of slavery, any attempt by the Congress to stifle or compromise away discussion of important moral issues only further inflames emotions on both sides and leads ultimately to even more social disruption and disunity.

So, tonight, I would ask that the Congress discuss the issue of abortion openly and freely on the floors of the House and Senate. Let those who believe the practice of abortion to be a moral evil join us in taking this case to our fellow Americans. And let us do so rationally, calmly, and with an honest regard for our fellow Americans.

Speaking for myself, I believe that once implications of abortion on demand are fully aired and understood by the American people, they will resolutely seek its abolition. Now, I know there are many who sincerely believe that limiting the right of abortion violates the freedom of choice of the individual. But if the unborn child is a living entity, then there are two individuals, each with the right to life, liberty, and the pursuit of happiness. Unless and until someone can prove the unborn is not alive—and all medical evidence indicates it is—then we must concede the benefit of the doubt to the unborn infant.

But whether it's cutting spending and taxing, shrinking the size of the deficit, ending overregulation, inefficiency, fraud and waste in government, cracking down on career criminals, revitalizing American education, pressing for prayer and abortion legislation, I think you can see that the agenda we've put before America these past two years has been a conservative one. Oh, and there are two other matters that I think you'd be interested in. First, as part of our federalism effort, next week we will be sending to the Congress our proposal for four mega-block grants that will return vital prerogatives to the states where they belong. And second, the Office of Management and Budget will press ahead with new regulations prohibiting the use of federal tax dollars for purposes of political advocacy.

And these important domestic initiatives have been complemented by the conservative ideas we've brought to the pursuit of foreign policy. In the struggle now going on for the world, we have not been afraid to characterize our adversaries for what they are. We have focused world attention on forced labor on the Soviet pipeline and Soviet repression in Poland and all the other nations that make up what is called the "fourth world"—those living under totalitarian rule who long for freedom.

We publicized the evidence of chemical warfare and other atrocities in Cambodia, which we're now supposed to call Kampuchea, and Afghanistan. We pointed out that totalitarian powers hold a radically different view of morality and human dignity than we do. We must develop a forward strategy for freedom, one based on our hope that someday representative government will be enjoyed by all the people and all the nations of the earth.

We've been striving to give the world the facts about the international arms race. Ever since our nearly total demobilization after World War II, we in the West have been playing catch-up. Yes, there's been an international arms race, as some of the declared Democratic candidates for the presidency tell us. But let them also tell us, there's only been one side doing the racing.

Those of you in the frontline of the conservative movement can be of special assistance in furthering our strategy for freedom, our fight against totalitarianism. First of all, there is no more important foreign policy initiative in this administration, and none that frightens our adversaries more, than our attempts through our international radios to build constituencies for peace in nations dominated by totalitarian, militaristic regimes. We've proposed to the Congress modest but vitally important expenditures for the Voice of America, Radio Free Europe/Radio Liberty, and Radio Marti. These proposals stalled last year, but with your help we can get them through the Congress this year. And believe me, nothing could mean more to the Poles, Lithuanians, Cubans, and all the millions of others living in that fourth world.

Now, it would be also unconscionable during any discussion of the need for candor in our foreign policy not to mention here the tragic event that last year shocked the world—the attack on His Holiness, Pope John Paul II—an act of unspeakable evil, an assault on man and God. It was an international outrage and merits the fullest possible investigation. Tonight, I want to take this opportunity to applaud the courage and resourcefulness of the government of Italy in bringing this matter to the attention of the world. And, contrary to what some have suggested, you can depend on it, there is no one on our side that is acting embarrassed or feeling embarrassed because they're going ahead with that investigation. We mean to help them.

And, now, Cap, you can breathe easy, because here we come. We must continue to revitalize and strengthen our Armed Forces. Cap Weinberger's been waging a heroic battle on this front. I'm asking you, the conservative leaders here tonight, to make support for our defense buildup one of your top priorities.

But besides progress in furthering all of these items on the conservative agenda, something else is occurring—something that someday we conservatives may be very proud happened under our leadership. Even with all our recent economic hardships, I believe a feeling of optimism is now entering the American consciousness, a belief that the days of division and discord are behind us and that an era of unity and national renewal is upon us.

A vivid reminder of how our nation has learned and grown and transcended the tragedies of the past was given to us here in Washington only a few months ago. Last November, on the Mall, between the Lincoln Memorial and the Washington Monument, a new memorial was dedicated—one of dark, low-lying walls inscribed with the names of those who gave their lives in the Vietnam conflict. Soon, there will be added a sculpture of three infantrymen representing different racial and ethnic backgrounds.

During the dedication ceremonies, the rolls of the missing and dead were read for three days, morning till night, in a candlelight ceremony at the National Cathedral. And those veterans of Vietnam who never were welcomed home with speeches and bands, but who were defeated in battle and were heroes as surely as any whoever fought in a noble cause, staged their own parade on Constitution Avenue.

As America watched them, some in wheelchairs, all of them proud, there was a feeling that as a nation we were coming together, coming together again, and that we had at long last brought the boys home. "A lot of healing ... went on," said Jan Scruggs, the wounded combat veteran who helped organize support for the memorial. And then there was this newspaper account that appeared after the ceremonies. I'd like to read it to you.

"Yesterday, crowds returned to the memorial. Among them was Herbie Petit, a machinist and former marine from New Orleans. 'Last night,' he said, standing near the wall, 'I went out to dinner with some ex-marines. There was also a group of college students in the restaurant. We started talking to each other, and before we left, they stood up and cheered. The whole week,' Petit said, his eyes red, 'it was worth it just for that.'"

It has been worth it. We Americans have learned again to listen to each other, to trust each other. We've learned that government owes the people an explanation and needs their support for its actions at home and abroad. And we've learned—and pray this time for good—that we must never again send our young men to fight and die in conflicts that our leaders are not prepared to win.

Yet, the most valuable lesson of all, the preciousness of human freedom, has been relearned not just by Americans, but all the people of the world. It is the "stark lesson" that Truong Nhu Tang, one of the founders of the National Liberation Front, a former Viet Cong minister and vice minister of the postwar Vietnamese Communist government, spoke of recently when he explained why he fled Vietnam for freedom. "No previous regime in my country," he wrote about the concentration camps and boat people of Vietnam, "brought such numbers of people to such desperation. Not the military dictators, not the colonialists, not even the ancient Chinese warlords. It is a lesson that my compatriots and I learned through witnessing and through suffering in our own lives the fate of our countrymen. It is a lesson that must eventually move the conscience of the world." This man who had fought on the other side learned the value of freedom only after helping to destroy it and seeing those who had had to give it up.

The task that has fallen to us as Americans is to move the conscience of the world, to keep alive the hope and dream of freedom. For if we fail or falter, there'll be no place for the world's oppressed to flee to. This is not a role we sought. We preach no manifest destiny. But like the Americans who brought a new nation into the world two hundred years ago, history has asked much of us in our time. Much we've already given; much more we must be prepared to give. This is not a task we shrink from; it's a task we welcome. For with the privilege of living in this kindly, pleasant, greening land called America, this land of generous spirit and great ideals, there is also a destiny and a duty, a call to preserve and hold in sacred trust mankind's

age-old aspirations of peace and freedom and a better life for generations to come.

God bless you all and thank you for what you're doing.

Conservatives Take a Stand against #Resistance

Charlie Kirk

We Will Not Be Turned Back

In typical "Gipper" fashion, President Reagan exuded perpetual optimism and confidence in the future of America in his speech to CPAC in 1983. It is important to remember that during this time, Reagan was facing significant challenges both at home and abroad. Republicans had just suffered a twenty-seven-seat loss in Congress, skyrocketing inflation had eroded confidence in American markets, and the threat of nuclear war jeopardized the world while the Soviet Union continuously escalated its aggression. It fell to President Reagan to rally the conservative base and persuade them that giving up was not an option.

Reagan's optimism for the future was sharpened by an iron will to restore government's accountability to the American people. Reading his words today, I am struck by the massive waste throughout the levels of government he was targeting for cuts. Looking at the historic arc of conservatism, it is clear that President Reagan uniquely embodies the conservative critique of the modern welfare state and government waste. Before Reagan, Republican Presidents

Ford and Nixon were hyper-focused on duplicating government programs that stifled America's growth.

Reagan's insistence on restoring the proper role of government rewarded hardworking Americans who'd had too many of their tax dollars wasted on government's mismanagement. It also broadened the appeal of the 1980s Republican Party to include the growing coalition of libertarians who were inspired by limited government stalwarts like Senator Barry Goldwater and economist Milton Friedman.

As a young conservative, I was struck by the permanence of Reagan's words concerning the problems and challenges facing Americans in 1983 and drawn to the wisdom they offer us as we navigate many of those same challenges today. Democrats threaten to reverse historic tax cuts for American families and businesses; entitlement spending consumes two-thirds of our national budget; federal bureaucracy is more focused on rewarding self-dealing and corruption than merit or common-sense policy.

Thirty-five years later, President Reagan would be smiling to see that his beliefs in a free market economy, low taxes, less regulation, and government accountability are very much alive and well within today's conservative movement. And as true today as it was then, the results speak for themselves. Reagan never sacrificed these ideals, even in the face of a growing minority in the House; Americans even grew in their support for his administration through his charming ability to communicate core conservative values to people who never described themselves as Republicans or conservatives.

In today's conservative movement, we've seen similar common-sense initiatives accelerating America's economic growth, including the largest, most successful enacting of a deregulation agenda and the largest tax cut in American history, second only to the Reagan tax cut of 1981. The ideas that Reagan laid out at CPAC that year are now the bedrock, dyed-in-the-wool ideas of the modern-day Republican Party and conservative base.

The final point I found most moving in this speech was the important and necessary focus on promoting freedom abroad. The threat of communism was understandably the biggest focus of the 1980s as the Soviet Union and United States exchanged countless threats to the point of risking an all-out nuclear war. Tensions reached a fever-pitch when the Soviet nuclear early-warning system incorrectly reported a NATO exercise as a U.S. missile launch targeting the USSR. The Soviets were preparing a counterstrike when they realized their error. Nuclear war was averted that day, but U.S.-Soviet relations continued to falter. But even when chaos mounted, Reagan was relentless in his rebukes of Soviet communism, which he called an "evil empire," and his willingness to engage in diplomacy with the Soviets.

After it all, it is heartwarming to reflect and say the two words: we won.

Thanks to President Reagan and the exceptionalism of American culture and people, communism was rebuked. The Berlin Wall fell, the Soviet Union crumbled, and freedom established a firmer foothold throughout the world. Just a few short years after this speech, the world witnessed the largest liberation of humanity since World War II.

President Reagan stands as a timeless inspiration for us all, not just for his remarkable ability to fight back in the face of evil and win, but also for leaving a legacy based on first principles that continues to drive our mission today. President Reagan's vision for a free society and a strong America are alive and well now more than ever. We must do everything in our power to defend and protect that vision for future generations.

Charlie Kirk is the founder and president of Turning Point USA.

Our Noble Vision:
An Opportunity Society
for All

1984

M r. Vice President, members of Congress, members of the cabinet, and distinguished ladies and gentlemen. I just want to say thank you to Mickey Edwards. I'm honored to stand beside this fine congressman from Oklahoma and ACU's great leader.

Seeing the size of your gathering here this evening, the exciting program that you've planned, and the media attention you're drawing, and seeing and feeling the drive, energy, and intellectual force that's coming to our cause from the American Conservative Union, Young Americans for Freedom, Human Events, and *National Review*, I believe the proof is undeniable: the conservative movement is alive and well, and you are giving America a new lease on life.

It is true that many of you are helping now in our administration. And we're going to add one more in the next few days, because coming to the West Wing, there on our staff, will be the man that organized the first four of these dinners—Frank Donatelli. We've been together through many struggles. We've known the agony of defeat. And recently, we've seen public support begin to swell behind our banner. What we worked so long and hard to win was good, but hardly good enough. So, in expressing my pride and affection for this good family, for our family, may I say not only happy anniversary, ACU, but also, long live the revolution.

The mission of this conference is a mission of principle: it is a mission of commitment, and it must and will be a mission of victory. Color our cause with courage and confidence. We offer an optimistic society. More than two hundred years after the patriots fired that first shot heard 'round the world, one revolutionary idea still burns in the hearts of men and women everywhere: a society where man is not beholden to government; government is beholden to man.

The difference between the path toward greater freedom or bigger government is the difference between success and failure; between opportunity and coercion; between faith in a glorious future and fear of mediocrity and despair; between respecting people as adults, each with a spark of greatness, and treating them as helpless children to be forever dependent; between a drab, materialistic world where Big Brother rules by promises to special interest groups, and a world of adventure where everyday people set their sights on impossible dreams, distant stars, and the Kingdom of God. We have the true message of hope for America.

In *Year of Decision, 1846*, Bernard DeVoto explained what drove our ancestors to conquer the West, create a nation, and open up a continent. If you take away the dream, you take away the power of the spirit. If you take away the belief in a greater future, you cannot explain America—that we're a people who believed there was a promised land; we were a people who believed we were chosen by God to create a greater world.

Well, I think we're remembering those bedrock beliefs which motivate our progress. A spirit of renewal is spreading across this land. We even have a pro-conservative newspaper in the nation's capital [the *Washington Times*]. And, if I may just interject, I understand that [*Times* Editor and Publisher] Jim Whalen will be honored by your group tomorrow night, and that's wonderful news and well-deserved.

I think America is better off than we were three years ago because we've stopped placing our faith in more government programs. We're restoring our faith in the greatest resource this nation has—the mighty spirit of free people under God. It was you who reminded Washington that we are a government of, by, and for the people, not the other way around. It was you who said it is time to put earnings back in the hands of the people, time to put trust back in the hands of the people, time to put America back in the hands of the people.

And this is what we're trying to do. Our critics are not pleased, but I hope we'll be forgiven this small observation: the spendthrifts who mangled America with the nightmare of double-digit inflation, record interest rates, unfair tax increases, too much regulation, credit controls, farm embargoes, gas lines, no growth at home, weakness abroad, and phony excuses about "malaise" are the last people who should be giving sermonettes about fairness and compassion.

Their failures were not caused by erratic weather patterns, unusual rotations of the moon, or by the personality of my predecessor. They were caused by misguided policies and misunderstanding human nature. Believe me, you cannot create a desert, hand a person a cup of water, and call that compassion. You cannot pour billions of dollars into make-work jobs while destroying the economy that supports them and call that opportunity. And you cannot build up years of dependence on government and dare call that hope.

But apparently nothing bothers our liberal friends. The same expertise that told them their policies must succeed convinced them that our program spelled economic Armageddon. First, they blamed the recession on our tax cuts. The trouble is, our tax cuts hadn't started yet. They also warned that when our tax program passed, America would face runaway inflation, record interest rates, and a collapse of confidence. Well, at least they got part of it right. Our program passed, and we witnessed a collapse all right. A collapse of inflation from 12.4 down to about four percent; a collapse of the prime interest rate from over twenty-one percent to eleven; and a new surge of confidence in stocks and bonds.

They warned that decontrolling the price of oil would send the cost of gas at the pumps skyrocketing. We decontrolled, and the price is lower today than it was three years ago when we decontrolled.

And then they said that recovery couldn't come or would be too feeble to notice. Well, from strong growth in housing to autos, construction, and high technology, from a rebirth of productivity to the fastest drop in unemployment in over thirty years, we have one of the strongest recoveries in decades. And we'll keep it strong if they'll get out of the way.

Pardon me if I add something here. You know, I did get a kick out of watching on TV the door-to-door campaigning in New Hampshire. I got to see some of the homes the people have been able to buy since we brought interest rates down. Incidentally, I'm sure all of you have read or seen on the air that in the month of January our sale of new houses dropped, and dropped to a great percent—about a nine percent drop below what it was the previous month. Only 688,000 new homes were sold in January. But they didn't add that that drop was only from the sales in December, and beyond that it was the highest number that had been sold since 1979 in a single month.

But our critics moan the recovery can't last. Those awful tax cuts haven't sparked business investment; private borrowers are being crowded out of the capital markets. Well, if that's true, how did the venture capital industry raise four times as much capital in 1983 as it did in 1980? How could real, fixed business investment increase by a thirteen-percent rate last year, the fastest rate in any recovery in the past thirty years? And how could funds raised in the equity markets zoom from $16.8 billion in 1983—or in 1982, to $36.6 billion in 1983? Still another record.

Now, all this means more growth, more jobs, more opportunities, and a more competitive America. Now, lately, the pessimists have been sounding a new alarm: the dollar is so strong, they say, that exporters can't export, and we'll have no chance for lasting growth.

Well, the facts are—as Secretary [of the Treasury] Don Regan has pointed out—the dollar is strong because of people's confidence in our currency, our low rate of inflation, and the incentives to invest in the United States. No American should undermine confidence in the nation's currency. A strong dollar is one of our greatest weapons against inflation. Anyone who doubts the value of a strong currency should look at the postwar performances of Japan, Switzerland, and West Germany. Yes, we have a trade deficit, but this isn't entirely new. The United States had a merchandise trade deficit in almost all of the years between 1790 and 1875. I remember them well. 'Course, I was only a boy at the time.

But that was when our economy grew into one of the largest and strongest in the world. Rising incomes have given us the ability to increase purchases from abroad. The U.S. economy is serving as an engine for worldwide recovery, and this will translate into greater demands for our own goods. But even with our current trade deficits, exports of goods and services have made a greater contribution to this recovery than to any previous recovery in the postwar period.

The critics were wrong on inflation, wrong on interest rates, wrong on the recovery, and I believe they'll be wrong on the deficit, too, if the Congress will get spending under control. If optimism were a national disease, they'd be immune for life. Isn't it time that we said no to those who keep saying no to America? If the sourpuss set cannot believe in our nation and her people, then let them stand aside and we will get the job done.

In fairness, I'll admit our critics are worried sick about the future of the economy. They're worried it might keep getting better and better.

Now, those who deal in a world of numbers cannot predict the progress of the human mind, the drive and energy of the spirit, or the power of incentives. We're beginning an industrial renaissance which most experts never saw coming. It started with the 1978 capital gains tax reduction—passed over the objections of the last administration—and which was then made greater by our own tax reductions in 1981.

Incentives laid the seeds for the great growth in venture capital which helped set off the revolution in high technology. Sunrise industries, such as computers, micro-electronics, robotics, and fiber optics—all are creating a new world of opportunities. And as our knowledge expands, business investment is stimulated to modernize older industries with the newer technologies.

Dr. Robert Jastrow, chairman of the first NASA lunar exploration committee, believes the potential in our high-tech industries for new jobs and economic growth is mind-boggling. A year ago, he predicted the computer industry would double in size by 1986, becoming America's biggest business. And now we're seeing the knowledge and benefits of high technology being put to use in medicine, bringing new hope to millions who suffer handicaps and disabilities.

Visionaries see infinite possibilities for new economic growth in America's next frontier—space. Our challenge of building a permanently manned space station, and of further exploration, can open up entire new industries. Products from metal alloys to lifesaving medicines—these can immensely improve our environment and life on Earth.

All our space-related activities must begin with the transportation to get there. This is an area of American technological leadership, and I intend to make sure we keep that edge. That's why I've asked Transportation Secretary Elizabeth Dole to start immediately promoting private sector investment in commercial, unmanned space boosters—the powerful rockets that carry satellites into orbit. With these boosters, and a thriving commercial launch industry, American private enterprise will be blasting off toward new horizons of hope, adventure, and progress—a future that will dazzle our imaginations and lift our spirits.

An opportunity society awaits us. We need only believe in ourselves and give men and women of faith, courage, and vision the freedom to build it. Let others run down America and seek to punish success. Let them call you greedy for not wanting government to take more and more of your earnings. Let them defend their tombstone society of wage and price guidelines, mandatory quotas, tax increases, planned shortages, and shared sacrifices.

We want no part of that mess, thank you very much. We will encourage all Americans—men and women, young and old, individuals of every race, creed, and color—to succeed and be healthy, happy, and whole. This is our goal. We see America not falling behind, but moving ahead; our citizens not fearful and divided, but confident and united by shared values of faith, family, work, neighborhood, peace, and freedom.

An opportunity society begins with growth, and that means incentives. As I told the people of Iowa last week, my sympathies are with the taxpayers, not the tax spenders. I consider stopping them from taking more of your earnings an economic responsibility and a moral obligation. I will not permit an anti-growth coalition to jeopardize this recovery. If they get their way, they'll charge everything on your "Taxpayers Express Card." And believe me, they never leave home without it.

As good conservatives, we were brought up to oppose deficits. But sometimes I think some have forgotten why. We were against deficit spending. Those who would be heroes trying to reduce deficits by raising taxes are not heroes. They have not addressed the point I made in the State of the Union: whether government borrows or increases taxes, it will be taking the same amount of money from the private economy and, either way, that's too much.

We must bring down government spending to a level where it cannot interfere with the ability of the economy to grow. The Congress must stop fiddling and pass a constitutional amendment requiring a balanced federal budget. With strong support from many of you here, we nearly scored a great victory in 1982. It's time to try again. We also seek a line-item veto to prevent pork barrel projects from passing just because they're attached to otherwise good legislation. I'm sure we're united by one goal. The Grace Commission identified billions of dollars in wasteful government spending. And I believe the Congress has a responsibility to work with us and eliminate that waste wherever it exists.

Combining these spending restraints with another key reform will make America's economy the undisputed leader for innovation, growth, and opportunity. I'm talking about simplification of the entire tax system. We can make taxes more fair, easier to understand, and, more important, we can greatly increase incentives by bringing personal tax rates down. If we can reduce personal tax rates as dramatically as we've reduced capital gains taxes, the underground economy will shrink, the whole world will beat a path to our door, and no one will hold America back. This is the real blueprint for a brighter future and declining deficits.

But economic opportunities can only flourish if the values at the foundation of our society and freedom remain strong and secure. Our families and friends must be able to live and work without always being afraid. Americans are sick and tired of law-abiding people getting mugged, robbed, and raped while dangerous criminals get off scot-free.

We have a comprehensive crime bill to correct this. It would put an end to the era of coddling criminals, and it's been passed by the Senate. But the legislation is bottled up in the House. Now, maybe it's time they heard from a few of you—a few million of you. You know, you don't have to make them see the light; just make them feel the heat. I hope you realize that in my comments about some of the shortcomings of the Congress, believe me, tonight present company is excepted.

Strengthening values also demands a national commitment to excellence in education. If we are to pioneer a revolution in technology, meet challenges of the space age, and preserve values of courage, responsibility, integrity, and love, then we can't afford a generation of children hooked on cocaine and unable to read or write. Conservatives have pointed out for years that while federal spending on education was soaring, aptitude scores were going steadily down. Look at the case of New Hampshire. It ranks dead last in state spending on education, but its students have the highest SAT scores among those states where at least half the students take the test. And they've maintained that honor for more than ten years. America's schools don't need new spending programs; they need tougher standards, more homework, merit pay for teachers, discipline, and parents back in charge.

Now, there's another important reform to be voted on soon in the Senate. ... Let us come together, citizens of all faiths, to pray, march, and mobilize every force we have so the God who loves us can be welcomed back into our children's classrooms. I'm gratified that Congressman Newt Gingrich is organizing a rally on the Capitol steps in support of our prayer in school amendment. Please be there if you can, and please send the message loud and clear that God never should have been expelled from America's schools in the first place. And maybe if we can get God and discipline back in our schools, we can get drugs and violence out.

Now, let me make it plain that we seek voluntary school prayer, not a moment of silence. We already have the right to remain silent; we can take the Fifth Amendment. But as we go on, we must redouble our efforts to redress a national tragedy. Since the Roe v. Wade decision, 15 million unborn children have been lost—15 million children who will never laugh, never sing, never know the joy of human love, will never strive to heal the sick or feed the poor or make peace among nations. They've been denied the most basic of human rights, and we're all the poorer for their loss.

Not long ago I received a letter from a young woman named Kim. She was born with the birth defect, spina bifida, and given little chance to live. But her parents were willing to try a difficult and risky operation on her spine. It worked. And Kim wrote me: "I am now twenty-four years old. I do have some medical problems due to my birth defect. I have a lot of problems with my legs. But I'm walking. I can talk. I went to grade and high school, plus one year of college. I thank God every day for my parents and my life."

And Kim said, "I wouldn't change it if I could."

Life was her greatest opportunity, and she's made the most of it. An opportunity society for all, reaching for its future with confidence, sustained by faith, fair play, and a conviction that good and courageous people flourish when they're free. This is the noble vision we share—a vision of a strong and prosperous America, at peace with itself and the world. Just as America has always been synonymous with freedom, so, too, should we become the symbol of peace across the Earth. I'm confident we can keep faith with that mission.

Peace with freedom is our highest aspiration—a lasting peace anchored by courage, realism, and unity. We've stressed our willingness to meet the Soviets halfway in talks on strategic weapons. But as commander in chief, I have an obligation to protect this country, and I will never allow political expediency to influence these crucial negotiations.

We should remember that our defense capability was allowed to deteriorate for many years. Only when our arms are certain beyond doubt can we be certain beyond doubt that they will never be used. President John F. Kennedy spoke those words in 1961. Too many who admired him have forgotten that the price of peace is dear. But some members of his party have not, and I am proud to have one of them, a brilliant patriot, Jeane Kirkpatrick, by my side.

And I deeply appreciate your patriotic support for rebuilding our defenses. We're just beginning to restore our capability to meet present and future security needs. I am open to suggestions for budget savings, but defense is not just another federal program. It is solely the responsibility of the federal government. It is its prime responsibility. So, our first responsibility is to keep America strong enough to remain free, secure, and at peace, and I intend to make sure that we do just that.

America's foreign policy supports freedom, democracy, and human dignity for all mankind, and we make no apologies for it. The opportunity society that we want for ourselves we also want for others, not because we're imposing our system on others, but because those opportunities belong to all people as God-given birthrights and because by promoting democracy and economic opportunity we make peace more secure.

Democratic nations do not wage war on their neighbors. But make no mistake, those who would hang a "do not disturb" sign on our shores, those who would weaken America or give Castro's terrorists free rein to bring violence closer and closer to our borders are doing no service to the cause of peace.

Fellow citizens, fellow conservatives, our time has come again. This is our moment. Let us unite, shoulder to shoulder, behind one mighty banner for freedom. And let us go forward from here not with some faint hope that our cause is not yet lost; let us go forward confident that the American people share our values, and that together we will be victorious.

And in those moments when we grow tired, when our struggle seems hard, remember what Eric Liddell, Scotland's Olympic champion runner, said in *Chariots of Fire*: "So where does the power come from to see the race to its end? From within. God made me for a purpose, and I will run for His pleasure."

If we trust in Him, keep His word, and live our lives for His pleasure, He'll give us the power we need—power to fight the good fight, to finish the race, and to keep the faith.

Thank you very much. God bless you and God bless America.

Reagan's Infectious Optimism

Steve Forbes

Our Noble Vision: An Opportunity Society for All

In the early 1980s, the United States desperately needed Ronald Reagan's faith in conservative values and, above all, his unbridled optimism for America's future. Those core convictions held by our fortieth president were perfectly expressed in his 1984 address to the Conservative Political Action Conference, a legendary Reagan speech known as *Our Noble Vision*. We need his faith and optimism just as badly now.

When Reagan spoke to CPAC in March of 1984, he was wrapping up his first term in office and beginning the campaign for a second. That campaign would culminate in one of the most lopsided victories in U.S. presidential history, with Reagan besting his Democratic opponent forty-nine states to one, winning 525 of 538 electoral votes. And it could have been more. His challenger, former Vice President Walter Mondale, running on a promise to raise taxes, carried his home state of Minnesota by less than 3,700 votes.

Reagan's optimism appealed to voters. He deeply believed in the American experiment, in part because he had seen it work for him. His optimism was the natural result of his quintessentially American experience, a life in which hard work and determination took him from very humble Midwestern beginnings to success and stardom, the governorship of his beloved adopted state, and the highest and most powerful office in the land.

Reagan believed the opportunities he had received should be available to all Americans, and that conservative policies were the best and surest way to grant them. *Our Noble Vision* outlines his support for a strong and stable dollar, robust national defense, and above all, a government that does not capriciously overregulate or tax the money its citizens work hard to earn. Early on in his address to CPAC, Reagan declared that conservatives offer an optimistic society "where man is not beholden to government; government is beholden to man."

Implementing the conservative policies expressed in *Our Noble Vision* dramatically improved the quality of American life. The 1970s had seen the U.S. on its heels internationally and struggling with a stagnant economy. The next decade, thanks to Reagan, saw the U.S. enjoy unprecedented prosperity.

The chronic unemployment and double-digit inflation Reagan inherited vanished under his tax cuts and regulatory streamlining. His conservative policies spurred a record-breaking peacetime economic recovery.

In no small part because of the two major tax cuts Reagan engineered, 20 million new U.S. jobs were created during his two-term administration. And those new employment opportunities were in no way limited to one segment of American society. For example, employment among African Americans increased more than twenty-five percent by the end of Reagan's second term. Their real incomes, which had dropped eleven percent from 1977 to 1982, were up seventeen percent by 1989. There was a forty percent increase in African American households earning more than $50,000 a year, black-owned businesses grew by almost forty percent, and African American college enrollments went up nearly thirty percent.

Most astonishing, against all expert expectations, Reagan laid the ground work for the U.S. winning the Cold War. Shortly after he left office, the Berlin Wall collapsed and the Soviet Union went to the ash heap of history without a shot being fired.

Reagan fully understood that when government gets out of the way, things get done. He was especially eager to empower innovation and growth in technology, citing his tax cuts as a stimulus for venture capital for "sunrise industries, such as computers, micro-electronics, robotics, and fiber optics," which he believed would create "a new world of opportunities." His optimism and enthusiasm for America's innovative future were right on track, foreseeing the high-tech marvels that have revolutionized our lives and created a seven trillion-dollar industry that employs over 18 million U.S. workers and accounts for nearly twenty-five percent of total U.S. economic output.

The Great Communicator's ability to turn a clever and memorable phrase was on full display at CPAC in 1986. Reagan's speech that year included such gems as:

> Believe me, you cannot create a desert, hand a person a cup of water, and call that compassion. You cannot pour billions of dollars into make-work jobs while destroying the economy that supports them and call that opportunity. And you cannot build up years of dependence on government and dare call that hope.

He took a number of jabs at his Democratic opponents, but he delivered them, as he always did, with subtlety and humor. Even the targets of his gibes must have been forced to smile when they heard them.

Reagan cared nothing for mean-spirited politics. That simply did not fit with his optimistic view of life and our nation's future, a viewpoint we need more than ever today. Reagan's infectious optimism and commitment to commonsense conservative values and policies made so clear throughout *Our Noble Vision* should be a guidepost to all political parties. They still have the power to make America the "shining city on a hill" that Ronald Reagan so deeply believed it was meant to be.

Steve Forbes is the chairman and editor-in-chief of Forbes Media.

Creators of
the Future

1985

T hank you all very much. Thank you, Vice Chairman [of the American Conservative Union James A.] Linen, for those very kind words. I'm grateful to the American Conservative Union, Young Americans for Freedom, *National Review*, Human Events, for organizing this wonderful evening. When you work in the White House, you don't get to see your old friends as much as you'd like. And I always see the Conservative Political Action Conference speech as my opportunity to "dance with the one that brung ya."

There's so much I want to talk about tonight. I've been thinking, in the weeks since the inauguration, that we are at an especially dramatic turning point in American history. And just putting it all together in my mind, I've been reviewing the elements that have led to this moment.

Ever since FDR and the New Deal, the opposition party, and particularly those of a liberal persuasion, have dominated the political debate. Their ideas were new; they had momentum; they

captured the imagination of the American people. The left held sway
for a long time. There was a right, but it was, by the '40s and '50s,
diffuse and scattered, without a unifying voice.

But in 1964 came a voice in the wilderness—Barry Goldwater;
the great Barry Goldwater, the first major party candidate of our time
who was a true-blue, undiluted conservative. He spoke from principle,
and he offered vision. Freedom—he spoke of freedom: freedom from
the government's increasing demands on the family purse, freedom
from the government's increasing usurpation of individual rights and
responsibilities, freedom from the leaders who told us the price of
world peace is continued acquiescence to totalitarianism. He was
ahead of his time. When he ran for president, he won six states and
lost forty-four. But his candidacy worked as a precursor of things to
come.

A new movement was stirring. And in the 1960s Young Americans for Freedom is born; *National Review* gains readership and
prestige in the intellectual community; Human Events becomes a
major voice on the cutting edge. In the '70s the anti-tax movement
begins. Actually, it was much more than an anti-tax movement, just
as the Boston Tea Party was much more than an anti-tax initiative.
In the late '70s, Proposition 13 and the Sagebrush Rebellion; in
1980, for the first time in twenty-eight years, a Republican Senate
is elected; so, may I say, is a conservative president. In 1984, that
conservative administration is reselected in a forty-nine-state sweep.
And the day the votes came in, I thought of Walt Whitman: "I hear
America singing."

This great turn from left to right was not just a case of the pen-
dulum swinging. First, the left hold sway and then the right, and here
comes the left again. The truth is, conservative thought is no longer
over here on the right; it's the mainstream now. And the tide of history
is moving irresistibly in our direction. Why? Because the other side is

virtually bankrupt of ideas. It has nothing more to say, nothing to add to the debate. It has spent its intellectual capital, such as it was, and it has done its deeds. Now, we're not in power because they failed to gain electoral support over the past fifty years. They did win support. And the result was chaos, weakness, and drift. Ultimately, though, their failures yielded one great thing—us guys. We in this room are not simply profiting from their bankruptcy; we are where we are because we're winning the contest of ideas. In fact, in the past decade, all of a sudden, quietly, mysteriously, the Republican Party has become the party of ideas.

We became the party of the most brilliant and dynamic young minds. I remember them, just a few years ago, running around scrawling Laffer curves on table napkins, going to symposia, and talking about how social programs did not eradicate poverty, but entrenched it; writing studies on why the latest weird and unnatural idea from the social engineers is weird and unnatural. You were there. They were your ideas, your symposia, your books, and usually somebody else's table napkins.

All of a sudden, Republicans were not defenders of the status quo, but creators of the future. They were looking at tomorrow with all the single-mindedness of an inventor. In fact, they reminded me of the American inventors of the nineteenth and twentieth centuries who filled the world with light and recorded sound.

The new conservatives made anew the connection between economic justice and economic growth. Growth in the economy would not only create jobs and paychecks, they said; it would enhance familial stability and encourage a healthy optimism about the future. Lower those tax rates, they said, and let the economy become the engine of our dreams. Pull back regulations and encourage free and open competition. Let the men and women of the marketplace decide what they want.

But along with that, perhaps the greatest triumph of modern conservatism has been to stop allowing the Left to put the average American on the moral defensive. By average American, I mean the good, decent, rambunctious, and creative people who raise the families, go to church, and help out when the local library holds a fundraiser; people who have a stake in the community because they are the community.

These people had held true to certain beliefs and principles that for twenty years the intelligentsia were telling us were hopelessly out of date, utterly trite, and reactionary. You want prayer in the schools? How primitive, they said. You oppose abortion? How oppressive, how antimodern. The normal was portrayed as eccentric, and only the abnormal was worthy of emulation. The irreverent was celebrated, but only irreverence about certain things: irreverence toward, say, organized religion, yes; irreverence toward established liberalism, not too much of that. They celebrated their courage in taking on safe targets and patted each other on the back for slinging stones at a confused Goliath, who was too demoralized and really too good to fight back. But now one simply senses it. The American people are no longer on the defensive. I believe the conservative movement deserves some credit for this. You spoke for the permanent against the merely prevalent, and ultimately you prevailed.

I believe we conservatives have captured the moment; captured the imagination of the American people. And what now? What are we to do with our success? Well, right now, with conservative thought accepted as mainstream thought and with the people of our country leading the fight to freedom, now we must move.

You remember your Shakespeare: "There is a tide in the affairs of men which, taken at the flood, leads on to fortune. Omitted, all the voyage of their life is bound in shallows and in miseries. On such a full sea are we now afloat. And we must take the current when it serves or lose our ventures." I spoke in the—[applause]. It's typical, isn't it? I just quoted a great writer, but as an actor, I get the bow. [Laughter]

I spoke in the State of the Union of a second American revolution, and now is the time to launch that revolution and see that it takes hold. If we move decisively, these years will not be just a passing era of good feeling, not just a few good years, but a true golden age of freedom.

The moment is ours, and we must seize it. There's work to do. We must prolong and protect our growing prosperity so that it doesn't become just a passing phase, a natural adjustment between periods of recession. We must move further to provide incentives and make America the investment capital of the world.

We must institute a fair tax system and turn the current one on its ear. I believe there is natural support in our country for a simplified tax system, with still lower tax rates but a broader base, with everyone paying their fair share and no more. We must eliminate unproductive tax shelters. Again, there is natural support among Americans, because Americans are a fair-minded people.

We must institute enterprise zones and a lower youth minimum wage so we can revitalize distressed areas and teenagers can get jobs. We're going to take our revolution to the people, all of the people. We're going to go to black Americans and members of all minority groups, and we're going to make our case.

Part of being a revolutionary is knowing that you don't have to acquiesce to the tired, old ideas of the past. One such idea is that the opposition party has black America and minority America locked up, that they own black America. Well, let me tell you, they own nothing but the past. The old alignments are no longer legitimate, if they ever were.

We're going to reach out, and we need your help. Conservatives were brought up to hate deficits, and justifiably so. We've long thought there are two things in Washington that are unbalanced—the budget and the liberals.

But we cannot reduce the deficit by raising taxes. And just so that every "i" is dotted and every "t" is crossed, let me repeat tonight for the benefit of those who never seem to get the message: we will not reduce the deficit by raising taxes. We need more taxes like John McLaughlin [Washington executive editor of *National Review*] needs assertiveness training.

Now, whether government borrows or increases taxes, it will be taking the same amount of money from the private economy, and either way, that's too much. We must bring down government spending. We need a constitutional amendment requiring a balanced budget. It's something that forty-nine states already require—no reason the federal government should be any different.

We need the line-item veto, which forty-three governors have—no reason that the president shouldn't. And we have to cut waste. The Grace Commission has identified billions of dollars that are wasted and that we can save.

But the domestic side isn't the only area where we need your help. All of us in this room grew up, or came to adulthood, in a time when the doctrine of Marx and Lenin was coming to divide the world. Ultimately, it came to dominate remorselessly whole parts of it. The Soviet attempt to give legitimacy to its tyranny is expressed in the infamous Brezhnev doctrine, which contends that once a country has fallen into communist darkness, it can never again be allowed to see the light of freedom. Well, it occurs to me that history has already begun to repeal that doctrine. It started one day in Grenada. We only did our duty, as a responsible neighbor and a lover of peace, the day we went in and returned the government to the people and rescued our own students. We restored that island to liberty. Yes, it's only a small island, but that's what the world is made of—small islands yearning for freedom.

There's much more to do. Throughout the world the Soviet Union and its agents, client states, and satellites are on the defensive—on the moral defensive, the intellectual defensive, and the political and economic defensive. Freedom movements arise and assert themselves. They're doing so on almost every continent populated by man—in the hills of Afghanistan, in Angola, in Kampuchea, in Central America. In making mention of freedom fighters, all of us are privileged to have in our midst tonight one of the brave commanders who lead the Afghan freedom fighters—Abdul Haq. Abdul Haq, we are with you.

They are our brothers, these freedom fighters, and we owe them our help. I've spoken recently of the freedom fighters of Nicaragua. You know the truth about them. You know who they're fighting and why. They are the moral equal of our Founding Fathers and the brave men and women of the French Resistance. We cannot turn away from them, for the struggle here is not right versus left; it is right versus wrong.

Now I am against sending troops to Central America. They are simply not needed. Given a chance and the resources the people of the area can fight their own fight. They have the men and women. They're capable of doing it. They have the people of their country behind them. All they need is our support. All they need is proof that we care as much about the fight for freedom seven hundred miles from our shores as the Soviets care about the fight against freedom five thousand miles from theirs. And they need to know that the U.S. supports them with more than just pretty words and good wishes. We need your help on this and I mean each of you—involved, active, strong, and vocal. And we need more.

All of you know that we're researching nonnuclear technologies that may enable us to prevent nuclear ballistic missiles from reaching U.S. soil or that of our allies. I happen to believe—logic forces me to believe—that this new defense system, the Strategic Defense Initiative, is the most hopeful possibility of our time. Its primary virtue is clear. If anyone ever attacked us Strategic Defense would be there to protect us. It could conceivably save millions of lives.

SDI has been criticized on the grounds that it might upset any chance of an arms control agreement with the Soviets. But SDI is arms control. If SDI is, say, eighty percent effective, then it will make any Soviet attack folly. Even partial success in SDI would strengthen deterrence and keep the peace. And if our SDI research is successful, the prospects for real reduction in U.S. and Soviet offensive nuclear forces will be greatly enhanced.

It is said that SDI would deal a blow to the so-called East-West balance of power. Well let's think about that. The Soviets already are investing roughly as much on strategic defenses as they are on their offensive nuclear forces. This could quickly tip the East-West balance if we had no defense of our own. Would a situation of comparable defenses threaten us? No, for we're not planning on being the first to use force. As we strive for our goal of eventual elimination of nuclear weapons, each side would retain a certain amount of defensive—or of, I should say, destructive power—a certain number of missiles. But it would not be in our interest, or theirs, to build more and more of them.

Now, one would think our critics on the left would quickly embrace, or at least be open-minded about a system that promises to reduce the size of nuclear missile forces on both sides and to greatly enhance the prospects for real arms reductions. And yet we hear SDI belittled by some with nicknames, or demagogued with charges that it will bring war to the heavens.

They complain that it won't work, which is odd from people who profess to believe in the perfectibility of man-machines after all. And man-machines are so much easier to manipulate. They say it won't be one hundred percent effective, which is odd since they don't ask for one hundred percent effectiveness in their social experiments. They say SDI is only in the research stage and won't be realized in time to change things. To which, as I said last month, the only reply is: then let's get started.

Now, my point here is not to question the motives of others. But it's difficult to understand how critics can object to exploring the possibility of moving away from exclusive reliance upon nuclear weapons. The truth is, I believe that they find it difficult to embrace any idea that breaks with the past, that breaks with consensus thinking and the common establishment wisdom. In short, they find it difficult and frightening to alter the status quo.

And what are we to do when these so-called opinion leaders of an outworn philosophy are out there on television and in the newspapers with their steady drumbeat of doubt and distaste? Well, when all you have to do to win is rely on the good judgment of the American people, then you're in good shape, because the American people have good judgment. I know it isn't becoming of me, but I like to think that maybe forty-nine of our fifty states displayed that judgment just a few months ago.

What we have to do, all of us in this room, is get out there and talk about SDI. Explain it, debate it, tell the American people the facts. It may well be the most important work we do in the next few years. And if we try, we'll succeed. So, we have great work ahead of us, big work. But if we do it together and with complete commitment, we can change our country and history forever.

Once during the campaign, I said, "This is a wonderful time to be alive," and I meant that. I meant that we're lucky not to live in pale and timid times. We've been blessed with the opportunity to stand for something—for liberty and freedom and fairness. And these are things worth fighting for, worth devoting our lives to. And we have good reason to be hopeful and optimistic.

We've made much progress already. So, let us go forth with good cheer and stout hearts—happy warriors out to seize back a country and a world to freedom.

Thank you, and God bless you. Thank you very much.

The Revolutionary Power of Conservative Ideas

Senator Ted Cruz

COMMENTARY ON

Creators of the Future

When Ronald Reagan ascended the stage to speak at CPAC in March of 1985, he stood at one of the highest points of his presidency. Six weeks before, he had taken the presidential oath at his second inauguration, a feat earned through a landslide victory of forty-nine states in the Electoral College and a higher share of the popular vote than any candidate, Republican or Democrat, has managed since.

Reagan won on renewed national confidence in our economy and America's standing in the world. Whether it was blue-collar workers and blue-dog Democrats celebrating an energetic departure from Jimmy Carter's "malaise" economy, or patriots from New York to Texas to California appreciating Reagan's bold stand against communist regimes across the globe, everyone knew there was a change in the air, and they liked which way the wind was blowing.

Though Reagan rightly tips his hat to the candidacy of Senator Barry Goldwater as kicking off the movement that culminated in his administration, he had cemented his transition from actor to statesman in his famous address on behalf of Goldwater, *A Time for Choosing*. His focus was on the youthful energy of a movement that finally had a voice in Washington.

Perhaps this was a wink to the dolorous Walter Mondale, whose ill-fated campaign to unseat Reagan attempted to make an issue of Reagan's age. It backfired terribly. Always the Great Communicator, Reagan rejoined that he wouldn't make an issue of Mondale's "youth and inexperience."

The vibrancy of the Reagan coalition was on full display at CPAC. Defense hawks, pro-lifers, Second Amendment allies, and free marketers had joined with an overwhelming majority of the country and driven a stake through the heart of Lionel Trilling's famed but specious characterization of conservatism as "irritable mental gestures which seek to resemble ideas."

Indeed, there were real ideas aplenty in conservatism, and Reagan was prescient to entertain them.

The concept that a free and booming economy was a better guarantor of individual prosperity and equality than the nanny state should have been obvious since Lyndon Johnson's Great Society programs had failed to save America's big cities from themselves. But Reagan's was the first administration to take the lesson to heart.

Reagan's exhortation to support the Strategic Defense Initiative—spaced based missile defense—was so cutting edge that defeatist critics mocked it as fantastical "Star Wars." But if the idea had one flaw, it was simply a couple decades ahead of its time. Today, critics of missile defense no longer have the argument that we lack the technology. Instead, they have retreated to the stalest leftist arguments from the depths of the Cold War: that an America with too much defensive power is unfair to the rest of the world.

As Reagan later showed by beating the USSR in an arms buildup that ultimately led to the fall of the Berlin Wall, a strong America strengthens freedom around the world without even firing a shot.

Reagan also challenged the notion that the Left has a stranglehold on the vote of black America and other minority communities. As we see from today's #WalkAway movement—the vitriol leveled at black celebrities who dare meet with the president—and the lowest black and Hispanic unemployment in half a century, liberals are finally desperately realizing that their presumed monopoly on the hearts and minds of minority Americans is crumbling—or, indeed, that they never really had one.

Reagan warns of the errors of Lenin and Marx dividing the world. I wonder what he would say today, when this philosophy of ashes still oppresses not only unfortunate people in Latin America, Africa, and Asia, but has come to "dominate remorselessly" in American academia, celebrity culture, and the rhetoric of radical politicians, who now are not embarrassed by the label of "socialist."

But this is no reason for despair. We have a coalition of our own today. It may look different. It may work differently. It may be even younger than Reagan's. But it is full of fire and ready to spark the flame of freedom wherever its light is needed.

There are still those upstarts of whom Reagan spoke, running around with Laffer curves scrawled on table napkins.

Mine is on the wall of my Senate office.

To borrow from his speech, we have many reasons to go forth with good cheer and stout hearts.

This is a wonderful time to be alive.

Ted Cruz is a United States senator from Texas serving since 2012.

Forward for Freedom

1986

T hank you all very much, and may I just say that every bit of
show business instinct that is within me says that perhaps
it would be better if the entertainment followed the speaker.
You are a tough act to follow. [The president was referring to the
comic routine of Yakov Smirnoff.]

But let me begin by saying how appropriate it is that we honor
tonight the Shuttle Seven; all of them were heroes. Each of us is in
their debt. And we know now that God holds them close, and we
pray He'll comfort their grieving loved ones. And we're aware, too,
of our own duty to them and to their memory. We must continue.
Other brave Americans must go now where they so valiantly tried
to lead—a fitting place, I've always thought, for Americans—"the
stars and beyond."

And in some closed societies, a tragedy of this sort would be
permanently disheartening, a fatal setback to any such program,
followed not by mourning and national recommitment, but by
attempts to evade responsibility. Well, not so in a democracy, and

not so in America. John Glenn said the other day that after the pad fire that killed three astronauts in 1967, support for the space program skyrocketed among the American people. And that's because here the government does not rule the people; it is the people. And ultimately what happens to programs of this sort, and what follows tragedies of this kind, are decisions that belong not to government, but to the people.

The tragedy of the Shuttle Seven will only serve to strengthen the resolve of America to pursue their dream of "the stars and beyond." And anyone who doubts this does not know the history of our land, the wonder of America and her free people, or the meaning of the words "the right stuff."

You know, I called the families yesterday of those seven heroes. Every one of them concluded the remarks between us by saying, "The program must continue; they would have wanted it that way." And it will.

Well, I'm delighted to be here tonight. And I want to extend my heartfelt thanks to the American Conservative Union, along with Human Events, *National Review*, and Young Americans for Freedom for putting on this conference and for extending the invitation.

Tonight, my thoughts cannot help but drift back to another conservative audience of more than twenty years ago and a presidential campaign that the pundits and opinion-makers said then was the death knell for our movement. But just as the opinion leaders had been stunned by Barry Goldwater's nomination, so too they would be shocked by the resiliency of his cause and the political drama to unfold around it: the rise of the New Right and the religious revival of the mid-'70s and the final, triumphant march to Washington in 1980 by conservatives.

And you know, that last event really did come as a shock of seismic proportions to this city. I can remember reading about a poll that was taken at a Washington National Press Club luncheon in January of 1980 on the eve of the primary season. Those in attendance were asked who would be the next president of the United States. Well, Jimmy Carter got a large number of votes, and so did Teddy Kennedy. But there was one candidate on the Republican side who got so few votes from the wise men of Washington that it wasn't even reported in the lineup. I think it had to do with his conservative leanings. Well, I hope they know I'm not about to change.

But while official Washington always underestimated our cause, some of the shrewder journalists did over the years sense something astir in America. Theodore White said openly, just after Barry Goldwater's campaign: "Some see this as a last adventure in the politics of nostalgia. Others see this Arizonan as a symbol, cast up by the first crest of an early tide, thrown back this once, but bound to come again in greater strength."

And you know, to be here tonight and to be a part of this historic conference, your biggest attention-getter, to look at your program for the next two days and all the important people and discussions, to stand here now with the presidential seal on this podium, to feel the energy, the almost festive air of this audience, I think you've provided an answer to Teddy White's implicit question about the fate of our movement, the state of our cause. Fellow conservatives, it took us more than twenty years, but who can deny it? We're rockin' and rollin'.

Now, I know a few liberal observers will try to downplay all this. But don't you think they're going to sound a little bit like Yogi Berra on that famous occasion when he said of a restaurant, "It's so crowded, nobody goes there anymore?" And as for those liberals who finally are catching on to the idea that there is a conservative movement, they kind of remind me of a cowboy who was out hiking in the desert one day and came across the Grand Canyon. And he said, "Wow, something sure happened here!"

Well, something has happened in America. In five short years, we have seen the kind of political change rarely seen in a generation on nearly every issue: federal spending, tax cuts, deregulation, the fight against career criminals and for tough judges, military readiness, resistance to Soviet expansionism, and the need for candor about the struggle between freedom and totalitarianism. The old taboos and superstitions of liberalism have collapsed and all but blown away, to be replaced by a robust and enlightened conservatism; a conservatism that brings with it economic prosperity, personal opportunity, and a shining hope that someday all the peoples of the world—from Afghanistan to Nicaragua to Poland and, yes, to Angola—will know the blessings of liberty and live in the light of freedom.

Those in this room know how often we were told the odds of accomplishing even a small part of this were all against us. I remember my own first visit up to the Hill after the 1980 election, when issues like the tax cuts came up. I met a congressman there. He was a kind of a big fellow, as I recall—had lots of white hair. He was from the Boston area, I think. Maybe you know him. He smiled very indulgently and told me not to expect too much because I was, to use his words, "in the big leagues now.

But you know, as a conservative, I had an advantage. Back in the hard years, the lean years, when we were forming our political PACs, sending out our fundraising letters, and working for candidate after candidate in campaign after campaign, all of us learned something vital, something important about our country. Something became an article of faith, a faith that sustained us through all the setbacks and the heartache.

You see, we knew then what we know now: that the real big leaguers aren't here in Washington at all; they're out there in the heartland, out in the real America, where folks go to work every day and church every week, where they raise their families and help their neighbors, where they build America and increase her bounty and pass on to each succeeding generation her goodness and splendor. And we knew something else, too: that the folks out there in real America pretty much see things our way and that all we ever have to do to get them involved is to be brave enough to trust them with the truth and bold enough to ask for their help.

And it's here we find the explanation for the success of the last five years, the reason why on issue after issue the liberals in this town have lost and are still losing: they've forgotten who's in charge, who the big leaguers really are.

It reminds me of a favorite little story of mine about a career naval officer who finally got his four stripes, became a captain, and then was given command of a giant battleship. And one night he was out steaming around the Atlantic when he was called from his quarters to the bridge and told about a signal light in the distance. And the captain told the signalman, "Signal them to bear to starboard." And back came the signal from ahead asking, or saying, "You bear to starboard." Well, as I say, the captain was very aware that he was commander of a battleship, the biggest thing afloat, the pride of the fleet; and he said, "Signal that light again to bear to starboard now." Well, the captain decided to give his unknown counterpart a lesson in seagoing humility, so he said, "Signal them again and tell them to bear to starboard. I am a battleship." And back came the signal, "Bear to starboard yourself. I'm a lighthouse."

Well, the American people have turned out to be just what the forefathers thought they would be when they made them the final arbiter of political power: a lighthouse to the ship of state, a source of good judgment and common sense signaling a course to starboard. But you who are not nautical-minded know that starboard is to the right, don't you?

But I come here tonight not just to celebrate these successes of our past, but also to strike a serious, even somber, note to remind each of you not only of how far we have come together, but how tragic it would be if we suddenly cast aside in a moment of dreadful folly all our hopes for a safe America and a freer world. My fellow conservatives, I want to speak to you tonight about our movement and a great danger that lies ahead.

Now, some of you may think I'm reacting here to claims that 1985 was a disappointing or, at best, a mediocre year for conservatives. In fact, I want to take sharp issue with this, suggest to you that those claims themselves are evidence of the broader problem I'm talking about: the danger of growing soft with victory, of losing perspective when things go our way too often, of failing to appreciate success when it occurs or seeing danger when it looms.

First, let's talk about 1985 and three legislative victories whose strategic significance were both enormous and largely overlooked. Now, some of you who go back with me to that campaign in 1964 can remember how easily the liberals dismissed our warnings then about the dangers of deficit spending. We were told it would bring prosperity. Others of you know how passionately the liberals believed in the use of high and punitive tax rates to redistribute income. And finally, all of us can remember how liberals found in the post-Vietnam syndrome a form of religious exercise, a kind of spiritual ecstasy, however much of that syndrome paralyzed American foreign policy and jeopardized freedom.

Now, let me ask you: if someone had come up to you even as late as a few years ago and told you that by 1985, all of these cherished doctrines—a belief in deficit spending, the politics of envy via high tax rates, and the refusal to help those resisting communist dictatorship—would be formally and publicly rejected in a single twelve-month period by the liberal Democrats themselves, wouldn't you have thought that person prone to acute shortages of oxygen in the cerebral hemispheres? That's a kind of bureaucratese for meaning playing without a full deck.

But consider 1985. We saw a de facto balanced budget amendment passed by both houses of the Congress. We saw a House of Representatives under liberal leadership agree to cut the top marginal tax rate to the thirty-five to thirty-eight-percent range. And we even saw that same House not only approve funds for an insurgency against a communist government, but spontaneously repeal that symbol of liberal isolationism, the Clark Amendment.

So, friends and neighbors, salute Halley's Comet. Salute that space shot "U-ra-nus"—I'm too old-fashioned to call it " Ur-a-nus." I just remember politics in 1985 was also a celestial phenomenon, Steven Spielberg all the way.

Actually, the remarkable year of 1985 at home was a reflection of a broader, even brighter strategic picture. In Europe and Asia, statism and socialism are dying, and the free market is; and all across the world, the march of democracy continues. Yet, even as I think the tide of history is all but irreversibly turned our way and this strategic picture will continue to improve, we must guard at all costs against an unnecessary but costly tactical defeat ahead. I'm talking, of course, about the election in November.

Now, this isn't going to happen as long as we conservatives will shoulder the burden of our recent successes, if we'll realize how much is at stake this November, forget for the moment the flowers and the sunshine, and summon once again those deep reserves of will and stamina that won for us our first victories. And bear in mind, this will require a supreme effort; our job is going to be even tougher this year. The very years of prosperity and peace that conservative programs have given America may in a strange way actually help those who fought the hardest against them. Good times, after all, tend to favor incumbents and fortify the status quo.

Yet, you and I know how unacceptable that status quo is, how much—on everything from right to life, prayer in the schools,

enterprise zones, aid to the anti-communist insurgents—still waits to
be done. So, we must go to the record, get the facts to the American
people.

The Speaker of the House has already indicated a tax increase is
the solution to our problems, and recently, another important member
of the House leadership echoed his sentiments. Not much has changed
on the federal spending either. Sure, the liberals are angry about
Gramm-Rudman, but they aren't looking realistically at our bloated
expenditures, only talking nonsense about shutting down the FBI and
the IRS—though I do admit that in mentioning that last point they
may be tempting me beyond my strength. And as for defense, let me
assure you the liberals haven't changed a bit; they're still looking at
America's defense budget with lust in their hearts. A lust to strip it
bare and use the funds for more of their social experiments.

Yet, this year we have to work even harder at summoning the vigor
to tell the American people the truth and the vigor to ask their help, to
remind them that what they do this November will decide whether the
days of high taxes and higher spending, the days of economic stagnation
and skyrocketing inflation, the days of national malaise and international humiliation, the days of "blame America first" and "inordinate
fear of communism" will all come roaring back at us once again.

More than that, we must tell the American people that the progress
that we've made thus far is not enough, that it'll never be enough until
the conservative agenda is enacted—and that means enterprise zones,
prayer in the public schools, and protection of the unborn.

And that's why, my fellow conservatives, we have to stop limiting
ourselves to talking about holding on to our strength in the Senate
and start talking about conservative control of the House of Representatives. That House has been in the hands of our opponents for
virtually half a century. Never forget that for those nearly fifty years

the liberals had it all their own way in this city and that the loss of such great power is rarely accompanied with graceful acquiescence.

Well, since the liberals are feeling pretty sorry for themselves, and that's why they're anxious about this election, they know that unless they deliver a telling blow this year to conservatism, the 1988 Conservative Political Action Conference will see major presidential candidates from both parties demanding a chance to appear here and claim the mantle of conservatism.

So, this is our break point; our opponents are pulling out all the stops. And you know, I think it's going to be worthwhile reminding the American people of how desperate the liberals are, how so much of their strength in the House of Representatives, as many as eighteen to twenty-three seats, is due to gerrymandering on a scale unprecedented in modern history. And this is not to mention the outrageous episode in which a legitimately elected member of the Congress and the people of Indiana's 8th District were disenfranchised in the House of Representatives.

But there's another issue that I also believe vividly illustrates how seriously out of touch the liberals are with the American people. We sometimes forget that no one is more realistic about the nature of the threat to our freedom than the American people themselves. In fact, their intuitive realism is why that "Bear in the Woods" ad some of you can remember from the 1984 campaign was so successful. Yes, the American people want an administration that pursues every path to peace, but they also want an administration that is realistic about Soviet expansionism, committed to resisting it, and determined to advance the cause of freedom around the world.

Now, we know what happens when an administration that has illusions about the Soviets takes over. First, there are the illusions, then the surprise and anger when the Soviets do something like invading Afghanistan. Any way you look at it, it heightened tension and the prospects for conflict.

In fact, the liberal conduct of foreign policy reminds me of a little football game that was played at Notre Dame back in 1946, when Notre Dame player Bob Livingstone missed a tackle. And his team-mate, all-American Johnny Lujack, screamed, "Livingstone, you so-and-so you," and he went on and on. And then, Coach Frank Leahy said, "Another sacrilege like that, Jonathan Lujack, and you'll be disassociated from our fine Catholic university." Well, in the very next play, Livingstone missed another tackle, and Coach Leahy turned to the bench and said, "Lads, Jonathan Lujack was right about Robert Livingstone." And that's why it's important to go to the record.

I remember a little booklet that came out a few years back. Although it was by the Republican Study Committee and entitled "What's the Matter with Democratic Foreign Policy," it was really about a shrinking group of foreign policy liberals here in Washington. And I just think that if we were able to get some of those choice quotations on issues like Vietnam, Grenada, and Central America before the American people and they were able to see what the Washington liberals really believe about foreign policy, the naivete, and confusion of mind, I believe we would shock the American people into repudiating these views once and for all.

And let me interject here two points that I think can be important this year. First, the question of defense spending. During the last few weeks, there've been a number of columns, editorials, or speeches calling for a slash in the military budget and quoting President Eisenhower as justification. President Eisenhower did warn about large concentrations of power like the military-industrial complex, but what's being left out is the context of that quote. In his farewell address to the American people, yes, he did warn us about the danger of an all-powerful military-industrial complex, but he also reminded us America must always be vigilant because "we face a hostile ideology—global in scope, atheistic in character, ruthless in purpose, and insidious in method." The pundits haven't been quoting that part of his speech.

I know there's been a great deal of talk in the media recently about the situation in South West Africa and especially Angola. And I know also you'll be having a special guest here tomorrow evening, as I did this morning in the Oval Office. Well, let me just say now it would be inappropriate for me as president to get too specific tonight. But I do want to make a comment here on some recent history and let you draw your own conclusions.

Last September at the Lomba River in southern Angola, when a force of UNITA rebels met an overwhelmingly superior force of government troops directly supported by the Soviet bloc, the UNITA forces defeated the government troops and drove them and their communist allies from the field.

In the history of revolutionary struggles or movements for true national liberation, there is often a victory like this that electrifies the world and brings great sympathy and assistance from other nations to those struggling for freedom. Past American presidents, past American Congresses, and always, of course, the American people have offered help to others fighting in the freedom cause that we began. So, tonight, each of us joins in saluting the heroes of the Lomba River and their leader, the hope of Angola, Jonas Savimbi.

So, you see, like the Panama Canal in 1976, foreign policy issues like defense spending and aid to the freedom fighters may prove the sleeper issues of the year.

So, let me urge you all to return to your organizations and communities and to tell your volunteers and your contributors that the president said that they're needed now as never before, that the crucial hour is approaching, that the choice before the American people this year is of overwhelming importance: whether to hand the government back to the liberals or move forward with the conservative agenda into the 1990s.

My fellow conservatives, let's get the message out loud and clear. The Washington liberals and the San Francisco Democrats aren't extinct; they're just in hiding, waiting for another try. Well, let's make it clear to the American people that they must choose this year between those who are enemies of big government and the friends of the freedom fighters and, on the other hand, those who are advocates of federal power and a foreign policy of illusion. So, let the choice be clear. Will it be "blame America first," or will it be "on to democracy" and "forward for freedom"?

And freedom is the issue. The stakes are that high. You know, recently Nancy and I saw together a moving new film, the story of Eleni. It's a true story. A woman at the end of World War II, caught in the Greek Civil War, a mother who, because she smuggled her children out to safety, eventually to America, was tried, tortured, and shot by the Greek communists.

It is also the story of her son, Nicholas Gage, who grew up to become an investigative reporter with the *New York Times* and who, when he returned to Greece, secretly vowed to take vengeance on the man who had sent his mother to her death.

But at the dramatic end of the story, Nick Gage finds he cannot extract the vengeance he has promised himself. To do so, Mr. Gage writes, would have relieved the pain that had filled him for so many years, but it would also have broken the one bridge still connecting him to his mother and the part of him most like her. As he tells it: "...her final cry, before the bullets of the firing squad tore into her, was not a curse on her killers but an invocation of what she died for, a declaration"—how that cry was echoed across the centuries, her cry was a cry of love—"'My children!'" A cry for all the children of the world, a hope that all of them may someday live in peace and freedom.

And how many times have I heard it in the Oval Office while trying to comfort those who have lost a son in the service of our nation and the cause of freedom. "He didn't want to die," the wife of Major Nicholson said at Fort Belvoir last year about her husband, "and we didn't want to lose him, but he would gladly lay down his life again for America."

So, we owe something to them, you and I. To those who've gone before Major Nicholson, Eleni, the heroes at the Lomba River—and to the living as well—Andrei Sakharov, Lech Walesa, Adolfo Calero, Jonas Savimbi—their hopes reside in us as ours do in them.

Some twenty years ago, I told my fellow conservatives that, "You and I have a rendezvous with destiny." And tonight, that rendezvous is upon us. Our destiny is now. Our cause is still, as it was then, the cause of human freedom. Let us be proud that we serve together, and brave in our resolve to push on now toward that final victory so long sought by the heroes of our past and present and now so near at hand.

Thank you. God bless you.

The Future of Conservatism

Congressman Mark Meadows

COMMENTARY ON

Forward for Freedom

When President Ronald Reagan gave his *Forward for Freedom* speech at the Conservative Political Action Conference in 1986, he had already realized much of his vision to restore American prosperity by championing a conservative agenda. It is interesting that, when asked to reflect upon the future of the conservative movement, Reagan spoke so much about the past. Reagan saw the 1986 election as a chance for conservatives to fight to preserve the ground they had gained under his administration. Simply put, Reagan saw the future of the conservative movement as a fight to preserve his policies.

Reagan claimed three major political achievements in his speech to CPAC: his administration's accomplishments of cutting deficit spending and taxes and supporting the fight against communism across the globe. He believed the future of the conservative movement in America relied on the preservation of these achievements.

Reagan presented CPAC with a dichotomy: fight to preserve conservatism or allow the increasingly hostile liberal movement to roll back all of the administration's achievements. The dichotomy was real; Thomas "Tip" O'Neill, then the Democratic Speaker of the House under Reagan, wanted to increase taxes on the American people and abolish the FBI and IRS.

I believe conservatives in America are facing another form of that radicalism in 2018. After eight years of liberal leadership in the White House, President Trump, in his first two years in office, has followed Reagan's example of cutting government regulation and taxes drastically, and strengthening our military. But this has only fueled the fire for the liberal movement in America. More than ever, liberals want to use any means necessary to stop President Trump's successful conservative policies. The American people must decide whether they want to fight to preserve these changes or give up their hard-won personal freedom.

In his speech, Reagan told a story about his battle for tax cuts. He described how, when speaking with a House member about cutting taxes, the congressman told Reagan he was "in the big leagues now" and should not expect much. Little did this Congressman realize, his comments flew directly in the face of Reagan's political philosophy. Reagan abhorred the idea that the "big leagues" would refuse to work for the American people. At a time when the United States was constantly compared to the Soviet Union, it was paramount that the American people were the foremost consideration for the United States government.

Reagan's campaign ideology in 1980 was that "government is not the solution to our problem, government is the problem." For Reagan, the "big leagues" were the American people; the teachers, farmers, businessmen, and nurses working every day to make their own lives and the lives of those around them better. And this is still what the modern conservative movement is all about. We work to make life better in America, for ourselves and our posterity. The conservative movement in America today is a fight to preserve and extend President Trump's Reagan-like policies.

Reagan concluded his speech: "Well, let's make it clear to the American people that they must choose this year between those who are enemies of big government and the friends of the freedom fighters and, on the other hand, those who are advocates of federal power and a foreign policy of illusion." In recent years, I believe Americans have lost this choice. Too often, Americans vote for "conservative" politicians who, once in Washington, refuse to stand by their campaign promises. I work hard every day to make sure this cannot be said of me. I want to represent the conservative American who feels he has no real representation in Congress.

Americans in the twenty-first century must choose whether they want the federal government to give them more personal freedom, or whether they want that freedom taken from them. Reagan had an indestructible faith in the attitude and spirit of the American people to choose conservatism and freedom. I share that faith.

Mark Meadows is a U.S. congressman from North Carolina serving since 2013.

A Future
that Works

1987

T hank you all. Thank you. As Henry VIII said to each one
of his six wives, "I won't keep you long."

Fellow conservatives and dear friends, it's such a pleasure to be with you again. I see so many who've served our cause with such distinction over the years. David Keene and so many others of you deserve accolades for commitment and dedication.

What we've accomplished these last six years wouldn't have been possible without a solid foundation, one painstakingly laid. And much of that work was done by men and women who were content to make their contribution knowing their names would never be enshrined, individuals who didn't make the clips when the recent documentary about the conservative movement was made. Two centuries ago, the Americans who were the bulwark of the cause of liberty and independence—[who] backed up the Hancocks, the Jeffersons, and the Patrick Henrys—were of similar stock.

And so, today let me express my appreciation to all of you. You are truly freedom's team. The going may be a little rough at this moment, but let no one doubt our resolve. You know, these last several weeks, I've felt a little bit like that farmer that was driving his horse and wagon to town for some grain and had a head-on collision with a truck. And later was the litigation involving claims for his injuries, some of them permanent. And he was on the stand and a lawyer said to him, "Isn't it true that while you were lying there at the scene of the accident someone came over to you and asked you how you were feeling, and you said you never felt better in your life?" And he said, "Yes, I remember that."

Well, later he's on the stand and the witnesses were there—the lawyer for the other side is questioning—and he said, "When you gave that answer about how you felt, what were the circumstances?" "Well," he said, "I was lying there, and a car came up and a deputy sheriff got out." He said, "My horse was screaming with pain—had broken two legs. The deputy took out his gun, put it in the horse's ear, and finished him off." And he said, "My dog was whining with pain—had a broken back. And," he said, "he went over to him and put the gun in his ear. And then," he says, "he turned to me and says now, how are you feeling?"

But getting back to our resolve: six years ago, we won a great victory, and we don't intend to let anyone again drag our beloved country into the murky pit of collectivism and statism.

This is the two hundredth anniversary of our Constitution, and no cloud will dim the shining light of our remembrance. This year, we rededicate ourselves to the shared values and the common purpose that have given our nation unrivaled prosperity and freedom. We hear the cynics but pay them no mind. We pass by the pessimists and the doomsayers, knowing that they'll always be with us, but confident that they no longer can hold our country back unless we let them. We see before us a future worthy of our past and a tomorrow greater than all our yesterdays. If there's any message that I wish to convey today, it is: be of good cheer. We're coming back, and coming back strong.

Our confidence flows not from our skill at maneuvering through political mazes, not from our ability to make the right deal at the right time, nor from any idea of playing one interest group off against the other. Unlike our opponents, who find their glee in momentary political leverage, we [nourish] our strength of purpose from a commitment to ideals that we deeply believe are not only right, but that work.

Ludwig Von Mises, that great economist, once noted: "People must fight for something they want to achieve, not simply reject an evil." Well, the conservative movement remains in the ascendancy because we have a bold, forward-looking agenda. No longer can it be said that conservatives are just anti-communist. We are, and proudly so, but we are also the keepers of the flame of liberty. And as such, we believe that America should be a source of support, both moral and material, for all those on God's Earth who struggle for freedom. Our cause is their cause, whether it be in Nicaragua, Afghanistan, or Angola. When I came back from Iceland I said—and I meant it—American foreign policy is not simply focused on the prevention of war, but the expansion of freedom. Modern conservatism is an active, not a reactive, philosophy.

It's not just in opposition to those vices that debase character and community, but affirms values that are at the heart of civilization. We favor protecting and strengthening the family, an institution that was taken for granted during the decades of liberal domination of American government.

The family, as became clear in the not-too-distant past, is taken for granted at our peril. Victimized most were the least fortunate among us, those who sorely needed the strength and protection of the family. A federal welfare system, constructed in the name of helping those in poverty, wreaked havoc on the poor family—tearing it apart, eating away at the underpinnings of their community, creating fatherless children, and unprecedented despair. The liberal welfare state has been a tragedy beyond description for so many of our fellow citizens, a crime against less fortunate Americans. The welfare system cries out for reform and reformed it will be. And when it is, the number one question that must be asked of every change is: will this strengthen the family?

Now, personally, I think that criterion should guide our decisions, not just in welfare reform, but in the deliberations of every department and agency. And if the answer is negative, the proposal should be sent to the Heritage Foundation for study, and you can bet they'll know what to do with it.

Our positive stance on family and children is consistent with our heartfelt convictions on the issue of abortion. Here again, we're not just against an evil. We're not just anti-abortion; we're pro-life. Many who consider abortion the taking of human life understandably feel frustrated, and perhaps a sense of helplessness, in bringing about the legal changes that we all seek. Progress has been slow and painful, and all the while the taking of unborn lives continues. Well, while we keep up the pressure for a change of law, there is something that can be done. Those of us who oppose abortion can and should aggressively move forward with a positive adoption versus abortion campaign.

We must see to it that adoption is a readily available alternative and is an encouraged course of action. I would like to commend those in our movement, while not easing up on applying political pressure, who have been involved in providing counseling and services, especially to unwed mothers. Every time a choice is made to save an unborn baby's life, it is reason for joy. In the meantime, we in government will see to it that not one tax dollar goes to encouraging any woman to snuff out the life of her unborn child and that eventually the life of the unborn again comes within the protection of the law.

Last week, we sent to Congress legislation to enact on a permanent, government-wide basis the Hyde Amendment restriction on federal funding of abortion. Our proposal would also cut off funding, under Title X, to private organizations that refer or perform abortions except when the mother's life is in danger. I hope all of you will join in the bipartisan effort to enact this much-needed legislation.

Conservatives are working for a society where children are cherished and in school are taught not only reading, writing, and arithmetic, but fundamental values as well. And in striving for this, we will not compromise in our commitment to restore the right to pray to the school children of America. We want a strong America, and we know the truth behind President Eisenhower's words when he quoted a young Frenchman's observation that if America ceases to be good, America will cease to be great.

The moral underpinnings of our country must be able to bear the weight of today if we're to pass on to the next generation an America worth having. And again, we're positive, and our eyes are on the future. And that's why so many of today's young people are supporting our cause. And believe me, as I was running for reelection, I saw them at every stop—those young people full of life, enjoying their freedom, and enthusiastic about the United States of America. I have to tell you, you young people are a new experience for us. We went through some years when you weren't cheering us, and it's wonderful to have you on our side. Well, our greatest political challenge is to find the formula that will mobilize our broad support among young people. Clearly, they aren't just looking for youthful appearances. My birthday cake's beginning to look more and more like a bonfire every year.

We must offer a vision of a future that works, a positive agenda for positive results. And we must not be so much against big government and high taxes as we are in favor of higher take-home pay and more freedom. And we've proven it works. With an emphasis on enterprise, investment, and work, on jobs and opportunity, we turned around economic decline and national malaise and set in motion one of the longest periods of peacetime economic growth and job creation in postwar history.

The pundits, you know, the pundits told us that we couldn't expect to get anything accomplished, even before we got to Washington. Now, they're trying to bring the curtain down before the show is over. Well, I learned a lesson in my former profession. So, let me give you a tip: we're saving the best stuff for the last act. Thank you. Thank you very much. Thank you.

Thank you very much. Our game plan is still the best one in town. The notion that government controls, central planning, and bureaucracy can provide cost-free prosperity has now come and gone the way of the hula-hoop, the Nehru jackets, and the all-asparagus diet. Throughout the world the failure of socialism is evident.

There's an underground joke that's told in the Soviet Union, for example, about a teacher who asked one of the young students, Ivan, what life is like in the United States. And dutifully Ivan said, "Half the people are unemployed, and millions are hungry or starving." "Well, then," the teacher asks, "then what is the goal of the Soviet Union?" Ivan said, "To catch up with the United States."

Seriously though, today free enterprise is propelling us into a new technological era. Small businesses throughout our land now have computer capability, which a decade ago was available only to large corporations. The economic vitality pushing our country into the twenty-first century is broad-based and irreversible—and it's not coming from the top, but from the bottom. The creative talents of our citizenry, always America's greatest asset, are being magnified by state-of-the-art technology and put to work for our benefit as never before. We have every reason to be optimistic.

Our scientific advances offer us new methods of meeting the challenges we face as a people. One of the first significant questions to emerge as a result of our rapid progress deals with the Strategic

Defense Initiative. I see you know that that is our effort to develop a way of protecting mankind from the threat of ballistic missiles. It holds the promise of someday making those missiles, deadly weapons that have been the cause of such dread, obsolete.

We have offered to share the benefits of our SDI program with the Soviet Union, perhaps as part of an overall agreement to dramatically reduce our respective nuclear arsenals. But let me make this clear: a defense against ballistic missiles is just one of many new achievements that will be made possible by the incredible technological progress that we are enjoying.

Each step forward improves our lives, adding to our ability to produce and build and generate wealth. Yet, each step also has strategic implications. SDI, as I say, is one. Let there be no doubt, we have no intention of being held back because our adversary cannot keep up. We will use our scientific skills to make this a more prosperous world and to enhance the security of our own country. We must not and will not bargain our future away.

Six years ago, we came to Washington at a time of great national uncertainty. The vigor and confidence so evident in our land today reflect more than luck. They are the outgrowth of ideas that stress freedom for the individual and respect for the humane and decent values of family, God, and neighborhood.

We are giving our children the greatest gift that is within our power to give, the one we received from those who came before us: a strong, free, and opportunity-filled America. And I thank you for all that you have done and continue to do to make certain that we do just that.

And so, thank you, and God bless you all.

Our Renewed Commitment to Domestic Reform

Allie Beth Stuckey

COMMENTARY ON

A Future That Works

An eternal optimist, Ronald Reagan had a knack for instilling hope. In confusion, he offered clarity. In chaos, he infused calmness. In catastrophe, he demonstrated competence. And in controversy, he remained confident.

By February of 1987, President Reagan was no stranger to controversy. The Iran-Contra affair dominated the news cycle, challenging Reagan's sterling reputation of transparency and integrity. The Reykjavik Summit with Gorbachev took place in October of 1986 and had appeared to be a failure. Democrats took the Senate in November, marking the first time in Reagan's presidency that the opposing party led both chambers of Congress, introducing the potential of an uphill battle for his administration during the final two years of his leadership.

Conservatives had cause for concern, but they also had reason to celebrate. The Reagan administration, with the help of Congress, had just enacted the Tax Reform Act of 1986, the second of the "Reagan tax cuts," which significantly simplified the income tax code. Reagan's tax reforms are credited for the longest peacetime economic expansion in postwar America.

Reagan's 1987 CPAC address, *A Future That Works*, assured conservatives that, despite setbacks, their revolution had won significant battles. Neither his administration nor conservatism would be hindered, and their cause was more crucial than ever.

The title of the address displays Reagan's iconic wit, its meaning twofold: his administration's vision of America—one that centered on the advancement of liberty at home and abroad—would work effectively to foster a bright, successful future for Americans. That future centered on literal work that would ensure fewer people were dependent on welfare. To Reagan, the protection and perpetuation of work was central to the success of the conservative movement.

Reagan believed that work is not a necessary evil, but an essential virtue, inextricably intertwined with human dignity. Without work, Reagan often argued, men and women grow purposeless, and ultimately fail to reach their potential. The welfare state at home, as well as socialism and communism abroad, endangered human flourishing by rendering individual productivity meaningless. Reagan viewed this as much worse than failed policy; to him, it was evil.

Reagan's deeply held conviction was that human beings are meant to be free—free to pursue their own destiny, to produce something meaningful, and to be a part of something bigger than themselves. He opposed any system that stripped men and women of responsibility, and he fought hard to dismantle them. The president knew well the time-tested truth: government never helps a person without telling him what to do. He understood that tyranny is most effective when masked as compassion. That was the battle before conservatives.

In his 1987 CPAC address, President Reagan reminded his audience of the innate morality of the conservative cause by insisting that their purpose was not only to oppose bad policies, but to lend support for better ones. Theirs was not only a fight *against* evil, but a fight *for* goodness.

While his charge is timeless, there is, of course, a bit of despair that accompanies his speech. So optimistic was Reagan about the future of the country, and so sure was he about the end of socialism and the perpetuation of liberty. A little over two years after this CPAC address, the Berlin Wall would fall—an exclamation mark on Reagan's legacy. What would Reagan say now if he knew that fewer than thirty years later, we are inviting socialism onto our shores, thereby diminishing the importance of work and demeaning human dignity?

Surely, he would be astonished to know that being a "socialist" is no longer a scarlet letter in American politics, but a badge of honor. Surely, he would be shocked by our forgetfulness of the deadliness of totalitarianism. Surely, he would be disappointed by Americans' willingness to exchange freedom for government control.

But I would like to believe that, in true Reagan form, he would tell us still to not to lose hope. That though the future seems bleak, the American experiment appears precarious, and conservatives feel outmatched in their quest for the protection of liberty, there is light beyond the horizon—if only we are willing to pursue it. He would remind us that ours is a worthy, moral fight. It is a fight for the souls of men, which, when set aflame by freedom, cannot be snuffed out.

"Liberty," Reagan warned years earlier, "is never more than one generation away from extinction." Today, let us then fight this good fight, so freedom does not die when we do.

Allie Beth Stuckey is a writer, speaker, commentator, and the host of the CRTV podcast Relatable.

On the Frontier of
Freedom

1988

T hank you very much. It's great to be here tonight, and I'm
delighted to see so many old friends. And now let's get right
to it. First, there's the INF treaty. How do you think I felt
when Gorbachev called a week and a half ago and asked me if our
first group of on-site inspectors could be the Denver Broncos' pass
defense? [Laughter] And then along came the House vote on Contra aid—I felt so terrible, I nearly called Dan Reeves and John
Elway to tell them what a rough week I'd had.

But seriously, while the Denver Broncos are all terrific athletes
and people, each one of us has to congratulate the Washington
Redskins. Believe me, the House action on the Contra vote was a
missed chance at a victory for peace in Central America. It's great
to know there are some people in Washington who play to win.
And believe me, I'll be getting back to that topic in a few minutes.

By the way, something odd happened just before I got here
tonight that I think you should know about. I got a message from
Dave Keene reminding me that this was the eve of Lincoln's

birthday—and suggesting I go upstairs and check on the ghost in Lincoln's bedroom. I did. And what do you know, there was Stan Evans dressed as Abe Lincoln. And he kept saying, "Listen to Jesse Helms."

Actually, I do want to thank you for that warm welcome, but I hope tonight isn't going to be like what happened to that fellow I knew back in Hollywood in those movie days—and, oh, how I hope I haven't told you this one before.

We had an actor that was in Hollywood, and he was only there long enough to get enough money to go to Italy, because he aspired to an operatic career. And then after some time there, in Milan, Italy, where he was studying, he was invited to sing at La Scala, the very spiritual fountainhead of opera. They were doing Pagliacci, and he sang the beautiful aria, Vesti La Giuba.

And he received such thunderous and sustained applause from the balconies and the orchestra seats that he had to repeat the aria as an encore. And again, the same sustained, thunderous applause. And again, he sang Vesti La Giuba. And this went on until finally he motioned for quiet, and he tried to tell them how full his heart was at that reception—his first time out. But he said, "I have sung Vesti La Giuba nine times now. My voice is gone. I cannot do it again." And a voice from the balcony said, "You'll do it till you get it right." Well, let's get it right tonight. And let's start where we should start.

A couple of weeks ago, I talked about the state of our Union, and tonight I'd like to talk about something that I think in many ways is synonymous: the state of our movement. During the past year, plenty of questions have been asked about the conservative movement by some people who were surprised to find out back in 1980 that there was such a thing. I mean a powerful new political movement capable of running a victorious national campaign based on an unabashed appeal to the American people for conservative ideas and principles.

Well, we conservatives have been in Washington now for a while and we occasionally need to remind ourselves what brought us here in the first place: our unshakable, root-deep, all-encompassing skepticism about the capital city's answer to the UFO, that bizarre, ever-tottering but ever-flickering saucer in the sky called "The Prevailing Washington Wisdom."

And, right now, some of the Potomac seers are saying we conservatives are tired; or they're saying we don't have a candidate, some of those candidates in the other party saying how easy it's going to be to win the presidency for their liberal agenda because they can run on, of all things, this administration's economic record. Boy, have I got news for them. They're seeing flying saucers again. I've even got a quote for them. It's from Napoleon—the morning of Waterloo—at breakfast with his generals. This is true. He said, "I tell you what—Wellington is a bad general. The English are bad troops. We'll settle the matter by lunchtime."

Well, my fellow conservatives, I think that's exactly what this year is about—settling the matter by lunchtime. Letting the liberals in Washington discover once again the lesson they refuse to learn. Letting them know just how big our election year will be because of booming economic growth and individual opportunity; and how big an election year ball and chain they've given themselves with a seven-year record of opposition to the real record. But, most of all, letting them know that the real friends of the conservative movement aren't those entrenched in the capital city for fifty years; the real friends of the conservative movement are an entity that gets heard from in a big way every four years and who, I promise you, are going to be heard from this year. I'm talking about those who, if the case is aggressively put before them, will vote for limited government, family values, and a tough, strong foreign policy every single time. I'm talking about those believers in common sense and sound values, your friends and mine, the American people.

You see, those who underestimate the conservative movement are the same people who always underestimate the American people. Take the latest instance. As I mentioned, in recent months some people— and I'm not mentioning any names because I don't want to build up any candidacies before New Hampshire, but you know who they are—have actually taken it upon themselves to prove to the American people that they've been worse off under this administration than they were back in the Carter years of the '70s.

Now I agree with you, this takes some doing. How do they manage it? Well, you see, any statistical comparison of the two recent administrations would start with 1977 to 1981 as the budget years of the last administration, and 1981 to 1987 as the pertinent years for this one. Now, that sounds reasonable enough. But our opponents have a new approach, one that would have embarrassed even the emperor's tailors. They take the years 1977, to up to 1983—and then they stop. So, you see, not only do 1984 and 1985 not get counted in their data base, but they include in this administration's economic record four years of the last Democratic administration. As columnist Warren Brookes pointed out in an article published in the *Washington Times*, "All of the foreshortened Reagan gains are nullified by the Carter losses, so they look like no gains at all, or, worse, losses." Our successes, in short, are buried under the last administration's failures.

But the truth is otherwise. Because under the last administration, real per capita disposable income rose at only one percent annual rate, only half the two percent rate of increase under this administration's gain that has totaled 12.4 percent in six years. Under the last administration, median family income declined 6.8 percent, while under this administration it went up 9.1 percent. Or take the real after-tax labor income per hour: if you use the approach adopted by our liberal critics, you see a 4.5 percent decline. But the truth is that that figure fell 8.5 percent under the last administration and we turned this around and accounted for an 8.9 percent increase.

Under the last administration, the average weekly wage went down an incredible ten percent in real terms, which accounted for the worst drop in postwar history. Here again, we've stopped the decline. And that's not to mention what all this has meant in terms of opportunity for women, for blacks, and minorities, the very groups our opponents say they most want to help.

Well, since the recovery began, seventy percent of the new jobs have been translated into opportunities for women; and black and other minority employment has risen twice as fast as all other groups. Minority family income has also increased at a rate over forty percent faster than other groups. In addition, since 1983, 2.9 million people have climbed out of poverty, and the poverty rate has declined at the fastest rate in more than ten years.

So, think for a moment on what these statistics mean and the kind of political nerve and desperation it takes to try to sell the American people on the idea that in the 1980s, they never had it so bad. The truth is, we're in the sixty-third month of this non-stop expansion. Real Gross National Product growth for 1987 was 3.8 percent, defying the pessimists and even exceeding our own forecast—which was criticized as being too rosy at the time—by more than one half percent. Inflation is down from 13.5 per cent in 1980 to only around four percent or less this year. And there's over 15 million new jobs.

So, believe me, I welcome this approach by the opposition. And I promise you, every time they use it, I'll just tell the story of a friend of mine who was asked to a costume ball a short time ago—he slapped some egg on his face and went as a liberal economist. Now, the reason I spell out these statistics and stress this economic issue should be very clear. You know that some cynics like to say that the people vote their pocketbook. But that's not quite the point. Economic issues are important to the people not simply for reasons of self-interest. They know the whole body politic depends on economic stability; the great crises have come for democracies when taxes and inflation ran out of control and undermined social relations and basic institutions. The American people know what limited government, tax cuts, deregulation, and the move towards privatization have meant. It's meant the largest peacetime expansion in our history, and I can guarantee you they won't want to throw that away for a return to budgets beholden to the liberal special interests.

No, I think the economic record of conservatives in power is going to speak for itself. But now let's turn to another area. For two decades we've been talking about getting justices on the Supreme Court who cared less about criminals and more about the victims of crime; justices who knew that the words "original intent" referred to something more than New Year's resolutions and fad diets. And then, seven months ago a seat opened on the Supreme Court. And even before our first nominee was announced, a campaign was planned unlike any that has ever been waged for or against a judicial nominee in the history of our country. And let me acknowledge once again my admiration for one of the courageous defenders, not only in our time but in all time, of the principles of our Constitution, yes, of its original intent—Judge Robert Bork.

One of America's most cherished principles—the independence and integrity of our judiciary—was under siege. And the American people, who have always been with the ultimate guarantors of the Constitution, began to say with clarity and finality, it must never happen again. So, when I nominated a judge who could as easily have been my first nominee, there was hardly a peep of protest. And Judge Kennedy is now going to be Justice Kennedy. And since our opponents won't, I'll let you in on a secret—Judge Kennedy will be just the kind of justice that you and I've been determined to put on the Court. Anyway, any man who teaches law school in a tri-corner hat and a powdered wig is okay by me on original intent.

Let's look at how far and how successfully we've carried the battle into the lower courts. Just look at the statistics on criminal sentencing. In few places can you see more clearly the collapse of the liberal stranglehold on our courts. The most recent statistics show federal judges imposed prison sentences that averaged thirty-two percent longer than those handed down during 1979. Robbery sentences were ten percent longer; drug offenses, thirty-eight percent longer; and weapons offenses, forty-one percent longer.

The great legal debates of the past two decades over criminal justice have, at their root, been debates over a strict versus expansive construction of the Constitution. The Constitution, as originally intended by the framers, is itself tough on crime, and protective of the victims of crime. For so long, the liberal message to our national culture was tune in, turn on, let it all hang out. And now they see conservatives taking the lead as our nation says "no" to drugs, and "yes" to family, and "absolutely" to schools that teach basic skills, basic values, and basic discipline. And it's no wonder that our nation admires a man who believes in teaching values in education, and talks turkey to teachers, parents, and educators, such as our secretary of education, Bill Bennett.

And so, I say to you tonight that the vision and record that we will take aggressively to the American people this November is a vision that all Americans, except a few on the left, share. A vision of a nation that believes in the heroism of ordinary people living ordinary lives; of tough courts and safe streets; of a drug-free America where schools teach honesty, respect, love of learning, and, yes, love of country; a vision of a land where families can grow in love and safety and where dreams are made with opportunity. This is the vision; this is the record; this is the agenda for victory this year. Well, that's the record then on the economy and the social issues. Now, let's turn to foreign policy.

I want to be clear tonight about the vote on Contra aid. It was a setback to the national security interests of the United States, and a sad moment for the cause of peace and freedom in Central America. Until now, the carrot-and-stick approach has worked in forcing a communist regime to relax some of its repression. But now, the action by the House of Representatives removes one part of that formula and goes only with the carrot. The effect of this vote then was to trust the promises of democracy of the Sandinista communists—the kind of promises that no communist regime in history has ever carried out, and that this regime was likely to carry out only under continued pressure. The effect of this vote was to rest the hopes for peace and democracy in Central America purely and simply on the word of the communist regime in Managua. This course is, and I repeat, a risk to America's national security.

But you know, I read something the other day and it's worth a note here. One of those opposing aid to the freedom fighters said it was important to get a twenty-vote margin. Well, as you know, it was nothing like that—if we could have turned around four or five votes, we would have won. Last week's vote was not the final word, only a pause. Last week, the bad news was the lost vote in the House. But the good news was our support in the Senate and the overwhelming number of House Republicans who voted with us and those forty-seven Democrats who braved the threats of reprisals to vote for Contra aid.

So, let me make this pledge to you tonight: we're not giving up on those who are fighting for their freedom—and they aren't giving up either. I'll have more to say on this in a few weeks. For now, I'll leave it at this: get ready—the curtain hasn't fallen, the drama continues.

While we're on foreign policy, let me turn for just a moment to what I said in that December interview while Mr. Gorbachev was here. You know, Ben Wattenberg was one of the journalists there, and he brought up a speech I made back in 1982 to the British Parliament. And he asked me if what I really was saying was what I said in England: that if the West remained resolute, the Soviets would have to, at some point, deal with their own internal problems and crises, that the tides of history are shifting in favor of the cause of freedom. Well, I believed then, and I believe now, that we must consider what we're seeing—or the steps in that direction. This hardly means accepting the Soviets at face value. Few of us can forget what that has led to in the past. FDR was quoted as saying during his dealings with Stalin—with the Soviets in '44: "Stalin doesn't want anything but security for his country and I think that if I give him everything I possibly can and ask nothing from him in return, noblesse oblige, he won't try to annex anything and will work with me for a world democracy and peace."

Well, no, there is no room for illusion. Our guard is up, our watch is careful. We shall not be led by—or misled by—atmospherics. We came to Washington with a common-sense message that the world is a dangerous place where the only sure route to peace and the protection of freedom is through American strength. In no place has this thesis of peace through strength been tested more than on the matter of intermediate-range nuclear forces (INF). In deploying over four hundred SS-20s, with over 1,200 warheads, against our friends and allies in Europe and Asia over the past decade, the Soviets were playing a high-stakes game of geopolitical blackjack. The prize was Europe. The strategy: discredit America's deterrence and undermine the NATO alliance. But we and our allies turned over a winning hand, deploying in Europe Pershing II and ground-launched cruise missiles that provided an effective counter to the new Soviet missiles, and Moscow finally stopped upping the stakes.

What I would like to see is for some of those who've been praising our INF treaty to show they've learned its true lesson and vote to maintain an adequate defense budget, our work on a strategic defense against ballistic missiles, and, yes, aid to the freedom fighters in Nicaragua.

And while we're on the subject of our nation's defense—you know, there's a man I want to talk about tonight who said once that "the definition of happiness was service to a noble cause." No one has done that better, and tonight I salute Cap Weinberger for all he's done for America.

But at the same time, we must not look at any single step alone—we must see not just the INF treaty, but also the advance of SDI and, most important, the growing democratic revolution around the globe against totalitarian regimes. We should engage the Soviets in negotiations to deter war and keep the peace. But at the same time, we must make clear our own position, as I have throughout these negotiations. In sitting down to these negotiations, we accept no moral equivalency between the cause of freedom and the rule of totalitarianism.

And we understand that the most important change of all is this: that containment is no longer enough, that we no longer can be satisfied with an endless stalemate between liberty and repression. That arms reduction negotiations, development and testing of SDI, and our help for freedom fighters around the globe must express the clear goal of American foreign policy. To deter war, yes. To further world peace, yes. But, most of all, to advance and protect the cause of world freedom so that someday every man, woman, and child on this Earth has as a birthright the full blessings of liberty.

We've seen dramatic change in these seven years. Who would have guessed seven years ago that we would see tax rates drop from seventy percent to twenty-eight percent, the longest peacetime economic boom in our history, or a massive shift in world opinion toward the ideas of free enterprise and political freedom?

I know some of you are impatient with the pace of this change. But if I might repeat a story I told when I addressed you for the first time as president—I had the pleasure in appearing before a Senate committee once while I was still governor. And I was challenged there because there was a Republican president in the White House at the time, who'd been there for some time and why hadn't we corrected everything that had gone wrong. And the only way I could think to answer him is, I told him about a ranch many years ago that Nancy and I acquired. It had a barn with eight stalls in it, in which they kept cattle—cows. We wanted to keep horses. Well, the accumulation within the stalls had built up the floor to the place that it wasn't even tall enough for horses in there. And so there I was, day after day, with a pick and shovel, lowering the level of those stalls, which had accumulated over the years. And I told this senator who'd asked that question that I discovered that you didn't undo in a relatively short time what it had taken some fifteen years to accumulate.

We have not only been undoing the damage of the past; we've put this nation on the upward road again. And, in the process, the differences between the liberals and conservatives have become clear to the American people. We want to keep taxes low, they want to raise them; we send in budgets with spending cuts and they want to ignore them; we want the balanced budget amendment and the line-item veto, and they oppose them; we want tough judges and tough anti-crime legislation, they hold them both up in the Congress.

You'd be surprised how many judges are waiting out there before they—so that they have to pass on them before they can take their office, and they've been waiting for months. We want a prayer amendment, they won't let it come to a vote in the House; we stress firmness

with the Soviets, they try to pass legislation that would tie our hands
in arms negotiations and endanger our defenses. But I say, we have a
program and a plan for the American people—a program to protect
American jobs by fighting the menace of protectionism, to move
forward at flank speed with SDI, to call America to conscience on the
issue of abortion on demand, to mention, as I did in my State of the
Union Address, the overwhelming importance of family life and family values.

That's a case to take to the American people. That's a fighting
agenda. I intend to campaign vigorously for whoever our nominee is,
and tonight I ask each of you to join me in this important crusade.
Let's ask the American people to replenish our mandate. Let's tell
them if they want four more years of economic progress and the
march of world freedom, they must help us this year. Help us settle
the matter before lunchtime. Help make 1988 the year of the Waterloo liberal.

I just have to add here, when you look at the figures overall—that
they have the nerve even to still be out there and campaigning. (Laugh-
ter)

We mustn't just think that electing the president is enough. We've
been doing that for more than half-a-century. We have—in the fifty
years between 1931 and 1980, only four years in that period was there
a Republican majority in both houses of the Congress—two years in
Eisenhower's regime, two years in Truman's. But for forty-six of those
fifty years, they controlled the Congress. Every Democratic president,
except for those two years, had a Democratic Congress. Every Republican president had a Democratic Congress, except for those two years
in Eisenhower's regime. And now, in the last seven years added to
that—yes, for six of those years we had one House. But except for the
four years, for fifty-eight years it will be our opponents holding the
House of Representatives, where so much legislation and

authorization for spending and so forth comes in. And in all those fifty-eight years, there have only been eight single years in which there was a balanced budget. So, who's at fault for the deficit today?

Back when the great society—when the war on poverty began, which poverty won—from 1965 to 1980—in those fifteen years, the federal budget increased to five times what it had been in '65. And the deficit increased to thirty-eight times what it had been just fifteen years before. It's built-in, it's structural. And you and I need to get representatives not only in the executive branch, but out there in the legislature, so that we can change that structure that is so built-in, and that threatens us with so much harm.

Well, I've gone on too long for all of you here, but I just wanted to—I couldn't resist, because you're the troops. You're out there on the frontier of freedom. One young soldier over there in Korea—one of our men—saluted me when I visited there, and very proudly said, "Mr. President, we're on the frontier of freedom." Well, so are you.

Thank you. God bless you all.

The Battles of Belief That Lie Ahead

Bill Walton

COMMENTARY ON

On the Frontier of Freedom

Much has been made of late over how Ronald Reagan would have survived in this age of Twitter, or how he might have coped with today's hyper-partisanship. For doubters, look no further than his 1988 speech at CPAC. He would have done just fine.

We will never know if President Reagan would have used Twitter. His many stories would've defied 140-character limits, and that famous twinkle in his eye might have been lost. But many of Reagan's best quotes would have made splendid tweets, such as, "Man is not free unless government is limited," and, "We can't help everyone, but everyone can help someone."

And if Trump's worldview appeals to so many Republicans today, Reagan's would be off the charts.

Reagan's 1988 speech at CPAC—his last such address as president—serves as another iron-wrought example of oration for American leaders. Whether inspiration has been intentionally sought from or naturally engrained by Reagan's towering yet humble legacy, Trump's speeches today emulate Reagan's undeniable kinship with the American people.

Real Americans, Reagan said that night, are not those who have been entrenched in the capital city for the last fifty years. The real conservative movement, he said, is a "big entity that gets heard from every four years, and I promise you they are going to be heard from this year."

Real conservatives, he said, are "those who, when the case is aggressively put before them, will vote for limited government, family values, and a tough, strong foreign policy every single time."

He talked at length about how a campaign to derail the nomination of Judge Robert Bork—one of the most qualified jurists ever to the Supreme Court—was "unlike any that has been waged against a judicial nominee in the history of our country." Unlike Trump, whose nominees have endured, Reagan's nominee was voted down in the Senate.

Reagan's lifelong journey to bend the course of history toward freedom continues today, as America's role in ending tyranny throughout the world changes and we rededicate our support to those fighting to be free.

Reagan understood, as does Trump, the importance of dealing with other nations from a position of strength, not sentiment. Sentiment told him to abandon missile defense because it made the Russians uncomfortable; common sense told him this wholly defensive weapon was a game-changer. It proved to be in the Soviet Union, and now, perhaps, will be prove likewise in North Korea.

"There is no room for illusion," Reagan said in the 1988 speech. "Our guard is up. Our watch is careful. We shall not be misled by atmospherics. We came to Washington with a common-sense message that the world is a dangerous place where the only sure route to peace, protection, and freedom is through American strength."

Like our renewed conservative movement, Reagan sought to expand the economy and prosperity through deregulation and pro-growth tax policy.

"We've seen dramatic change in these seven years," he said that night. "Who'd have thought in these last seven years, we'd see taxes drop from seventy to twenty-eight percent, the longest peacetime recovery in our history and a massive shift in world opinion toward the idea of free enterprise and political freedom?"

Our economy is again expanding rapidly thanks to pro-growth conservative tax policy. Changes in leadership in Brazil, Hungary, Austria, and elsewhere, as well as Brexit and other measures, show how world opinion is again responding to America and moving toward the idea of free enterprise and political freedom.

Reagan viewed the media with a gimlet eye and, like Trump, sought to bypass its bias and communicate directly with the American people. His speech even recounts an example of fake news (although it wasn't called that then) that will seem familiar to news-watchers today.

Reagan said Democrats and their friends in the media tried to diminish and distort his economic accomplishments by comparing the last three years of the Jimmy Carter administration with just the first two years of his own, when the economy suffered from the left-over effects of Carter's policies. Reagan pushed back, hard. It's a pleasure to watch him take their distortions apart.

He also shared with the current president a talent for portraying himself as a happy and humorous warrior through it all. At the end of his story about the economic comparison, Reagan talked about a barn he had bought with Nancy. The previous owners had kept cows in the barn, and the accumulation of cow waste on the bottom of the barn made it too short for horses. So, he had to clean out the barn, he said, and, as he explained to a Senate committee, "That which took fifteen years to accumulate will not be removed overnight."

The policy fights conservatives fought in 1988 remain crucial battles today, and we must fight hard if we are to realize John Winthrop's vision of America as a "shining city upon a hill," for which Reagan is an eternal champion. Reagan proved in his 1988 CPAC speech that freedom has much more than a fighting chance when a U.S. President is grounded in conservative fundamentals and delivers that message in a way that speaks to Americans and their desire to be free.

Bill Walton is the host of The Bill Walton Show, managing partner of Rappahannock Ventures, and a member of the Board of the American Conservative Union.

Afterword

Edwin Meese III

Reagan at CPAC is a remarkable collection of commentaries on the speeches of President Ronald Reagan at the annual Conservative Political Action Conference and provides for current and future generations a review of his exceptional impact on conservatism in America. I appreciate this opportunity to offer a few reflections on those speeches and their continuing relevance today.

What is considered the modern conservative movement developed in three overlapping phases: intellectual, political, and governing. Each phase had an important relationship to Ronald Reagan's speeches.

Shortly after the end of World War II, a number of leading scholars such as Friedrich Hayek and Milton Friedman became concerned about the spread of socialism and similar collectivist doctrines in both academic and political circles. To provide a counter force to such harmful concepts, they worked together to pursue a vigorous program of writing and speaking in support of "classical liberalism," the philosophy of free market economics and individual liberty. In 1947, they organized the *Mont Pelerin Society,* which became a rallying point for similar thinkers throughout the world. Hayek's famous book condemning socialism, *The Road to Serfdom,* became widely read and an abridged version was published in *Reader's Digest.*

In the 1950s, the more senior scholars were joined by a brilliant young Yale graduate, William F. Buckley, who popularized the conservative message through articles, books, speeches, and a television debate show, *Firing Line.* One of Bill Buckley's most significant achievements was the founding of *National Review,* a highly literate but informative and entertaining journal of conservative ideas.

Through these efforts, conservatism became an intellectual movement which spread from the institutions of higher learning to widespread forums of public discussion and debate. Ronald Reagan was a voracious reader and became interested in a variety of books on liberty, constitutionalism, free market economics, and similar topics. His views turned away from liberalism and the products of conservative thought became the foundation of his political principles and philosophy, and ultimately, the content of his speeches.

In 1964, Senator Barry Goldwater ran for the presidency as the Republican candidate on a staunchly conservative platform. Although he was not successful, his campaign established a series of robust policy positions as their ideological agenda. They also attracted a large body of adherents, including many young people, who were eager to support the politics of liberty and limited government. This became the base of conservatism as a political movement.

As described in *Reagan at CPAC,* one other result of the Goldwater campaign was the emergence of Ronald Reagan on the national political scene. In October of 1964, he gave a national television speech which electrified its viewers and raised over five million dollars for the Goldwater election effort. The speech, *A Time for Choosing* (also known as "Rendezvous with Destiny" and "The Speech"), dealt with the failure of big government with its oppressive bureaucracy, high taxes, and burdensome regulation. It extolled freedom, limited government, and citizen responsibility. The success of the speech encouraged political leaders in California to recognize Reagan's potential as a candidate for office and led to the next phase of conservatism.

In 1966, Ronald Reagan ran for governor of California, winning against a highly popular incumbent by nearly one million votes. By accomplishing two successful terms as governor, leading the National Governors' Association, and later serving two successful terms as president, he established conservatism as a governing movement. In these leadership positions, Ronald Reagan proved that conservative ideas and actions actually worked in practice. As both state and national leader, he entered office to face daunting challenges of fiscal and economic crisis, bureaucratic management failure, and the threat of high crime, as well as public discouragement. But in each position, Reagan's leadership ability, cheerful and optimistic spirit, and persuasive communication skills enabled him to rebuild financial stability, restore sound government, and re-establish public confidence in our institutions.

One challenge that is unique to the presidency is the responsibility for national security and the conduct of foreign affairs. When Ronald Reagan was inaugurated as president, major problems in these areas faced America and were often discussed in his CPAC speeches. As related in several of the commentaries, the president identified Marxism-Leninism as an evil force in the world and decried the plight of the captive nations and the oppression that so many suffered under totalitarian rule. But his remarks always included messages of optimism and hope as well as his commitment to work for positive change. He espoused a strategy of peace through strength, support for freedom fighters around the world, contention against Soviet aggression, and action to ultimately free those imprisoned behind the "iron curtain."

When he gave his last speech at CPAC as President of the United States, Ronald Reagan did not know when that day of victory and liberation would be achieved, but he was confident that his strategy and initiatives were moving the world toward the attainment of those goals. But it was not long before his steadfast actions resulted in the ultimate victory in the Cold War and the implosion of the Soviet Union.

Ronald Reagan's speeches at CPAC are part of the history of the modern conservative movement and are linked to the phases I have described. He reminded us of the ideals and values that have guided our republic through more than two centuries of progress and trial in our quest to preserve freedom and assure justice. His words have challenged us in the past and inspired us for the future. Ed Feulner, Founder of The Heritage Foundation, in his book, *The March of Freedom*, described the president this way:

"Ronald Reagan is called the 'Great Communicator,' and with good reason. He has a profound appreciation for the importance of rhetoric. ...He is persuasive because he is so deeply persuaded of [conservative] ideas himself. ...He boiled down politics to its most fundamental level and spoke a plain language of right and wrong."

Ronald Reagan has given us a legacy of great speeches which express the permanent convictions of the conservative movement and are an invaluable tribute to his continuing influence among lovers of freedom.

Acknowledgments

ACU would like to thank:

Jennifer Mandel, Michael Pinckney, and Amy Muller of the Ronald Reagan Presidential Library, whose tireless efforts illuminated Reagan's rich history with CPAC.

The thoughtful conservative leaders who volunteered their time and talent to contribute to this book.

Luke Schneider, without whose work this book would not have been possible. He rose to the challenge and completed a daunting task.

Ryan Cole, for his poignant insights.

The conservative thought leaders who had the vision in 1964 to unite liberty-minded people under the banner of a new organization, ACU, and who, a few years later, established CPAC as the place for conservatives to unite annually to set our agenda.

Ronald Reagan, who best articulated the ideas of conservatism and led the effort to restore our nation to greatness.

Mercedes and Gisella, who did not merely tolerate their husbands' long hours, but have been strong allies in the cause of freedom.

Each of the speeches included in this book are courtesy of the Ronald Reagan Presidential Library, except for excerpts from the fourth annual CPAC in 1979, which is courtesy of the Hoover Institute through the Brigham Young University Library.

Appendices

T he ACU has included Reagan's handwritten drafts of three
of his revolutionary speeches for the reader's benefit in this
section. Interested readers will be happy to know even more
annotated documents can be found on ACU's website, conservative.
org/Reagan.

Appendix 1

A Time For Choosing

1964

Ronald Reagan drafts the original handwritten copy of *A Time for Choosing*, which launched his political career and inspired conservatives to create ACU and host the first CPAC.

OFFICE MEMORANDUM • STANFORD UNIVERSITY • OFFICE MEMORANDUM

DATE: June 12, 1979

To   :   Cindy - Governor Reagan's Office

FROM :   Molly Sturges

SUBJECT: Transcript of 1964 Goldwater Speech

Attached is the only copy I have of the
Goldwater speech. I don't know whether it
is a transcription from the tape or whether
it is an annotated draft of the speech text.

I am almost positive that some of the annota-
tions on the copy are the Governor's own.

I hope that this is what you are looking for.

ANNOUNCER:

The following pre-recorded political program is sponsored by TV For
Goldwater-Miller on behalf of Barry Goldwater, Republican candidate for
President of the United States. Ladies and Gentlemen, we take pride in
presenting a thoughtful address by Ronald Reagan. Mr. Reagan....

RONALD REAGAN:

Thank you very much. Thank you, and good evening. The sponsor has been
identified, but unlike most television programs, the performer hasn't
been provided with a script. As a matter of fact, I have been permitted
to choose my own words and discuss my own ideas regarding the choice that
we face in the next few weeks.
I have spent most of my life as a Democrat. I recently have seen fit to
follow another course. I believe that the issues confronting us
cross party lines. Now one side in this campaign has been telling us that
the issues of this election are the maintenance of peace and prosperity.
The line has been used "We've never had it so good!"
But I have an uncomfortable feeling that this prosperity isn't something
upon which we can base our hopes for the future. No nation in history has
ever survived a tax burden that reached a third of it's national income.
Today 37 cents out of every dollar earned in this country is the tax
collector's share, and yet our government continues to spend   17 million
dollars a day more than the government takes in. We haven't balalnced our
budget 28 out of the last 34 years. We have raised our debt limit three
times in the last 12 months, and now our national debt is 1 ½ times bigger
than all the combined debts of all the nations of the world. We have 15
billion dollars in gold in our treasury - we don't own an ounce. Foreign claims
are 27.3 billion dollars, and we have just had announced that the dollar of
1939 will now purchase 45 cents in its total value. As for the peace we
would preserve, I wonder who among us would like to approach wife or
mother whose husband or son has died in Vietnam and ask them if they think this

-2-

is a peace that should be maintained indefinitely. Do they mean
peace, or do they mean we just want to be left in peace? There can
be no real peace ~~at~~ *while* one American is dying someplace in the world
for the rest ~~js~~ of us. We are at war with the most dangerous enemy that
has ever faced mankind in his long climb from the swamp to the stars,
and it has been said ~~that~~ if we lose that war, and in so doing lose
this way of freedom of ours, history will record ~~xxxxxxx~~ *with the greatest astonishment* that those
who had the most to lose did the least to prevent its happening.
Well, I think it's time ~~And~~ we ~~still~~ ask ourselves if we still know the freedoms that were
intended for us by the Founding Fathers. Not too long ago two friends
of mine were talking to a Cuban refugee, a business man who had escaped
from Castro, and in the midst of his story one of my friends turned to
the other and said, "we don't know how lucky we are." And the Cuban ~~jx~~ stopped and said,
"How lucky you are! I had someplace to escape to." In that sentence
he told us the entire story. If we lose freedom here, there is no
place to escape to. This is the last stand on earth. And this idea
that government is beholden to the people, that it has no ~~xxxxxx~~ other
source of power except the sovereign people, is still the newest and
most unique idea in all the long history of man's relation to man.
This is the issue of this election. Whether we believe in our capacity
for self ~~to~~ government or whether we abandon the American revolution and
confess that a little intellectual elite in a far-distant capital
can plan our lives for us better than we can ~~jxx~~ plan them ourselves.
You and I are told increasingly that we have to choose between a
left or right, but I would like to suggest that there is no such thing
as a left or right. There is only ~~xb~~ an up or down - *up to* man's ~~old~~ *age* .
dream - the ultimate in individual freedom consistent with law and
order, or down to the ant heap of totalitarian, and regardless of the

-3-

sincerity, their humanitarian motives, those who would trade our freedom
for security have embarked on this downward course. In this vote-harvesting
time they use terms like the great society, or as we were told a few days
ago by the president, we must accept a "greater government activity in the
affairs of the people." But they have been a little more explicit
explicit in the past and among themselves—and all of the things that
I now will quote have appeared in print. These are not Republican
accusations. For example, they have voices that say "cold war will end
through our acceptance of a not undemocratic socialism." Another voice
says that the profit motive has become outmoded; it must be replaced by
the incentives of the welfare state, or our traditional system of individual
freedom is incapable of solving the complex problems of the 20th century.
Senator Fullbright has said at Stanford University that the Constitution
is outmoded. He referred to the President as our moral teacher and our leader,
and he said he is hobbled in his task, by the restrictions of power
imposed on him by this antiquated document. He must be freed so that he can
do for us what he knows is best. And Sen. Clark of Penn., another articulate spokesman, defines liberalism as "meeting the material needs of the
masses through the full power of centralized government." Well, I for one
resent it when a representative of the people refers to you and me - the
free men and women of this country - as "the masses." This is a term we
haven't applied to ourselves in America. But beyond that, "the full power
of centralized government"- this was the very thing the Founding Fathers
sought to minimize. They knew that governments don't control things.
A government can't control the economy without controlling the people.
And they know when a government sets out to do that, it must use force and
coercion to achieve its purpose. They also knew, those Founding Fathers,
that outside of its legitimate function, government does nothing as well
or as economically as the private sector of the economy. Now, we have no better
example of this than the governments involvement in the farm & economy

-4-

over the last thirty years. Since 1955 the cost of this program has
nearly doubled. 1/4 of farming in America is responsible for 85% of the
farm surplus, 3/4's of farming is out on the free market and has known a
21% increase in the per capita consumption of all its produce. You
see, that 1/4 of farming that's regulated and controlled by the Federal
government. In the last three years we have spent 43 dollars in the feed
grain program for every dollar of corn we don't grow. Sen. Humphrey
last week charged that Barry Goldwater as president would seek to
eliminate farmers. He should do his homework a little better, because he
will find out that we have had a decline of 5 million in the farm
population under these government programs. He will also find that the
Democratic administration has sought to get from Congress an
extension of the farm program to include that 3/4's that is now free. He
will find that they have also asked for the right to imprison farmers
who wouldn't keep books as prescribed by the Federal government. The Secretary of
Agriculture ask for the right to seize farms thru condemnation and resell
them to other individuals. And contained in that same program was
a provision that would allow the Federal government to remove 2 million farmers
from the soil. At the same time there has been an increase in the Department
of Agriculture employees. There is now one for every 30 farms
in the U.S. and still they can't tell us how 66 shipments loads of grain
headed for Austria disappeared without a trace, and Billy Sol Estes never left
shore! Every responsible farmer and farm organization has repeatedly asked
the government to free the farm economy, but who are farmers to know
what is best for them? The wheat farmers voted against a wheat program.
The government passed it anyway. Now the price of bread goes up; the price
of wheat to the farmer goes down. Meanwhile, back in the city, under urban renewal
the assault on freedom carries on. Private property rights are so diluted

-5-

that public interest is almost anything that a few government planners
decide it should be. In a program that takes from the needy and gives
to the greedy,we see such spectacles as in Cleveland, Ohio, a million—
and—a-half-dollar building completed only three years ago must be destroyed
to make way for what government officials call a "more compatible use of
the land." The President tells us he is now going to start building
public housing units in the thousands where heretofore we have only
built them in the hundreds. But FHA and the Veterans Administration
tell us that they have 120 thousand housing units they've taken back
through mortgage foreclosures. For three decades we have sought to
solve the problems of unemployment through government planning, and the
more the plans fail, the more the planners plan. The latest is
the Area Redevelopment Agency. They have just declared
Rice County, Kansas a depressed area. Rice County, Kansas has two
hundred oil wells, and the 14,000 people there have over 30,000,000 thirty million
dollars on deposit in personal savings in their banks. When the
government tells you you are depressed, lie down and be
depressed!

We have so many people who can't see a fat man standing beside a
thin one without coming to the conclusion that the fat man got that
way by taking advantage of the thin one! So they are going to solve
all the problems of human misery through government and government
planning. Well, now if government planning and welfare had the
answer, and they've had almost thirty years of it,shouldn't we
expect government to read the score to us once in a while?
Shouldn't they be telling us about the decline each year in the
number of people needing help?.... the reduction in the need for
public housing? But the reverse is true. Each year the need
grows greater, the program grows greater. We were told four years
ago that seventeen million people went to bed hungry each night.

-6

Well, that was probably true. They were all on a diet! But now we
are told that 9.3 million families in this country are poverty-stricken
on the basis of earning less than $3,000 dollars a year. Welfare spending
is ten times greater than the dark depths of the depression. We are
spending 45 billion dollars on welfare. Now do a little arithmetic,
and you will find that if we divided the 45 billion dollars up equally
among those 9.3 million poor families, we would be able to give each
family $4,600 dollars a year, and this added to their present income
should eliminate poverty!

Direct aid to the poor, however, is running only about $600 per family.
It seems that someplace there must be some overhead.

So now we "declare" war on poverty, or "you too can be a Bobby Baker!"
Do they honestly expect us to believe that if we add one billion dollars
to the forty-five billion we are spending, one more program to the
thirty-odd we have, (and remember this new program doesn't replace any,
it just duplicates existing programs)....do they believe that poverty
is suddenly going to disappear by magic? Well, in all fairness I should
explain that there is one part of the new program that isn't duplicated.
This is the youth feature. We are now going to solve the drop-out
problem, juvenile delinquency, by reinstituting something like the old
CCC camps, and we are going to put our young people in camps, but
again we do some arithmetic, and we find that we are going to spend
each year just on room and board for each young person that we help
$4,700 a year! We can send them to Harvard for $2700! Don't get me
wrong. I'm not suggesting that Harvard is the answer to juvenile
delinquency!

But seriously, what are we doing to those we seek to help? NOt too
long ago, a judge called me here in Los Angeles. He told me of a
young woman who had come before him for a divorce'

She had six children, was pregnant with her seventh. Under his
questioning, she revealed her husband was a laborer earning $250
a month. She wanted a divorce so that she could get an $80.00
raise. She is eligible for $330 a month in Aid to Dependent Children
program. She got the idea from two women in her neighborhood who
had already done that very thing. Yet anytime you and I question the
schemes of the do-gooders, we are denounced as being against their
humanitarian goals. They say we are always "against" things, never
"for" anything. Well, the trouble with our liberal friends is not
that they are ignorant, but that they know so much that isn't so!
We are for a provision that destitution should not follow unemployment
by reason of old-age, and to that end we have accepted Social Security
as a step toward meeting the problem. But we are against those
entrusted with this program when they practice deception regarding
its fiscal shortcomings, when they charge that any criticism of the
program means that we want to end payments to those people who depend
upon them for a livlihood. They have called it insurance to us and
a hundred million people in their literature. But then they appeared
before the Supreme Court and they testified that it was a welfare
program. They only use the term "insurance" to sell it to the people.
And they said Social Security dues are a tax for the general use of the
government, and the government has used that tax. There is no fund, because
Robert Byers, the actuarial head, appeared before a Congressional Committee
and admitted that Social Security as of this moment is two hundred
ninety-eight billion dollars in the hole! But he said there should be
no cause for worry because as long as they have the power to tax, they
could always take away from the people whatever they needed to bail
them out of trouble! And they are doing just that. A young man,
twenty-one years of age, working at an average salary... his social
security contribution would, in the open market, buy him an insurance
policy that would guarante...

two hundred twenty dollars a month at age 65. The government promises
a hundred and twenty-seven! He could live it up until he is 31 and
then take out a policy that would pay more than social security.
Now are we so lacking in business sense that we can't put this program
on a sound basis so that people who do require those payments will
find that they can get them when they are due... that the cupboard
isn't bare? Barry Goldwater thinks we can. At the same time, can't
we introduce voluntary features that would permit a citizen to do
better on his own, to be excused upon presentation of evidence that
he had made provisions for the non-earning years? Should we not allow
a widow with children to work, and not lose the benefits supposedly
paid for by her deceased husband? Shouldn't you and I be allowed
to declare who our beneficiaries will be under these programs, which
we cannot do? I think we are for telling our senior citizens that
no one in this country should be denied medical care, because of a
lack of funds. But I think we are against forcing all citizens
regardless of need, into a compulsory government program, especially
when we have such examples, as announced last week, when President
France admitted that their medicare program was now bankrupt. They've
come to the end of the road. IN addition, was Barry Goldwater so
irresponsible when he suggested that our government give up its program
of deliberate planned inflation so that when you do get your social
security pension, a dollar will buy a dollar's worth, and not 45 cents
worth? I think we are for the international organization, where the
nations of the world can seek peace. But I think we are against
subordinating American interests to an organization that has become
so structurally unsound that today you can muster a 2/3 vote on the
floor of the General Assembly among nations that represent less than
10% of the world's population. I think we are against the hypocrisy
of assailing our allies because here and there they cling to a colony,

while we engage in a conspiracy of ~~xxxxxx~~ silence and never open our
mouths about the millions of people enslaved in Soviet colonies in the
satellite nations. I think we are ~~fore~~ aiding our allies by sharing
of our material blessings with ^three^ nations ~~that share~~ in our fundamental
beliefs, but we are against doling out money government to government,
creating bureacracy, if not socialism, all over the world. We set
out to help 19 countries. We are helping 107. We spent one hundred
forty-six billion ^dollars.^ With that money, we bought a two-million-dollar
yacht for Hailie Selassee. We bought dress suits for Greek undertakers,
extra wives for Kenya government officials. We bought a thousand
TV sets for a place where they have no electricity. In the last
six years, fifty ^two^ nations have bought seven billion dollars of our
gold, and all fifty-two are receiving foreign aid from us. No
government ever voluntarily reduces itself in size. Government
programs, once launched, never disappear. Actually, a government
bureau is the nearest thing to eternal life we'll ever see on this
earth!
Federal employees number two and one-half million and federal, state
and local, one out of six in the nation's work force is employed
by government. These proliferating bureaus with their thousands of
regulations have cost us many of our Constitutional safeguards.
How many of us realize that today Federal agents can invade a man's
property without a warrant? They can impose a fine without a formal
hearing, let alone a trial by jury, and they can seize and sell
his property in auction to enforce ^the^ payment of that fine. In Chico
County, Arkansas, James W~~ee~~ ^ier^ overplanted his rice allotment. The
government obtained a $17,000 ~~xxx~~ judgment, and a U.S. Marshal sold
his 950-acre farm at auction. The government said it was necessary
as a warning to others to make the system work!

1 δ

Last February 19th, at the University of Minnesota, Norman Thomas,
times candidate for President on the Socialist Party Ticket, said
"If Barry Goldwater ~~ever~~ became President, he would stop the advance
of Socialism in the United States." I think that's exactly what
he ~~izgaingxdexxbexxx~~ will do!

As a former Democrat, I can tell you Norman Thomas isn't the only
man who has drawn this parallel to Socialism with the present
administration. Back in 1936, Mr. Democrat, himself, Al Smith, the
great American, came before the American people and charged that
the leadership of his party was taking the party of Jefferson,
Jackson, and Cleveland, down the road under the banners of ~~Marxism~~ Lenin
and Stalin. And he walked away from his party, and he never returned
~~tit~~ to the day he died, because to this day, the leadership of that
party has been taking that party, that honorable party, down the
road in the image of the labor socialist party of England. Now it
doesn't require expropriation or confiscation of private property
or business to impose Socialism upon a people. What does it mean
whetheryou hold the deed or the title to your business property, if
the government holds the power of life and death over that business
or ~~pax~~ property? Such machinery already exists. The government can
find some charge to bring against ~~you~~ any concern it chooses to
prosecute. Every businessman has his own tale of harrassment. Somewhere a perversion has taken place. Our natural, inalienable rights
are now considered to be a dispensation from government, and freedom
has never been so fragile, so close to slipping from our grasp as
it is at this moment. Our Democratic opponents seem unwilling to
debate these issues. They want to make you and I think that this
is a contest between two men... that we are to choose just between
two personalities. Well, what of this man they would destroy?
And in destroying, they would destroy that which he represents, the
ideas that you and I hold dear.

11

Is he the brash and shallow and trigger-happy man they say he is?
Well, I have been privileged to know him "when." I knew him long
before he ever dreamed of trying for high office, and I can tell you
personally, I have never known a man in my life I believe so incapable
of doing a dishonest or dishonorable thing.
This is a many who in this his own business, before he entered politics,
instituted a profit-sharing plan, before unions had ever thought of it.
He put in health and medical insurance for all his employees. He took
50% of the profits before taxes and xxxxx set up a retirement plan,
and a pension plan for all his employees. He sent monthly checks for
life to an employee who was ill and couldn't work. He provides nursing
care for the children of mothers who work in his the stores. When
Mexico was ravaged by floods from the Rio Grande, he climbed in his
airplane and flew xxxxx medicine and supplies down there. An ex-GI
xxxxx told me how he met him. It was the week before Christmas during
the Korean War, and he was at the Los Angeles airport trying to get a
ride home to Arizona, and he said that there were a lot of service men
there and no seats available on the planes. Then a voice came over the
loudspeaker and said, "Any men in uniform wanting a ride to Arizona,
go to Runway runway such-and-such," and they went down there, and there
was a fellow named Barry Goldwater sitting in his plane. Everyday
in the weeks before Christmas, all day long, he would load up the
plane, fly to Arizona, fly them to their homes, flyzthemz then fly
back over to get another load. During the hectic split-second timing
of a campaign, this is a man who took time out to sit beside an old
friend who was dying of cancer. His campaign managers were understandably
impatient, but he said, "There aren't many left who care what happens
to her. I'd like her to know that I care." This is a man who said to
his 19-year-mik old son, "There is no foundation like the rock of
honesty and fairness, and when you begin to build your life upon

/2

that rock, with the cement of the faith in God that you have, then you
have a real start!" This is not a man who could carelessly send other
people's sons to war. And that is the issue of this campaign that makes
all of the other problems I have discussed academic, unless we realize
that we are in a war that must be won. Those who would trade our
freedom for the soup kitchen of the welfare state have told us that they
have a utopian solution of peace without victory. They call their
policy "accommodation." And they say if we only avoid any direct
confrontation with the enemy, he will forget his evil ways and learn
to love us. All who oppose them are indicted as warmongers. They
say we offer simple answers to complex problems. Well, perhaps there
is a simple answer.... not an easy one... but a simple one. If you
and I have the courage to tell our elected officials that we want
our national policy based upon what we know in our hearts is morally
right. We cannot buy our security, our freedom from the threat of the
bomb by committing an immorality so great as saying to a billion human
beings now in slavery behind the Iron Curtain, "Give up your dreams
of freedom because to save our own skin, we are willing to make a deal
with your slave-masters." Alexander Hamilton said "A nation which
can prefer disgrace to danger is prepared for a master, and deserves
one!" Let's set the record straight. There is no argument over the
choice between peace and war, but there is only one guaranteed way
you can have peace... and you can have it in the next second....
surrender! Admittedly there is a risk in any course we follow other
than this, but every lesson in history tells us that the greater
risk lies in appeasement, and this is the spector our well-meaning
liberal friends refuse to face.... that their policy of accommodation
is appeasement, and it gives no choice between peace and war, only
between fighting or surrender. If we continue to accommodate, continue
to back and retreat, eventually we have to face the final demand — The
                                                            ultimatum.

13

And what then, when Nikita Khrushchev has told his people he knows what
our answer will be, he has told them that we are retreating under the
pressure of the cold war and someday when the time comes to deliver
the ultimatum, our surrender will be voluntary because by that time
we will have weakened from within spiritually, morally and economically.
He believes this because from our side he has heard voices pleading
for "peace at any price," or "better Red than dead," or as one
commentator put it, he would rather "live on his knees than die on
his feet." And therein lies the road to war, because those voices
don't speak for the rest of us. You and I know and do not believe
that life is so dear and peace so sweet as to be purchased at the price
of chains and slavery. If nothing in life is worth dying for
dying for, when did this begin.... just in the face of this enemy...
or should Moses have told the children of Israel to live in
slavery under the Pharoahs? Should Christ have refused the cross?
Should the patriots at Concord Bridge have thrown down their guns
and refused to fire the shot heard round the world? The martyrs
of history were not fools, and our honored dead who gave their
lives to stop the advance of the Nazis didn't die in vain! Where
then is the road to peace? Well, it's a simple answer after all.
You and I have the courage to say to our enemies, "There is a price
we will not pay." There is a point beyond which they must not advance!"
This is the meaning in the phrase of Barry Goldwater's "Peace through
strength!" Winston Churchill said that destiny of man is not
measured by material computation. When great forces are on the move
in the world, we learn we are spirits, not animals. And he said
there is something going on in time and space, and beyond time and
space which, whether we like it or not, spells duty. You and I
have a rendezvous with destiny. We will preserve for our children
this, the last best hope of man on earth, or we will sentence them
totake the last step into a thousand years of darkness.

14

We will keep in mind and remember that Barry Goldwater has faith in us.
He has faith in you and I, that we have the ability and the dignity
and the right to make our own decisions and determine our own destiny.

Thank you.

America's Purpose in the World

1978

draft---ACU speech for 3/17/78

As a ~~part-time~~ part-time journalist ~~with~~ FACED WITH PRODUCING A syndicated daily radio broadcast~~s~~ and twice-a-week newspaper column~~,~~ I find ~~I am~~ BEING on the mailing list~~s~~ of an almost endless ~~list~~ ARRAY of organizations. ~~Because~~ A MOST HELPFUL. NOW Some of the ~~of this, a~~ flood of material crosses my desk ~~every week. Not~~ VERY SWIFTLY, BUT NOT all of it, ~~inxfxxxxxxxxx fxxxxxxx~~ ~~rivets my attention, of course,~~ ~~but some of it does and~~ One thick handout I got late last year was especially fascinating, ~~not only because of content but it was~~ JUST BECAUSE it was MAILED TO ME AT RCC.

It was from the White House Press Office, ~~and it was headed~~ UNDER THE TITLE "Domestic and Foreign Policy Accomplishments". IT TOLD ME IN 21 single-spaced pages it ~~sought to tell editors and news directors~~ of the wonders of the Carter Administration's first year, ~~beginning~~

~~It started out~~ Beginning with the modest statement that ~~the Pres~~ --QUOTE-- "The President tackled directly and comprehensively major domestic problems that had been almost completely ~~ignored~~ ignored in previous years." -- UNQUOTE ~~It then recited an impressive list of major accomplishments~~ ~~------~~ ~~Oh, ------~~ True ~~meant~~ hadn't the White House claimed to find a way to control ~~everything from~~ the weather ~~or to eliminate~~ crab grass ~~but it~~ on the White House lawn, but it did think it had, --or nearly solved-- solved our energy problems, social security's 17 million ~~does seem to think it~~ (we added 52,000 new employees in the 1st 10 months of 1977) ~~dollar deficit~~ the size of big government, the welfare mess and a host of other problems that have been ~~at~~ center stage in American life for quite some time.

Tonight, ~~I would like to share~~ perhaps we should discuss some of those White House claims ~~of accomplishment with you~~ and see if they have stood the test of even ~~a brief period of time~~ --the three months that have passed since they were made. I know that's a little cruel - like checking up on some one's new year's resolutions, - After all the administration.

~~But, rather than concentrate on domestic issues, where it seems~~

2-2-2

pretty clear to everyone, ~~Democrats and Republicans, liberals and~~
~~nonsensical conservatives~~ independents, ~~and newspapers~~ ~~that~~ President

STET ~~Carter~~ has scarcely gotten a single *domestic* program worth noting through
Congress. ~~I would like to~~ concentrate on the Administration's handling
of foreign affairs, ~~and~~ national security *and it's sense of priorities.*

On priorities ~~It is tempting to stop and wonder about an Administration's~~
There is the matter of issuing the
~~sense of priorities when it issues its~~ former budget director ~~who~~
~~is under federal investigation~~ a diplomatic passport; *The taking of*
depositions from bartenders
~~to consider what priorities are being neglected when the White House~~
~~scrambles around interviewing bartenders~~ and issuing a 33-page denial
that the President's chief aide *expectorated at or in the direction of* a young woman. *It boggle*
the mind ~~what they would have done if he'd spit on the sidewalk.~~
~~It is tempting to where the White House' priorities are when~~
Then there was the solemn oath
~~it solemnly swears~~ to apppoint and retain U.S. attorneys on the merit
Obviously there is no merit in a U.S. attorney who goes
system, ~~but manages to fire a crusading one when he begins~~ investigating
A
~~some Congressmen in the President's own party.~~
suspected fraud on the part of congressmen who belong to the President own party.
~~But, rather than yield to those temptations, I would like to~~
Moving
~~move~~ on to the Carter Administration's record in foreign affairs.

~~First~~, let me say a few words about Panama and our canal there.
And I do mean a few words.

(following will be short fill-in, commenting on Senate vote on
Neutrality treaty which will have been taken day before).

3-3-3

hand to Paul Laxalt

My purpose tonight, however, is not to repeat my views on this
questions. Panama _is_ an important issue. The final outcome is not
yet certain, and certainly the matter won't end with the final vote
in the Senate. In a way, that will only begin it.

But, Whatever the outcome on Capitol Hill, the smug assumptions of
many of the treaties' proponents have been successfully and vigorously
challenged.

Few Americans accept the belief of some of those now in positions
of importance in guiding our foreign policy that America's purpose in
the world is to appease the mighty ~~~~ out
of a sense of fear or to appease the weak out of a sense of guilt,
~~~~.

But a question remains. Is the faulty thinking that has led us
to these particular treaties an isolated particle, or is it part of
a much larger whole? *Does the admin. know the difference between being a diplomat and a doormat!*
In reviewing the foreign policy of this administration, *one can only* ~~I have~~
come to the conclusion that ~~~~ the mistaken assumptions that led
~~~~ to its course on the Panama Canal treaties are being duplicated
around the world.

~~~~ Its policy is rooted in well-meaning intentions,
but it shows a woeful uncertainty as to America's purpose in the world.

The administration _means_ to do good by espousing a human rights
doctrine it cannot define, much less implement. ~~~~ In the process,
this policy has ~~been~~ *met* with scorn *from* our enemies and ~~~~
~~with~~ alarm from our friends. That self-graded White House report
card ~~I mentioned said about~~ *said, with regard to* human rights, "The President has strengthened
our human rights policy and we are letting it be known clearly that
the United States stands with the victims of repression." --UNQUOTE,

4 - 4 - 4 *in the face of a final report that contained not one word about Russian violations of the Human Rights provisions in the Helsinki Agreement?*

Now, that's quite a mouthful, but if the ~~Democratic administration~~

If the

Carter Administration "stands with the victims of repression", the people of Cuba, Panama, Vietnam, Cambodia and the mainland of China have yet to hear about it. The fact is, the Carter human rights policy is whatever ~~the middle-men-appointees~~ his appointees who guide it want it to be. In practice, they have ceaselessly scolded authoritarian governments ~~are~~ of ~~which are friendly nations~~ *countries that are friendly* and ignored authoritarian and totalitarian countries that are not.

~~The Administration has fabricated a vague~~

Mr. Carter ~~wishing~~ might find a reading of the historian Charles Beard informative. Nearly 40 years ago, Beard concluded that the defect of a foreign policy based on what he called "the ~~self-~~ selfless sacrifice required by an absolute morality" was the inability to understand "the limited nature of American powers to relieve, restore and maintain life beyond its own ~~proper~~ sphere of interest and control--a recognition of the hard fact that the United States...did not possess the power...to assure the establishment of democratic and pacific government."

But, *by* using a combination of heavy-handed moves against allied countries, on the one hand, and ~~engaging in what I call~~ *making* "pre-emptive concessions" toward unfriendly or potentially unfriendly ~~nations~~ *on the other* countries, the Carter Administration has managed to convey the view

~~that if only it wishes hard enough, it too will make democracy~~
~~it desperately wants all the world to have liberty by the~~
~~reality everywhere.~~
~~principles~~

that it desparately wants the whole world to have democratic institutions ~~and~~ that would *be the envy of* the most ardent A.C.L.U. lawyer, ~~somehow~~ and ~~that~~ wishing ~~it so~~ will make it so.

That view of the world ranks along with belief in the Tooth
of
~~. . . . . and a false sense of guilt are not~~

5-5-5

the only elements in this Administration's foreign policy.

Too often, President ~~Carter~~ the is advised by men and women who are forever trapped in the tragic, but still fresh memory of a lost war. And, from Vietnam, they have drawn all the wrong lessons.

~~In saying,~~ When they say "never again", they mean the United States should never again resist communist aggression.

In saying "never again", they ~~do imply~~ imply that the war should have been lost; that it is alright for the victors to conduct a brutal campaign against their own people, violating even minimal ~~~~ human rights;

...That it is alright to ignore these massive violations ~~while~~ and all right ~~seeking~~ for us to seek better relations with the governments responsible. That White House document, ~~in fact~~, lists as an "accomplishment" the fact that "the Administration has started the process of normalizing relations" with ~~Vietnam.~~ the communist conquerors of S. Vietnam. The lesson we should have learned from Vietnam is that never again will Americans be asked to fight and die unless they are permitted to win.

~~I do not share the assumptions of Mr. Carter and his advisors.~~

~~I believe the great majority of Americans don't share them either.~~

We need a foreign policy stripped of platitudes, cant and mere moral earnestness--an earnestness fatally compromised by the massive crimes of some of the communist world's newer members. This pattern of Communist violations of human rights ~~None of this~~ should come as no surprise to us. Over and over again, newly established Marxist regimes have committed them. ~~It was the~~ It was the Soviet Union In the 1920's and '30's; in the late 40's the new Iron Curtain countries; ~~~~ China in the '50's and it was Communist China of Cuba through the Cultural Revolution of the '60's it is ~~It was also Cuba~~ ~~in the '60's~~; and now Vietnam and Cambodia.

The problem with much of the Carter team is that they know too little, not too much of history. And, they have lost faith in their ~~~~ own country's past and traditions.

6-6-6

Too often, that team has operated under the assumption that the United States must prove and reprove and prove again its goodness to the world. ~~In our world~~ Proving that we are civilized in a world that is often ~~unapologetically,~~ uncivilized ─and unapologetically so─ is hardly necessary. ~~But, just what should we be doing?~~

The themes of a sound foreign policy should be no mystery, nor the result of endless agonizing reappraisals. They are rooted in our past; in our very betginnings as a nation.

The founding fathers established a system which meant a radical break ~~with~~ from ~~that~~ that which preceded it. A written constitution would provide a permanent form of government, limited in scope, but effective in providing both ~~liberary~~ liberty and order.

Government was not to be a matter of self-appointed rulers, governing by whim or harsh ideology. It was not to be government by the strongest or for the few.

~~These~~ Our principles were revolutionary. ~~and~~ We began as a small, weak republic. But we survived. Our ~~every~~ example inspired others, imperfectly at times, but it inspired them nevertheless.

~~Undoubtedly~~ This constitutional republic, conceived in liberty and dedicated to the proposition that all men are created equal, ~~--~~ prospered and grew strong. ~~Remaining faithful to our principles~~

To this day, America ~~has remained~~ is still ~~is the~~ the abiding alternative to tyranny. That is our purpose in the world--nothing more and nothing less.

To carry out that purpose our fundamental aim in foreign policy must be to insure our own survival and to protect those ~~and have~~ others who share our values.

x 7-7-7

Under no ~~one~~ circumstances should we have any illusions about

the intentions of those who ~~is~~ are enemies of freedom. Our communist

adversaries have little regard for human rights because they have

little interest in human freedom. The ruling elite of those countries

wish only one thing: to preserve their privileges and to eliminate

the nagging reminder that others have done and are doing better

under freedom.

Every American President since World War II has known or

quickly learned that the Soviet Union, for example, ~~was~~ is not ~~and~~

~~~~ benign in its intentions.

The Soviet Union has no interest in maintaining the status

quo. It does not ~~except~~ accept our soft definition of "detente". "Detente", [To the Soviet U.]

~~to the Soviets is a breather~~, Union, is an opportunity to expand ~~their~~ its

sphere of influence around the world, ~~another easier form of conquest.~~

The Soviet Union has steadily increased is capacity for such

expansion. That capability has grown enormously since 1945 and, above

all, since 1962 when the Cold War was first declared over by the

hopeful and naïve.

Today, the U.S.S.R. continues its drive to dominate the world

in ~~its~~ military capability: on the land, on water and in the air.

Meanwhile, the Carter ~~~~ Administration seems confused

and torn, partly believing the realities and partly listening to

those who believe that pre-emptive concessions by us will result in

MATCHING concessions by the Soviets. ~~The Russians~~ But they don't bargain that way.

They understand strength; they exploit weakness + take advantage of inexperience

MAYBE ~~Some of this confusion can be credited to inexperience. Mr.~~

WHATEVER THE REASON

8-8-8

And possibly it was inexperience that led the Pres.

~~Carter, apparently~~ to placate the most dovish members of his party, *by scuttling* ~~cut out to scuttle~~ the B-1 bomber ~~program~~ --one of his bargaining chips-- even before the SALT II negotiations began.

~~But~~, While confusion and conflicting advice seem to tug and pull at the White House, the Soviet Union continues to build up its capability for world domination. It has even gone so far as to put entire factories underground and to disperse much of its ~~industry~~ industrial capacity -- the most sophisticated civil defense program ever developed. ~~This insisted of, would damage square~~ The knowledge that our strategic missiles, if they ever had to be used, would inflict minimal damage on the ~~Soviets~~ Soviets, compared to *the* havoc their's would produce on our continent, ~~would in itself~~ should, in itself, be sufficient to spur the Administration to making certain that we *be positive* ~~assure the United States~~ ~~and remain~~ Number One in ~~national defense in~~ the world in terms of national defense capabilities. ~~So far, this does not seem though, the White House acts as if it is dealing~~ *this does not seem to have sank in* *So far though this does not seem to be a White House priority.* ~~from weakness, not strength, with the Soviets.~~

Today, ~~For example~~, we can ~~now~~ see the brunt of the Soviet Union's capabilities at work in the Horn of AFrica.

To most Americans, that part of the world seems remote, ~~for many unfortunate reasons~~ *as* ~~but so were~~ *SEEMED REMOTE, along with* Korea and Vietnam ~~and all~~ the other places *where* the Soviets have sought advtange. ~~~~

In Ethiopia, formerly a close friend of the United States, the Soviets with their Cuban foreign legion have turned that country into a free fire zone in order to subdue Ethiopia's two principal ~~war~~ enemies, Somalia and the Eritrean rebels.

The Soviet goal is obvious: to secure a permanent foot hold for itself on the Red Sea. ~~In this sequence: If it is successful, and~~

Insert P. 8

One of the reasons given for cancellation of the B-1 was economy and even here there was ~~was meant~~ a lack of accuracy. First of all the price given ~~cost~~ for the aircraft was what the price will be in 1986 if inflation continues – which ~~incidentally~~ ~~indicates~~ suggests a lack of resolve in the admin's anti-inflation fight. Second we were told the B-52 or the F-111 could be modified to do the ~~B~~ job the B-1 was supposed to do. Here the cost differential shrinks sizeably when we look at the facts. The modification itself is quite costly & we can ~~double that cost.~~ It will take 2 planes to substitute for the B-1 because the ~~B-1~~ ever B-1 will carry twice the payload the others will. It will carry that load twice as fast in a plane only half the size of a B-52 and it's far less vulnerable to the Soviet defense system.

9-9-9

If the Soviets are successful--and it ~~is looking~~ (looks more & more) as if they will
be--then the entire Horn of Africa will be under their influence,
if not their control. From there, they can threaten the sea lanes
carrying oil to Western Europe and the United *States,* if and when they
choose.

More immediately, control of the Horn of Africa would give
~~the Soviet Union~~ Moscow the ability to destabilize those governments on
the Arabian peninsula which have proven themselves strongly
anti-communist. Among ~~these~~ are *them* ~~~~ some of the
world's principal oil exporters.

Moscow can also turn its full attention south if it can insure
its po^siton in the Horn of Africa. It takes no great stretch of
the imagination to see that Rhodesia is ~~the~~ a tempting target.
Cuban leaders now boast that it is.

What are we doing about it? Apparently, our response to the
~~and~~ Rhodesian settlement proposed by the moderate black leaders
and Prime Minister Ian Smith is not to tell the Soviets--behind
the scenes--to get lost or risk pressures *that* they won't like elsewhere.
No, our response seems to be best summed up by ~~Mr. Andrew Young,~~
~~Mr. Carter's~~ *own* ambassador to the United Nations, who is unhappy with
the moderate, democratic solution in Rhodesia because he's afraid (HE SAYS)
it will bring on a massive Soviet arms buildup. ~~How~~ WHAT DOES HE THINK
WE'RE HAVING NOW?
~~He seems to have a understanding of foreign affairs~~
He seems to believe that the only Rhodesian plan we can afford
to support is one to the liking of the two terrorist guerrilla
leaders. But if they ~~had~~ *have* their way, one or the other of them ~~would~~ *will*
become the sole power in Rhodesia, fronting of course for the
Soviet Union. Unless we want to make the world safe for terrorist

10-10-10

guerrillas, the only sensible course is for us to support the moderate

solution in Rhodesia and quietly tell MOscow to keep its hand off---

unless,of course, we are too ▓▓ weak to do that. Is that what Mr.

Young is trying to tell us? I hope not, for a Marxist Rhodesia would

lead to ~~{~~more tempting targets for Moscow in Africa. ^Djibouti, Sudan,
         even   *perhaps*

Chad, the old Spanish Sahara\where guerrillas are already in operation).

And one other which will cost us dearly.

~~And, future, make no mistake,~~ Whatever we may think of South

Africa's internal policies,\its mineral riches and its strategic
                    ~~control of~~ it

position are the Soviet Union's ultimate goal in Africa.

Unless the White House can bring itself to understand these

realities, it is not too much to say that in a few years we may be

faced with the prospect of a Soviet empire of proteges and dependancies

stretching from Addis Ababa to Capetown. Those who now reject that

possibility out of hand--and they seem to have the ear of the man

in the Oval office--have yet to explain Angola, MOzambique, the

situation in the ▓ Horn of AFrica or the terrorists in Rhodesia.

One thing is certain: Soviet successes will not breed caution in

the Kremlin. Rather, the reverse.

Those in the Carter Administration who are not even inclined to

protest ▓▓▓▓▓▓▓▓▓▓ the recent Soviet moves assure us that,

sooner or later, the Soviets will make serious mistakes and our doing

nothing will hasten that day.

But to say, as they do, that all is well because the Soviets are

creating their own Vietnam is ▓▓▓▓▓▓▓▓▓▓▓▓▓▓ nonsense. These

Carter advisers seem to forget that the Soviets won in Vietnam and

they intend to win again--this time in Africa. They learned the true

lesson of the Vietnam war; certainty of purpose and ruthlessness of

11--11--11

execution wins wars. ~~No.~~ Vietnam held no terror for the Soviets
as it did for so many Americans, And adventures in Africa hold no
terror for ~~them either~~ the Soviets, them either.

To say, as some in the Administration do, that African nationalism
will stop the Soviets is the weakest reed of all. The reason is simple:
African nationalism, as such, does not exist. No African government
has yet condemned the Russians, nor do the halls of the Organization
of African Unity ring with anti-Soviet slogans. Perhaps ~~they in~~ because
those halls happen to be in Addis Ababa, the capital of Ethiopia.

The criticism by African states of the Soviets that the Administration
seems to be so desperately hoping for will not materialize. After all, There is
in Africa, as around the world, a healthy respect for power and the
determined use of power.

One veteran West European diplomat put the African situation in
perspective recently. He was quoted as saying, "This situation is
going to make the leaders of a lot of these small, ~~weak~~ weak nations
stop and think. And what do they see on the American side? Apparent
indecision, attempts to talk, a reluctance to give weapons to ~~their~~
friends _~~and a belief that there are nasty, immoral wars~~_ " And, he might have added:
and a belief that there are nasty, immoral wars of aggression imperialist
& nice clean wars of national liberation. ~~On this point, of purpose isn't confined to the White House.~~

The Administration's uncertainty of purpose isn't confined to
the world's current ~~many~~ hot spots. It is apparent even in our own
hemisphere.

That White House ~~memo~~ tally sheet I mentioned listed its "accomplishments"
in Latin America. It said, "The Administration has developed a new
global approach to Latin America..." ~~—~~

Well, what it has done from ~~its~~ the beginning was to accept the
notions fashionable in the most liberal circles that surround of

12--12--12

the Panama Canal and <u>rapprochement</u> with Cuba were the keys to successful
relations with Latin America.

Nothing could have been further from the truth. Of Panama, I
have already had a good deal to say. But let me say again, we have
earned no respect or lasting affection in Latin America with <u>these</u>
treaties.

Nor does friendship with Castro make any sense. It never did.
His intentions toward us remain fixed. We are the enemy; a threat
to him and all loyal supporters of Moscow. There is not now nor ever
will be a place for a free America in his vision of the world.

Unfortunately, our policy toward Latin America has not only
entailed friendship for one dictator who is a sworn enemy and for
another who routinely suppresses human rights and may be involved
in the worst sort of ~~a~~ corruption -- that policy has also entailed
Hostility
~~enmity~~ toward our ~~few~~ friends.

Let me cite just one example, Brazil. An ally in World War II,
(contributing a division which saw hard action in ~~Italy)~~ Europe),
a friend through most of the '60's and now a great hope for contributing
          industrial
to the future ^strength of the West, Brazil now finds itself turned
on by us~~,~~ with a vengeance. Whatever the motives, ~~human~~ human rights
         worries over
or ~~nuclear proliferation~~, the ends ~~nonviolation~~ did not justify the
means . The result is that we have very nearly lost a ~~firm~~ friend
                          Administration's
without achieving any of the ~~White House~~' professed objectives.

~~Isn't~~ It's time to try another approach, an approach based on
reality and not the slogans and romantic notions of ~~liberal~~ ideologues
who just happen to have access to the Oval Office?

First, let us end this cycle of American indifference, followed
by frenzied activity in Latin America (as it has been elsewhere). ~~a~~

13-13-13

The cycle *It* leaves our southern neighbors ■ bewildered *and* cynical .
Instead, I propose a steadier course in which Latin America's growing
importance is recognized not as an act of charity, but in our own
self-interest.

Latin America, with all its resources and vitality, should be
encouraged to join not the Third World, much less the communist's
Second World, but the First World--that community of stable,
prosperous and free nations of Western Europe, North America and
Japan.

Today, there is hope that much of Latin American might do so.
First, many nations have learned the cost of Socialist experimentation.
Argentina under the Perons. Chile under Allende. Peru under ~~Junta~~
Velasco. Mexcio under Echeverria. All suffered economic catastrophe.
~~Their mar~~ Their successors learned the bitter truth ~~of~~ that defying
the laws ~~mor~~ of economics benefits no one and, in fact, hurts most
the poor whose cause those *earlier* leaders so demagogically espoused.

Today, as a result of those experiments which went so badly
out of control, more and more of our neighbors are turning to the
free market as a model ~~windowl~~ of development. Their acceptance of
economic rationality should be neither ignored nor penalized, but
actively encouraged.

At the same time, we must ~~remember~~ *recognize* that Latin America is
~~gradually~~ once again leaving a period of strictly military rule and
entering a more democratic phase. But in this case, the United States
is doing too much, *pushing* rather than too little.

Unhappily, the change from military to civilian rule is not a
an easy one. Nor can it be rushed. If it is, we will only succeed in
creating weak and vulnerable democratic governments that will soon be
swept out of power by yet another generation of military strongmen

14-14-14

even more convinced of the defects of democracy.

Above all, we want a free and prosperous Latin America. And, to
obtain that, we cannot continue to reward our self-declared enemies
and then ~~to~~ turn around and punish our friends.

~~That~~ That leads me again to Panama. The treaties that have occupied
so much of our attention in recent months represent both the ~~best~~ *good instincts* and
the ~~worst~~ *bad ~~impulses~~ impulses* of American diplomacy.

The ~~worst~~ *bad,* for reasons I have repeated on many occasions, ~~but they~~
~~can be summarized as follows~~: the ~~sick~~ feeling that we ~~must~~ *are* ~~somehow~~ ~~be~~
guilty of some ~~nameless~~ sin for which we must now atone; and, our
inability to say "no" ~~when~~ "~~no~~ ~~should have been said.~~ ~~That was the proper thing to say~~
~~I do not mean we should have said "no"~~ out of truculence *but* *not*
because it was the proper thing to say
~~but rather~~ to secure our interests and to ~~reassure~~ *reaffirm* our
~~most~~ greater responsibility, which is leadership of ~~what~~ *all that* remains of
the free world.

As ~~I said, however,~~ *Yes* the treaties represent the good i~~mpulses~~ *instincts .* ~~always~~
of American diplomacy, too, ~~They are represented by~~ *They* a spirit of
generosity and ~~a~~ willingness to change with the times. A good foreign
policy must have both elements~--the need to say "no" and the willingness
to change--in just the right proportions. Unfortunately, ~~the latter~~
~~which has been allowed to dominate~~ *seems today to dominate*
latter element ~~has dominated our~~
~~foreign policy, so there remains but one~~ --accepting change
because it seems fashionable to do so, with little real regard for
the consequences *seems to dominate our foreign policy today.*

someone in positions of importance seems
Too many ~~in important positions~~ believe that through generosity
and self-effacement we can avoid trouble, whether it's *with* Panama and
the Canal~~ ~~ or the Soviet Union and SALT.

15-15-15

But, like it or not, trouble will not be avoided. The American people and their elected leaders will continue to be faced with hard choices and difficult moments, for our resolve is continually being tested by those who envy us our prosperity and begrudge us our freedom. ~~Our destiny is not be aloof or~~ ~~actioned~~ neutral.

America will remain great and act responsibly so long as ~~they~~ it exercises power--wisely, ~~to be sure,~~ *and not* ~~and not power~~ in the bullying sense- ~~but power exercised, nonetheless.~~

Leadership is a great burden. We grow weary of ~~they~~ it at times. And the Carter Administration, despite the ~~clumsy~~ its own cheerful propaganda about accomplishments, reflects that weariness.

But if we are not to shoulder the burdens of leadership in the free world, then who will?

The alternatives are neither pleasant nor acceptable. ~~for the hard fact is that~~ (Great nations which *fail to* ~~do not~~ meet their responsbilities *ARE* ~~will be~~ consigned to the dustbin of history. ~~_____~~ We grew from that small, weak republic which ~~had~~ *HW as its assets* spirit, ~~drive~~ *OPTIMISM, FAITH |* *OUR GOD an* ~~and~~ unshakable belief that ~~we could~~ free men and women could govern themselves wisely. *we* ~~to~~ became the leader of the free world, *an* ~~the~~ example for all those who cherish freedom. ~~to look to.~~

IF WE ARE ~~_____~~ To continue to be that example, *If we are to* ~~as well as to~~ preserve our own freedom, we must ~~develop policies that~~ understand ~~the qualities of other~~ those who would dominate us and deal with them ~~firmly and~~ with determination.

WE MUST ~~If we~~ shoulder our burden with ~~my~~ our eyes fixed on the future, *but* *recognizing* ~~need to~~ the realities of today, ~~and~~ not counting on *mere* ~~vague~~ hopes or wishes *WE MUST BE WILLING TO CARRY OUT OUR RESPONSIBILITY AS* ~~to carry out our responsibilities we can~~ ~~back again be~~ *THE CUSTODIAN OF INDIVIDUAL FREEDOM. Then WE WILL ACHIEVE OUR DESTINY TO BE AS A,* ~~for all the world to see,~~ that shining city on a hill *FOR ALL MANKIND TO SEE.*

####

"Our Time Is Now. Our Moment Has Arrived."

1981

P resident Reagan infuses his timeless wit into a draft of his speech at CPAC since winning the White House.

THE WHITE HOUSE

WASHINGTON

March 18, 1981

MEMORANDUM FOR THE PRESIDENT

FROM: KENNETH L. KHACHIGIAN

Herewith a draft of the speech for the Conservative Political Action Conference, drafted by Tony Dolan.

I wanted you to have it this evening so you might begin
review. There are two points I wanted to raise with you
regarding the draft:

(1) You'll note the reference on the top of page 3 to the
campaigns of Taft, MacArthur, and Knowland. I'm not
absolutely sure that these reflected your political
preference at the time -- and if they do not ring true, they
probably ought to be cut.

(2) We are making sure -- with Vin Scully -- that this
Leo Durocher story, on page 6, has at least the ring of
truth to it.

Still, I wanted to let you have it as early as possible
because tomorrow's schedule is especially heavy. There is
left aside in Friday's schedule a chunk of time for speech
preparation.

(Dolan)   March 18, 1981
                                           First Draft

CONSERVATIVE POLITICAL ACTION CONFERENCE DINNER
FRIDAY, MARCH 20, 1981

It has been said that anyone who seeks success or
greatness should first forget about both and seek only the
truth . . . and the rest will follow.

Well, fellow truth-seekers, none of us here tonight --
contemplating the seal on this podium and a balanced budget
in 1984 -- can argue with that kind of logic. For whatever
history does finally say about our cause, it must say:
that the Conservative movement in ~~twentieth~~ 20th century America
held fast through hard and difficult years to its vision of
the truth.

And history must also say that our victory, when
it was achieved, was not so much a victory of politics as
it was a victory of ideas; not so much a victory for any
one man or party as it was a victory for a set of
principles -- principles that were protected and nourished
through many grim and heartbreaking defeats by a few
unselfish Americans.

~~Many of you -- most of you here tonight -- are exactly~~
you are
those Americans I am talking about, ~~and~~ I wanted to be here
not just to acknowledge your efforts on my behalf, not
just to remark that last November's victory was singularly
your victory; not just to mention that the new Administration
in Washington is a testimony to your perseverance and
devotion to principle -- but to say, simply, "Thank you",
I
~~and to~~ say those words not as a President or even as a
Conservative, but as an American.

Page 2

I say this knowing there are many in this room whose
talents might have entitled them to a life of affluence
but who chose another career out of a higher sense of duty
to country. And I know, too, that the story of their
selflessness will never be written up in <u>Time</u> or <u>Newsweek</u>
or go down in the history books.

And I suppose there are even a few people here
tonight that Penn James hasn't managed to get a job for yet in
the new Administration.

Well, I want you to know, we're working on it. (In)
fact, Penn was in the Oval Office only the other day to
discuss a job opportunity for John Lofton.

"Mr. President," he began, "as you know, we have an
opening in our embassy in Kabul, Afghanistan."

Actually, I told Penn I thought that was quite an
idea. Can anyone here think of a faster way to get the
Soviets out of Afghanistan than to send John Lofton over
there with his tape recorder and a fresh supply of batteries?

Well, John is tireless and dedicated and I like to
think that words like that describe so many who have
contributed to the conservative movement during the past
few decades.

Which is why on an occasion like this it's a little
hard not to reminisce -- not to think back and realize just
how far we have come. The ~~Spanish~~ Portugese have a word for such
recollection -- "saudade" -- a term ~~one of their poets~~ (poetic) rich
~~used when he spoke of~~ with the dreams of yesterday.

Page 3

And surely in our past there was many a dream that
went a glimmering and many a field littered with
broken lances: "MacArthur for President," "Taft for
President," "Knowland for President," -- and though we
made it at least halfway home with this one -- "Goldwater
for President."

And who can forget that hot July night in San Francisco
when Barry Goldwater told us that we must set the tides
running again in the cause of freedom "until our cause
has won the day, inspired the world, and shown the way to
a tomorrow worthy of all our yesteryears."

And there are those of you who will remember an
enterprise we embarked on together that climaxed in Kansas
City in 1976. In fact, looking around this room I can't
resist telling you about something that happened to me not
long after that convention. I was out on the mashed
potato circuit again and was seated next to a man who
had been very active in my campaign. He told me a story about
Robert E. Lee. It seems that some years after the end of
the Civil War the general was at a similar dinner when
the man seated next to him -- an old grizzled veteran of
the Army of Northern Virginia -- leaned over and said:
"You know general, if you ever want to give it another
go . . . "

But our memories are not just political ones.

I like to think back about a small, artfully written
magazine named National Review -- founded in 1955 and
laughed at by the intellectual establishment because it

Page 4

published an editorial that said it would stand athwart
the course of history yelling "stop."

And then there was a spritely written newsweekly
coming out of Washington named Human Events that many said
would never be taken seriously but would later become "must
reading" not only for Capitol Hill insiders but for all
of those in public life.

And I hope, too, you will forgive me if I think back
about a representative of an electric company who used to
stand on cafeteria tables and talk to workers in G.E. plants,
and then go home and wonder -- deep into the night -- whether
this much loved land might go the way of other great nations
that lost a sense of mission and a passion for freedom.

There are so many others -- people and institutions --
who come to mind for their role in the success we celebrate
tonight. I cannot try to enumerate them, some of them
are now only memories -- it is especially hard to believe
that it was only a decade ago, on a cold March day on a
small hill in upstate New York, that one of our great
intellectual leaders, Frank Meyer, was buried.

He had made the awful journey that so many others made:
He pulled himself from the clutches of "the God that Failed,"
and then in his writing fashioned a vigorous new synthesis
of traditional and libertarian thought -- a synthesis
that is recognized today as modern conservatism.

It was Frank Meyer who reminded us that the robust
individualism of the American experience was part of the
deeper current of Western learning and culture.

Page 5

He pointed out that a respect for the law, an
appreciation for tradition, and regard for the social
consensus that gives stability to our public and private
institutions -- these civilized ideas -- must still motivate
us even as we seek a new economic prosperity based on
reducing Government interference in the marketplace.

Our goals complement each other -- we are not cutting
the budget simply for the sake of sounder financial
management. This is only a first step toward returning
power to the States and communities, only a first step
towards reordering the relationship between citizen and
Government. We can make Government again responsive to
people but only by cutting its size and scope and thereby
insuring that its legitimate functions are performed
efficiently and justly.

Because ours is a consistent philosophy of government
we can be very clear: we do not have a separate social agenda,
a separate economic agenda and a separate foreign agenda,
We have one agenda. Just as surely as we seek to put our
financial house in order and rebuild our Nation's defenses,
so too we seek to protect the unborn, to end the
manipulation of school children by utopian planners and
permit the acknowledgement of a Supreme Being in our
classrooms just as we allow such acknowledgements in
other public institutions.

Page 6

Now obviously we are not going to be able to accomplish
all this at once. The American people are patient. I
think they realize that the wrongs done over several decades
cannot be corrected instantly.

But I also believe we (conservatives, if we mean to
continue governing, must realize that it will not always
be so easy to place the blame on the past for our national
difficulties.

You know, one day Leo Durocher sent a rookie out to
play center field -- the rookie promptly dropped the first
fly ball hit to him. Then Durocher sent a veteran out
to replace him who also dropped his first fly ball. At
which point, Durocher rushed down to the end of the bench,
grabbed the rookie, shook him violently and yelled: "You've
got center field so screwed up nobody can play it."

The point is we must lead a Nation, that means more
than criticizing the past -- indeed as T.S. Elliot once
said, it is only in accepting the past that we can hope to
understand it.

During our political efforts, we were the subject of
much indifference and often times intolerance -- that is
why I hope our political victory will be remembered as a
generous one and our time in power will be recalled for
the tolerance we showed those with whom we disagreed.

But beyond this, we have to offer America and the
world a larger vision. We must remove (Government's

Page 7

smothering hand from where it does harm; we must seek to
revitalize the proper functions of (Government. But we
do these things to set loose again the energy and ingenuity
of the America people. We do these things to reinvigorate
those social and economic institutions which serve as a
buffer and a bridge between the individual and the state --
and which remain the real source of our progress as a people.

And we must hold out this exciting prospect of an
orderly, compassionate, pluralistic society -- an Archipaelgo
of prospering communities and divergent institutions --
a place where a free and energetic people can work out
their own destiny under God.

I know that some will think about the perilous world
we live in and the dangerous decade before us and ask what
practical effect this conservative vision can have today.

When Prime Minister Thatcher was here recently we both
remarked on the sudden, overwhelming changes that had come
recently to politics in both our countries.

At our last offical function, I told the Prime
Minister that everywhere we look in the world the cult of
the state is dying. And I held out the hope that it would not
be long before those of our adversaries who preached the
supremacy of the state were remembered only for their role
in a sad, rather bizarre chapter in human history.

The cliches of (communism -- their claims to inevitable
victory -- that bubble of self-confidence they keep around
themselves -- have always been the chief attraction of
Marxism-Leninism for the rest of the world.

Page 8

But is was another great figure in the conservative
movement, Whittaker Chambers, who described the fragility
of that self-confidence and the threat that even a glimpse
of reality poses to the most dedicated communist.

In his unforgettable book, <u>Witness</u>, he described a
fashionable young intellectual who tried to explain her
father's sudden defection from the party:

"He was immensely pro-Soviet," she said, "and
then -- you will laugh at me -- but you must
not laugh at my father -- and then -- one night --
in Moscow -- he heard screams. That's all.
Simply one night he heard screams."

And then Chambers wrote in one of the most moving
passages in modern autobiography about one reason for his
own break with the party:

What Communist has not heard those screams?
They come from husbands torn forever from their
wives in midnight arrests. They come, muffled,
from the execution cellars of the secret police,
from the torture chambers of the Lubianka, from
the citadels of terror now stretching from Berlin
to Canton. They come from those freight cars
loaded with men, women and children, the enemies
of the Communist State, locked in, packed in,
left on remote sidings to freeze to death at
night in the Russian winter. They come from
minds driven mad by the horrors of mass starvation
ordered and enforced as a policy of the Communist

Page 9

State. They come from the starved skeletons,
worked to death, or flogged to death (as an
example to others) in the freezing filth of
sub-arctic labor camps. They come from children
whose parents are suddenly, inexplicably, taken
away from them -- parents they will never see
again.

What Communist has not heard those screams?

But it is important for us to understand that Chambers
was not calling the brutality of Communism its greatest
weakness. He was talking instead about Communism's attempt
to deny the human soul -- that spark of the divine that
is so quickly enflamed by the sounds of anguish from
those suffering under totalitarian rule.

We have heard in our century, far too much of those
sounds -- of anguish -- they have come from stark forbidding
monuments to the emptiness of the Communist faith --
monuments to brutal inhumanity, monuments to rehearsed
cruelty, monuments to concentrated evil -- monuments made
not of marble or stone but of barbed wire and terror.

But from these terrible places have come survivors --
witnesses to the triumph of the human spirit over the
mystique of state power; prisoners whose spiritual values
made them the rulers of their guards. With their survival,
they brought us "the secret of the camps" -- a lesson for

our time and for any age: evil is powerlss if the good
are unafraid.

That is why the communist vision of man without
God must eventually be seen as an empty and a false
faith -- the second oldest in the world -- first proclaimed
in the Garden of Eden with whispered words of temptation
"Ye shall be as Gods."

The crisis of the Western World, Whittaker Chambers
reminded us, exists to the degree in which it is indifferent
to God. "The Western World does not know it," he said
about our struggle, "but it already possesses the answer
to this problem but only provided its faith in God is as
great as communisms' faith in man."

And this is the real task before us: to reassert
our commitment as a Nation to a law higher than our own,
to renew our spiritual strength. For only by building a
wall of such spiritual resolve can we, as a free people,
hope to protect our own heritage and make it someday
the birthright of all men.

What then do I think we can look to in the years
ahead?

Another spring in Prague -- this time one that
endures?

Solzhenitsyn at the Finland Station?

The doors of the Lubianka opened wide?

High Mass again in Gorki Square?

Page 11

These are not just our dreams -- they belong to those
who live today without freedom but with irrepressible hope.

So while we celebrate our recent political victory,
we must understand there is much work before us: to gain
control again of government, to reward personal initiative
and risk-taking in the marketplace, to revitalize our
system of federalism, to strengthen the private institutions
that make up the independent sector of our society and to
make our own spirirtual affirmation in the face of those
who would deny man his place before God.

Not easy tasks perhaps. But I would remind you -- as
I did in my Inaugural *address* -- that we are, after all, Americans.
This year we will celebrate a victory won two centuries ago
at Yorktown -- a victory of a small fledgling Nation over
a mighty world power. The heritage from that long difficult
struggle is before our eyes today in this city -- in the
great halls of our Government and in the monuments to the
memory of our great men.

It is this heritage that evokes the images of a much
loved land -- a land of struggling settlers and lonely
immigrants, of giant cities and great frontiers -- images
of all that our country is and all that we want her to be.

This is the America entrusted to us -- let us stand by
her, protect her, lead her wisely.

This is our moment now -- our time together. And
while we are in the thickest of the fight, let us turn
its tide -- so that as long as men speak of freedom and

Page 12

those who have protected it, they will say of us: here,
were the brave and here, their place of honor.

Appendix 4

The Agenda Is Victory

1982

THE WHITE HOUSE

Office of the Press Secretary

_____

For Immediate Release   February 26, 1982

REMARKS OF THE PRESIDENT
BEFORE ENTERING
THE CONSERVATIVE POLITICAL ACTION
CONFERENCE

The East Room
The Mayflower Hotel

          THE PRESIDENT: Thank you. (Applause.) Thank you.
Thank you very much. And Nancy thanks you.

          Well, I wish it was a bigger room in there. But I assume
that you're going to see and hear the festivities in here? I haven't
been on prime time television for years.

          Anyway, I just want to thank you all for all that you've
done, and your very presence here and your willingness to be in the
overflow room is an indication of why we're going to keep on going
until these things we've believed in so many years and fought for from
the outside, we're going to make sure we on the inside, and we're going
to get them and we're going to accomplish them. (Applause.)

          I know we have to go in there so that dinner can continue
and we can keep on schedule, but you know, I can't help but be a little
-- well, it's a little ironic, and I'm a little amused that suddenly
our opponents have developed a real conscience about political action
committees. I don't remember them being that aroused when the only
ones that you knew about were on their side. Now they're on our side
and they want to do away with them.

          Well, they're not going to do away with you. And God
bless you all, and thanks. (Applause)

                              END

Forgive me
but I felt I had to shorten it.
RR

(Dolan/AB)
February 24, 1982

CONSERVATIVE POLITICAL ACTION CONFERENCE DINNER
FEBRUARY 26, 1982

Nancy and I are delighted to be here at the ninth
annual Conservative Political Action Conference. Anyone
looking at the exciting program you have scheduled over
these 4 days -- and the size of this gathering here tonight --
cannot help but be impressed with the energy and vitality of
the conservative movement in America. ~~And I think~~ we owe a
special debt of gratitude to the staffs of the American
Conservative Union, Young Americans for Freedom, Human
Events and National Review for making this year's conference
the most successful in the brief but impressive history of
this event.

You may remember that when I spoke to you last year I
said the election victory we enjoyed in November of 1980 was
not a victory of politics so much as it was a victory of
ideas; not a victory for any one man or party but a victory
for a set of principles -- principles that had been protected
and nourished during years of grim and heartbreaking defeats
by a few dedicated Americans.

You are those Americans -- and ~~tonight~~ I salute you.
~~But~~ I've also come here tonight to remind you of how much
remains to be done and to ask your help in turning into
reality even more of our hopes for America and the world.

The agenda for this conference is victory -- victory in
this year's crucial congressional, State and local elections.

The media coverage you have received this week and the
attention paid to you by so many distinguished Americans --
in and out of government, conservative and not so conservative --

Page 2

are testimony to the sea-change that you have already brought

about in American politics.

But despite the glitter of nights like this, ~~despite~~

~~the increasing attention paid to conservative~~ ideas ~~during~~

~~the last year,~~ ~~despite~~ the excitement we all still feel at

the thought of enacting reforms we were able only to talk

about a few years ago, we ~~conservatives~~ should ~~never forget~~ always remember

our strength still lies in our faith in the good sense of

the American people -- and that the climate in Washington is

still opposed to those enduring values, those "permanent

things" that we have always believed in.

But Washington's fascination with passing trends and

one-day headlines can sometimes cause ~~us~~ serious problems

over in the West Wing of the White House. ~~As you know,~~ There is the

~~we've had some~~ problem of ~~with~~ leaks ~~in our Administration.~~

~~In fact,~~ Before we even ~~made a decision~~ announced the ~~to~~ give away ~~the~~

of surplus cheese, ~~the mice in Government~~ the warehouse mice had hired

a lobbyist.

~~And~~ Then a few weeks ago, ~~you may recall~~, Those stories about the broke

~~tape recordings made in the Oval Office by President~~ Kennedy tapes.

~~were all the rage. I can't begin to tell you the price we~~

~~paid for that:~~ That caused a stir.

-- Al Haig came in to brief me on his trip to Europe; I

uncapped my pen and ~~he~~ stopped talking.

-- Up on the Hill they were saying: you need eloquence

in the State Dining Room, wit in the East Room and sign

language in the Oval Office.

-- It got so bad I found myself ~~assuring~~ telling every visitor

~~to the Oval Office that~~ there were absolutely no tape recordings

Page 3

being made -- and ~~then I told them that~~ if they wanted a
transcript of that remark ~~they could~~ [first] mention it to the
potted plant on their way out.

~~Well, that particular story faded like so many others --
but if it is important to remember that~~ Washington is a
place of fads and one-week stories, [it is also] ~~we should also remember
that this remains~~ a company town. [And the companies] ~~And there's only one
company, one business, one vested interest here -- its name~~
[are] is Government, Big Government.

~~You know,~~ I remember what Stan Evans used to call ~~a few
years ago~~ his "iron law of politics": "When our people get
someplace [WHERE] they can do us some good -- they stop being our
people." And it is easy to come here and forget our principles
and our constituents -- to start wanting to be an insider,
to start talking the conventional wisdom -- to forget that
there's a big country out there across the Potomac, a country
that sent us here with one job in mind: to cut the size and
burden of government not to increase it.

[Well] ~~Now~~ I don't think that's happened ~~in our Administration~~ [to me.]
~~In fact,~~ I have a sneaking suspicion that a few of you ~~here~~
[first might have agreed when we decided] ~~tonight agree with my recent decision~~ not to ask ~~the~~ Congress
for higher taxes. [And I hope you realize it's] ~~But let's be honest with ourselves: its~~
going to take more than 402 days to completely ~~transform the~~ [change what's
been going on for 40 years. I realized that the other day]
~~Federal bureaucracy. This came home to me the other day~~
when I learned about one private citizen in Louisiana who
~~wrote to HUD~~ [asked] ~~asking~~ for help in developing his property and
[got a letter back that said:] ~~received this letter back from the bureaucracy~~: "We have
observed that you have not traced the title prior to 1803.
Before final approval, it will be necessary that the title
be traced previous to that year."

Page 4

~~So this particular citizen wrote to Washington~~:
~~His answer was eloquent.~~
~~He wrote~~ "Gentlemen, I am unaware that any educated man failed to
know that Louisiana was purchased from France in 1803. The
title of the land was acquired by France by right of conquest
from Spain. The land came into possession of Spain in 1492
by right of discovery by an Italian sailor, Christopher
Columbus. The good Queen Isabella took the precaution of
receiving the blessing of the Pope . . . the Pope is emissary
of ~~Jesus Christ~~ the son of God, ~~And God~~ who made the world.
Therefore, I believe that it is safe to assume that He also
made the part of the United States called Louisiana. And I
hope to hell you're satisfied."

Changing the habits of four decades, is, as I say,
going to take more than 402 days. But change will come. ~~It
will come because~~ As we conservatives are in this ~~thing~~ for the
long haul. ~~We~~ As owe our first loyalty ~~not to the trends or
special interests that dominate Washington, but~~ to the ideas and
principles ~~that~~ we discussed, debated, developed and popularize
over ~~many~~ the years. ~~-- even as some in official Washington and
in the media, who are now so anxious to offer us advice,
rarely took notice.~~

Last year I pointed to these principles as the real
source of our strength as a political movement and mentioned
some of the intellectual giants who fostered and developed
them. Men like Frank Meyer who reminded us that the robust
individualism of America was part of deeper currents in
Western civilization, currents that dictated respect for the
law and the careful preservation of our political traditions.

Page 5

Only a short time ago, ~~and I can't help but see this as another astounding bit of change~~, conservatives filled this very room for a testimonial dinner ~~for~~ a great conservative intellect and scholar -- ~~the~~ author of The Conservative Mind ~~and the defender of "the permanent thing~~s" -- Russell Kirk.

In a recent speech, Dr. Kirk has offered some political advice for the upcoming elections -- he said ~~conservatives~~ now more than ever, *we* must seek out ~~what he calls~~ the "gift of audacity."

~~He has warned us~~ *We must* not ~~to~~ become too comfortable with our newfound status in Washington. ~~He has said in that special prose of his:~~ "When stern decisions must be reached, smugness and dullness may produce political ruin. When men are arming, a conservativism of complacency, ~~or of the disputed middle, cannot long endure.~~ When the walls of order are breached, the vigorous conservative must exclaim: Arm me, audacity, from head to foot."

It was Napoleon, ~~he has reminded us, that~~ master of the huge battalions, who once said "it is imagination that rules the human race" and Disraeli who mentioned that "success is the child of audacity."

~~That is why~~ We must approach the upcoming elections with a forthright and direct message for the American people. ~~We must challenge our opponents, we must go straight to the matter,~~ We must remind ~~the American people~~ *them* of the economic catastrophe that we faced ~~before this Administration took over~~ *on Jan. 20 1981;*: millions out of work, inflation in double digits for 2 years in a row, interest rates ~~reaching~~ *at* 21 and one-half percent, productivity and the rate of growth in the GNP down

Page 6

for the third year in a row, the money supply increasing by

a ~~rate of 9~~ ^13^ percent.

~~This economic mess had~~ And all this due to one overriding cause: Government

was too big and it spent too much money. Federal spending

in the last decade ~~has gone up by~~ ^up^ nearly 300 percent. In

1980 alone, ~~spending~~ ^it^ increased by 17 percent. Almost three

quarters of the Federal budget ~~was being~~ routinely referred

to as "uncontrollable" largely due to increases in programs

like food stamps, which ~~had grown by a staggering~~ ^in 15 years had increased^ 16,000

percent ~~in the last 15 years~~ or medicare and medicaid, ~~which~~

~~had grown~^up^~ by more than 500 percent in just 10 years. Our

national debt was approaching an ~~incredible~~ $1 trillion and

we were paying nearly $100 billion a year in interest on

that debt -- ^MORE THAN^ enough money to run the entire Federal Government

~~in 1960.~~ ^only 20 yrs ago.^

^In an effort to keep force taxes^

~~Attending to this spending space was a tax burden that~~

had increased by 168 percent in just 10 years. ~~Not only~~

~~that -- when this Administration came into office~~ ^1 and^ we were

looking at a tax increase from 1980 to 1984 of more than

$300 billion.

I~~t was clear where all of this was leading~~ -- Unless we

stopped the spending juggernaut, ~~unless we~~ ^and^ reversed the

trend towards ~~higher and~~ ^even^ higher taxes, Government by 1984

would ~~consume~~ ^be taking^ nearly one quarter of the gross national

product. Inflation and interest rates, according to several

studies, would be heading towards 25 percent -- levels that

would stifle enterprise and initiative and plunge the Nation

into even deeper economic crisis.

Page 7

~~It was essential for any conservative government to~~
address this economic problem first. ~~Our very strength as a
nation -- our very ability to protect our political freedom --
depended on it.~~ History tells us of great nations brought
to their knees by unchecked inflation and wild government
spending.

Brooks Adams once put it this way: "Nature has cast
the United States into the vortex of the fiercest struggle
which the world has ever known. She has become the heart of
the economic system of the age, and she must maintain her
supremacy by wit and force, or share the fate of the discarded."

~~You may remember that~~ At this point last year much of
the smart money in Washington was betting -- as it is today --
on the failure of our proposals for restoring the economy;
~~It was said~~ that we could never assemble the votes we needed
to get our program for economic recovery through the Congress.

But assemble the votes we did:

-- For the first time in nearly 25 years we slowed the
spending juggernaut and got the taxpayers out from under the
Federal steamroller.

-- We cut the rate of growth in Federal spending almost
in half. Lowered inflation to a single digit rate & it's still going down. It was 8.4% for 1981 but by Dec. the
~~-- We didn't just slow the $200 billion tax increase~~ figure on an annualized rate was only 3.5%. By reducing inflation
~~the last Democratic administration planned for the next~~ we increased the purchasing power of the average family and more than
~~three years.~~ We cut taxes for businesses and individuals ~~on
a sweeping scale and we've~~ and indexed taxes to inflation.
This last step ended once and for all that hidden profit on
inflation that had made the Federal bureaucracy America's
largest growth industry.

Page 8

-- We've moved against waste and fraud -- ~~our Inspectors~~ with a task force
~~in our inspection~~ who have already found thousands of people who've
~~Generals have estimated that they have saved the Government~~
been dead for as t years still receiving benefit checks.
~~some $2 billion in just 6 months last year.~~ We've concentrated
on criminal prosecutions and we've cut back in other areas
like the multitude of films, pamphlets and public relations
experts -- or as we sometimes call them "the Federal flood
of flicks, flacks, and fold-outs."

-- We're cutting the size of the Federal payroll by
75,000 over the next few years -- and ~~make no mistake about~~ are fighting
~~this -- we will figh~~t to dismantle two ~~cabinet~~ departments,
the Department of Energy and the Department of Education,
agencies whose policies have frequently been exactly the
opposite of what we need for real energy growth and sound,
~~rigorous~~ education for our children.

Even now -- less than 5 months after our program took
full effect -- we've seen the first signs of recovery:
~~inflation has dropped dramatically by nearly 30 percen~~t. In
January, leading economic indicators like housing permits
showed an upturn. By 1983, we will begin bringing down the
percentage of the gross national product consumed by both
the Federal deficit and by Federal spending and taxes.

Our situation now is ~~actually~~ in some ways similar to
that which confronted the United States and other Western
nations shortly after World War II. Many economists then
were predicting a return to depression once the stimulus of
war-time spending was ended. But people were weary of
wartime government controls -- and here and in other nations
like West Germany, those controls were eliminated ~~over~~ against the
advice of ~~some~~ experts. At first there was a period of

Page 9

hardship, ~~that saw~~ higher unemployment and declining growth --
in fact, in 1946, our gross national product dropped 15
percent. But by 1947 ~~the gross national product~~ was holding
steady, and ~~then~~ in 1948 ~~it~~ increased by 4 percent. Unemployment
dropped 2 years in a row and in 1949, consumer prices were
~~actually~~ decreasing.

A lot of the experts ~~were wrong -- they~~ underestimated
the economic growth that occurs once Government stops meddling
and the people take over -- they were wrong then and they're
wrong now.

~~It is now~~ The job of this Administration and of the
Congress is to move forward with additional cuts in the growth
of Federal spending and thereby insure America's economic
recovery. *We have proposed budget cuts for 1983 and our proposals*
crys are equally anguished because there will be a budget deficit.
~~I want to be clear about this Administration's position~~
They are a little like a dog sitting on a short tick-thorn twice pain
On the spending cuts now before the Congress and those tax
reductions we have already passed for the American people *LET*
ArE ; we are standing by our program, we will not turn back, ~~or~~
~~will not run for cover, we will not~~ sound retreat just as we
near certain victory.

~~Now,~~ In the discussion of Federal spending ~~I think~~ the
time has come to put to rest *the sob sister* ~~one little bit of budget bunkum~~
~~that has been making the rounds all too frequently lately.~~
~~I'm speaking of~~ attempts to portray our desire to get Government
spending under control as a hardhearted attack on the poor
people of America.

In the first place, even with the economies we have
proposed, spending for entitlements -- benefits paid directly
to individuals -- will actually increase by one-third over

Page 10

the next 5 years, and in 1983, non-defense items ~~investment~~
~~will amount to more~~ ~~budget will consume more~~ than 70 percent of total spending.

As Dave Stockman pointed out the other day, we are
still providing 95 million meals a day. We are still providing
$70 billion in health care to the elderly and the poor. ~~We~~ some 47 mil. peop.
~~More than 10 mil. are living in subsidized housing and~~
~~are still providing an increasing level of income transfer~~
~~payments to those households who are without income.~~ We are
still providing scholarships for a million to a million and
one-half students.

~~Only here in Wonderland on the Potomac,~~ Only here in
~~the~~ THIS city of Oz, would a budget this big and this generous be
characterized as a miserly attack on the poor.

~~But let's understand~~ Where do some of these attacks originate?
They are coming from the very people whose past policies --
all done in the name of compassion -- brought us the current
recession. ~~It was~~ Their policies ~~of tax and tax, spend and~~
~~spend that~~ drove up inflation and interest rates. And ~~it~~
~~was~~ their policies ~~that~~ stifled incentive, ~~and~~ creativity and
halted the movement of the poor up the economic ladder.

Some of ~~this~~ THEIR criticism is perfectly sincere. But let's
also understand that some of ~~this~~ THEIR criticism comes from those
who have a vested interest in a permanent welfare constituency
and in ~~the~~ government programs that reinforce ~~that~~ the dependency ~~of~~
~~our people.~~
~~Well,~~ I would suggest ~~tonight~~ that no one should have a
vested interest in poverty or dependency -- that these
tragedies must never be looked at as a source of votes for
politicians or paychecks for bureaucrats -- they are blights
on our society, ~~blights~~ that we must work to eliminate, not
institutionalize. There are those who will always require
help from the rest of us on a permanent basis & we'll
provide that help. To those with temporary need we should
have concern and ...

Page 11

~~possible~~ .

~~You know in listening to some of these attacks, I~~
~~Sometimes ask myself~~: How can limited government and fiscal
restraint be equated with lack of compassion for the poor?
How can a tax break that puts a little more money in the
weekly paychecks of working people be seen as an attack on
the needy? Since when do we in America believe that our
society is made up of two diametrically opposed classes --
one rich, one poor -- both in a permanent state of conflict
and neither able to get ahead except at the expense of the
other? Since when do we in America accept this alien and
discredited theory of social and class warfare? Since when
do we in America endorse the politics of envy and division?

~~As the young boy in the New Yorker cartoon put it when~~
~~he saw his dinner plate. "I say it's spinach and I say the~~
(heck)
~~hell with it~~."

~~We've heard these tired arguments before. I remember~~
~~how loudly they were made~~ When we reformed the welfare
system in California and got the cheaters and the undeserving
off the welfare rolls. ~~And~~ instead of hurting the poor we
                                        by more than 40%.
were able to increase their benefits ~~to the truly needy 1 percent~~.

By reducing the cost of Government we can continue
bringing down inflation -- the cruelest of all economic
exploitations of the poor and the elderly. And by getting
the economy moving again we can create a vastly expanded job
market that will offer the poor a way out of permanent
dependency.

So let's tell the American people the truth tonight and
next fall about our economic recovery program: it isn't for

Page 12

one class or group -- its for all Americans: working
people, the truly needy, the rich and the poor.

One man who held this office, a President vastly underrated
by history, Calvin Coolidge, pointed out that a nation that
is united in its belief in the work ethic, and its desire
for commercial success and economic progress is usually a
healthy nation -- a nation where it is easier to pursue the
higher things in life like the development of science, the
cultivation of the arts, the exploration of the great truths
of religion and higher learning.

In arguing for "economy" in government, President
Coolidge spoke of the burden of excessive government.

> "I favor a policy of economy," he said, "not because
> I wish to save money, but because I wish to save people.
> The men and women of this country who toil are the
> ones who bear the cost of the Government. Every dollar
> that we carelessly waste means that their life will be
> so much the more meager. Every dollar that we save
> means that their life will be so much the more abundant.
> Economy is idealism in its most practical form."

And this is the message we conservatives can bring to
the American people about our economic program. Higher
productivity, a larger gross national product, a healthy Dow
Jones average, they are our goals and they are worthy ones.
But our real concern are not statistical goals or material
gain. -- it goes far beyond these -- it concerns those conservative
ideas and principles, those "permanent things," I spoke of
earlier:

We want to expand personal freedom, to renew the American
dream for every American. We seek to restore opportunity
and reward, we seek to value again personal achievement and
individual excellence. We seek to rely on the ingenuity and

Page 13

energy of the American people to better their own lives and

those of millions of others around the world.

~~It is~~ By accomplishing these goals ~~that~~ we can reunite

America with the great wisdom with which she began her

nationhood -- the realization that Government can be ~~the~~

~~enemy as well as~~ the protector of freedom ~~or it can be the enemy~~.

~~Now I think~~ We can be proud of the fact that a conservative

administration has pursued these goals by confronting the

Nation's economic problems head-on. ~~But it should not be~~

AT THE SAME TIME ~~forgotten that~~ we ~~also~~ dealt with one other less publicized,

but equally grave problem: the serious state of disrepair

in our national defenses. The last Democratic administration

had increased real defense spending at a rate of 3.3 percent

a year. -- THAT WAS NO INCREASE AT ALL -- NOT WHEN INFLATION WAS 3 OR 4 TIMES 3.3%. ~~not even enough to keep up with inflation. I~~

~~don't think I have to recount for you again all the horror~~

BY 1980 WE HAD ~~stories of 1980:~~ ~~the~~ fighter planes that couldn't fly; ~~the~~

navy ships that couldn't leave port; ~~the~~ rapid deployment

force that was neither rapid, nor deployable, AND NOT MUCH OF A FORCE. ~~nor a force.~~

The protection of this Nation's security is the most

solemn duty of any President: that is why I have asked for

substantial increases ~~this year~~ in our defense budget - SUBSTANTIAL BUT NOT EXCESSIVE.

ARE THESE ~~Those who think these increases are excessive?~~ ~~should contemplate~~

~~the erosion that has taken place in defense spending during~~

~~the past two decades.~~ In 1962, President Kennedy's budget

~~called for~~ defense AMOUNTED TO ~~spending that accounted for~~ 43.8 percent

of the entire budget. ~~even with our increases, the defense~~

~~spending this year will account for~~ OURS is only 28.5 percent. ~~of the~~

~~budget -- just two-thirds of that figure 20 years ago. In~~

In 1962, President Kennedy's request for military spending

Page 14

~~accounted for~~ was for 8.6 percent of the gross national product;
~~even with our increases, the figure today is~~ OURS IS only 6.3 percent.
~~of the gross national product.~~

~~Those who call for defense spending cuts should think
long and hard about the reaction they are likely to get from
the American people.~~ The Soviet Union outspends us by 50 ON DEFENSE

percent ~~on defense which consumes~~ AN AMOUNT EQUAL TO 15 percent of their gross

national product. ~~Opinion poll after opinion poll shows~~ During the campaign I was asked any number
of times, if I were faced with a choice of balancing the budget or
~~that the American people are well aware of the danger of~~
restoring our Nat. defenses what would I do. Every time I said
~~neglecting our defenses; and that they are in no mood to~~
I would restore our defenses & every time I was applauded for
~~gamble with the readiness of our armed forces or the security~~
giving that answer.
~~of our nation.~~

So let ~~us~~ me be very clear; ~~about the course this Administration
is taking~~: we will press for further cuts in Federal spending,
we will protect the tax reductions already passed, we will ~~spend~~
~~what~~ bolster spending ~~on national~~ on defense what is necessary for our nat. security.
~~And if the Congress hesitates, we will take our case to~~ it becomes necessary
~~the American people.~~

~~There will be no about-faces -- let me assure you, I do~~
I have no intention of leading the
~~not intend to lead~~ a Republican Party into next fall's
on a platform of
election ~~that stands for~~ higher taxes and cut-rate defense.

~~But let me also assure you. If the other major party~~
If our opponents
wants to go to the American people next fall and say:
~~"Elect our candidates to the Congress -- give us the ball~~ --
we're the party that refused to cut spending, we're the
party that tried to take away your tax cuts, we're the party
that wanted a bargain basement military and held a fire sale
on national security" ~~-- believe me, if the other party~~
~~wants to be that candid with the voters~~ -- we'll give them
all the running room they want.

Page 15

    There are other matters on the political agenda for
this coming year -- matters I know that you have been discussing
during the course of this conference.

~~Surely~~ *I hope* one of them will be ~~this Administration's~~ *Our* attempt
to give Government back to the people.-- ~~not just by controlling~~
~~Federal taxes and spending but by returning control over~~
~~Government's everyday decisions to our states and localities.~~
~~Thirty-Two~~ Federal grants in aid ~~have grown from 32 programs in~~
IN 1960, *HAVE GROWN* to over 500 ~~programs~~ in 1981. Our Federalism proposal
would ~~cut through this jungle of grants and~~ return the bulk
of these programs to State and local governments where they
can be made more responsive to the people.

~~This week, in our talks with the governors, we have~~
~~already made progress by starting a dialogue and I believe~~
~~we will eventually see the Congress pass this program largely~~
~~in the form we have proposed.~~

~~But we will need your help. Already there are those~~
~~who are saying that our Federalism proposal is just a short-~~
~~term wonder, a temporary enthusiasm of just one more administration~~
~~in Washington. But I think they are forgetting we are~~
We are deeply committed to this program because it has its roots
deep in conservative principles. We have talked a long time
about revitalizing our system of Federalism. Now with a
single bold stroke we can restore the vigor and health of
our State and local governments, ~~we can get government back~~
~~to the people. Let me assure you:~~ This proposal lies at
the heart of our legislative agenda for the next year and we
will need your active support in getting it passed.

Page 16

There are other issues before us. ~~As you know, this~~
This Administration is unalterably opposed to the forced busing
of school children; just as we also support constitutional
protection for the right of prayer in our schools.

And there is the matter of abortion.-- ~~perhaps the most
serious moral question and the most potentially divisive
issue to face this Nation since slavery.~~ I support a
~~prohibition of abortions~~ -- but I believe we must also
~~realize that a great educational dialogue lies before us in
achieving this goal.~~ We must with calmness and resolve help
the vast majority of our fellow Americans understand that
~~less~~ *more than (1½* million abortions performed in America last year amount
to a great moral evil, an assault on the sacredness of human
life.

Finally, there is the problem of crime -- a problem
whose gravity cannot be underestimated. ~~As you know,~~ This
Administration has moved, in its appointments to the Federal
bench and in its legislative proposals for bail and parole
reform, to assist in the battle against the lawless. But we
must *always remember* ~~never forget~~ that our legal system does not need reform
so much as it needs transformation -- and this cannot occur
at just the Federal level -- it can really occur only when
society as a whole acknowledges principles that lie at the
heart of modern conservatism: right and wrong matters,
individuals are responsible for their actions, society has a
right to be protected from those who prey on the innocent.

This then is the political agenda before us -- perhaps
more than any group, your grassroots leadership, your candidate

Page 17

recruitment and training programs, your long years of hard work and dedication have brought us to this point and made this agenda possible..

But let us never forget that even more is at stake in the next few years than just these issues -- more than spending cuts, military readiness, a sound economy or a conservative House and Senate.

We live today in a time of a ~~great~~ climatic struggle for the human spirit -- a time that will tell whether the great civilized ideas of individual liberty, representative Government and the rule of law under God will perish or endure.

Whittaker Chambers, who sought idealism in Communism and found only disillusionment wrote movingly of the moment ~~that great, gallant man who stood as a witness for~~ "the permanent things" even as he was ~~ridiculed and dismissed by Washington's wisemen, reflected~~ It a was looking at the delicate ear of his tiny daughter suddenly he knew that could not be just an accident of nature and he ~~once upon this drama of our times.~~ said - he didn't realize it at the time but in that moment HAD touched his FOREHEAD WITH HIS FINGER after he wrote; "For in this century, within the next decades," ~~he said,~~ "will be decided for generations whether all mankind is to become communist, whether the whole world is to become free, or whether, in the struggle, civilization as we know it is to be completely destroyed or completely changed. It is our fate to live upon that turning point in history."

~~More recently, a scholar at the Hudson Institute reminded us that we are living today "in the most dramatic and important period in human history."~~

~~Max Singer sees the uniqueness of America in history as part of mankind's remarkable story of progress during the past two centuries.~~

February 24, 1982

~~Page 18, between paragraphs 1 and~~ 2:   *Insert . P. 18*

We have already come a long way together. ~~And, believe me, I speak from the bottom of my heart when I say~~ Thank you for all ~~that~~ you have done for me, and for the common values we cherish. ~~Together, we labored in the wilderness; together we marched to victory.~~

~~In that same spirit of unity, I ask you to~~ Join me in a new effort, a new crusade. Nostalgia has its time and place. Coming here tonight has been a sentimental journey for me as I'm sure it has been for ~~so~~ many of you.

But nostalgia isn't enough. The challenge is now. It's time we stopped looking backwards at how we got here ~~.-- how we won the last election. The other side made that mistake and look where it got them. What~~ We must ask ourselves tonight ~~is~~ how we can forge and weild a popular majority from one end of this countr to the other -- a majority united on basic, positive goals with a platform broad enough and deep enough to endure long into the future, far beyond the lifespan of any single issue o**R** personality

~~We have a firm foundation. We labored long and lovingly to create it. But it is a foundation~~ A*RE*~~to be built upon.~~

~~Conservatives must understand this. Our numbers and commitme swelled between 1976 and 1980, or I would not stand as President here tonight. In 1980 we succeeded in rallying millions of~~ '76. ~~Americans to our side who were not there in 1964 or 1960 or 1976. But we cannot take them for granted. It's time we stopped talkin to ourselves and started talking to America.~~

Page 2

~~For our movement to have a future -- and for our country to fulfill its destiny -- we cannot afford to turn inward~~. We
must reach out and appeal to the patriotic and fundamentally
~~conservative~~ ideals of average Americans who do not consider
themselves "movement" people, but who respond to the same
American ideals we do. I'm not talking about some vague notion
of an abstract, amorphous American mainstream. I'm talking
about Main Street Americans in their millions. They come in all
sizes, shapes and colors -- blue collar workers, blacks, Hispanics,
shopkeepers, scholars, service people, housewives and professional
men and women. They are the backbone of America, and we cannot
move America without moving their hearts and minds as well.

Page 18

"Up until 200 years ago," he wrote, "there were relatively few people in the world. All human societies were poor. Disease and early death dominated most people's lives. People were ignorant, and largely at the mercy of forces of nature. Now we are somewhere near the middle of a process of economic development that will take some 400 years. At the end of that process almost no one will live in a country as poor as the richest country of the past. There will be many more people, most living long, healthy lives, with immense knowledge and more to learn than anybody has time for -- largely able to cope with the forces of nature, and almost indifferent to distance."

This is the new age mankind can someday enjoy if today we Americans can but persevere in the cause of freedom. It is a vision worthy of us, of our great Nation, of our beginnings as a people.

Winston Churchill said once during the darkness of Britain's struggle for survival, "When great causes are on the move in the world . . . we learn that we are spirits, not animals, and that something is going on in space and time and beyond space and time, which, whether we like it or not, spells duty." ← INSERT →

Fellow Americans, ~~fellow conservatives~~, our duty, ~~America's duty~~, is before us tonight -- let us go forward determined to serve selflessly a vision of man with God, government for people and humanity at peace.

For it is now our task to tend and preserve -- through the darkest and coldest of nights -- that "sacred fire of liberty" that President Washington spoke of two centuries ago -- a fire that remains tonight a beacon to all the oppressed of the world, shining forth from this kindly pleasant greening land called America.

Appendix 5

We Will Not Be
Turned Back

1983

ACCOMPLISHMENTS?

1. Accomplishments -- What are your greatest ones? How will you be remembered in history? Will conservatives look back upon this Administration favorably?

In two years, we have accomplished a great deal that's not only good for the country but should also make conservatives proud. As fellow conservatives, let's take a look at just how far we've come:

General Themes

o   Legitimized and brought into center of national dialogue many key conservative issues. Turned the national debate around. Now the liberals are not proposing many new programs. They are debating how much we should increase defense; how much power should be returned to the States; and whether or not we should allow prayer in schools.

o   We have also credentialed many conservatives for future government service. For first time in our lifetime, large numbers of solid conservatives have had an opportunity to participate in the management of the Federal departments and agencies. They will be able to serve in government under future conservative administrations for many years to come.

o   Both of these changes have profound implications for the future.

Domestic Specifics

o   Overall, we have laid foundations for economic recovery and restoration of U.S. military strength.

o   Specifically, could name many things:

-- inflation at lowest levels since 1972 (when it was arti-ficially held down by wage and price controls) -- this time achieved the right way, through fiscal and monetary restraint so it can stay down;

-- Interest rates down because inflation is lower;

-- Spending growth still too high but -- at about 10% -- is down more than 1/3 from 1980 record rate of 17%;

-- Taxes will be over $735 billion lower in next 5 years as a result of our programs;

-- Defenses being restored -- have enacted over 90% of what we have sought; 600 ship Navy; morale and re-enlistment rates up; making up for decade of neglect.

o Other Domestic Accomplishments:

-- More than any administration in memory, we have kept the
   promises of our campaign (e.g.; taxes, spending, defense).

-- Despite the fact that one House of Congress in hands of other
   party, we have a substantial string of successes on Capitol
   Hill, proving that conservatives can govern effectively.

-- Have come farther than anyone thought possible in establish-
   ing Cabinet government.

-- Substantial progress in shrinking size of and intrusiveness of
   government; e.g. deregulation. Major success in preventing
   burdensome new regs from being imposed; repealing or reforming
   old regs more laborious but progress being made.

-- Through block grants, have begun the return of power to State
   and local governments.

-- Major cuts and reform of discretionary programs such as CETA.

-- Healthy changes in Federal policy toward disruptive issues
   such as forced school busing and reverse discrimination.

-- Major effort underway on tuition tax credit.

-- Support for any legitimate pro-life measure in Congress.

-- Proposed voluntary prayer amendment and committed to fight for
   it.

-- Proposed regulations to de-politicize Federal grants and
   contracts. No longer will it be legitimate for tax dollars to
   be used by grantees to lobby for bigger government.

-- On Justice Front, conservatives should especially appreciate
   how far we've come:

   * Proposed perhaps the most comprehensive package of tough-
      minded criminal law reform measures -- e.g.; bail reform,
      sentencing reform, increased penalties for narcotics
      traffickers. Also cracking down on organized crime and
      on drugs (e.g. South Florida);

   * Major, successful effort to appoint devotees of judicial
      restraint to the bench. Particularly distinguished
      appointments, in addition to Mrs. O'Connor, have been at
      Circuit court level: Professors Bork and Scalia (D.C.
      Court); Posner (7th Circuit) and Winter (2nd Circuit).

   * In antitrust area, AG and William Baxter (leading conser-
      vative professor) have been especially effective in

attacking "big is bad" mythology.

o   Let's also recognize that during entire 97th Congress, few
    proposals for massive new spending were even seriously discusse
    None was enacted. National Health insurance, government-run da
    care, other key items on the liberal agenda of the '70s have
    disappeared so far in the '80s.

Foreign Policy Initiatives

The accomplishments and initiatives here are equally lengthy, but
let's just name a few of special interest to conservatives:

-- Restoration of American defenses;
-- Shown a new direction in foreign policy, making it clear that
    America will no longer be a patsy for the other side. Won't si
    still anymore for abuse and double standards in international
    debate.
-- By proposing that we eliminate an entire class of weapons from
    the face of the earth, we are proving that we can not only hold
    the moral high ground but that we need not make any more uni-
    lateral disarmament concessions to the Soviets.
-- Know that conservatives are also pleased that we have taken the
    right stand on the Law of the Sea Treaty. Major European
    countries followed our lead despite dire predictions that we
    would have to stand alone.

I'm grateful to the Am. Conservative Union, Young Ams. for freedom,
Nat. Review & Human E wants for organizing this
3rd annual memorial service for the Dem.   (Dolan/AB)
platform of 1980. Someone asked me why I   February 17, 1983
wanted to make it 3 in a row. Well you know how   12:00 p.m.
the dried love makes.

PRESIDENTIAL ADDRESS: CONSERVATIVE POLITICAL ACTION
                         ~~CONFERENCE~~
                         FRIDAY, FEBRUARY 18, 1983

I am delighted to be back here with you, at your tenth
annual conference. In my last two addresses, I've talked about
our common perceptions and goals and I thought I might report to
you tonight on where we stand in achieving those goals -- a sort
of state of the Reagan report, if you will.

Now I'm the first to acknowledge that there is a good deal
left unfinished on the conservative agenda. Our clean-up crew
will need more than 2 years to deal with the mess left by others
over a half century. But I'm not disheartened. In fact, my
attitude about that unfinished agenda isn't very different from
that expressed in an anecdote about one of my favorite
Presidents, Calvin Coolidge. Some of you may know that after Cal
Coolidge was introduced to the sport of fishing by his Secret
Service detail, it got to be quite a passion with him, if you can
use that word about "Silent Cal". Anyway, he was once asked by
reporters how many fish were in one of his favorite angling
places, the River Brule. Coolidge said the waters were estimated
to carry 45,000 trout. "I haven't caught them all yet," Cal
added, "but I've intimidated them."

It's true we haven't brought about every change important to
the conscience of a conservative . . . but we conservatives can
take a great deal of honest pride in what we have achieved.

In a few minutes I want to talk about just how far we have
come and what we need to do to win further victories. But right
now I think a word or two on strategy is in order. You may

Page 2

remember I mentioned in the past that it was now our task as
conservatives not just to point out the mistakes made over all
those decades of liberal government -- not just to form an able
opposition -- but to govern, to lead a nation. And I noted this
would make new demands upon our movement, upon all of us.

For the first time in half a century, we've developed a
whole new cadre of young conservatives in government. We've
shown that conservatives can do more than criticize -- we've
shown that we can govern and move our legislation through the
Congress.

~~But~~ I know ~~that~~ there is concern over attempts to roll back
some of the gains we have made. And it seems to me that here we
ought to give some thought to strategy -- to making sure we
~~conservatives~~ stop and think before we act.

For example, some ~~prominent liberals~~ of our critics have been saying
recently that they want to take back the people's third-year tax
cut and abolish tax indexing. And some ~~conservatives and~~ others including members
of my staff wanted immediately to open up a verbal barrage
against them. Well, I hope you know that sometimes a President it's better if
~~doesn't~~ ~~can't always~~ say exactly what's on his mind. ~~In fact, right at~~ There's an
~~that moment, one of those~~ old ~~story~~ about ~~the~~ farmer and ~~the~~
lawyer ~~came to mind.~~ that illustrates my point.

It seems these two had a pretty bad traffic accident. They
both got out of their cars, the farmer took one look at the
lawyer, walked back to his car, and brought back a package with a
bottle inside. "Here," the farmer said, "take a ~~sip~~ nip of this.
You look pretty shook up -- it will steady your nerves." The
lawyer ~~took a sip~~ did. The farmer said, "You still look a bit pale,

Page 3

have another." ~~This~~ The lawyer ~~did~~ and at the farmer's urging *took another swallow* ~~took~~ another and another. Finally, the lawyer said that he was feeling better ~~but~~ *and* asked the farmer if he didn't want to take a little nip. *too* "~~No~~" ~~said~~ The farmer, *said "not me* I'm waiting for the state trooper."

~~And~~ I wonder if we ~~conservatives~~ can't learn something from that farmer. ~~After all, if the liberals~~ *If our liberal friends* really want to head into the next election under the banner of taking away from the American people their first real tax cut in nearly 20 years -- if, after peering into their heart of hearts, they ~~conclude that~~ *feel* they must tell the American people ~~they want~~ *that* over the next 6 years ~~to take $1,500 from~~ *they want to reduce the income of* an average family of four, ~~if they~~ *(by 1500) and they* ~~feel compelled~~ *want* to voice these ~~kinds of~~ deeply-held convictions in an election year; ~~I say to you~~ *Well*: Fellow conservatives, who are we to stifle the voices of conscience?

Now in talking about our legislative agenda I know some of you have been disturbed by the notion of stand-by tax increases in the so-called out years. Well, I wasn't wild about the idea myself. But the economy is getting better. And I believe these improvements are only the beginning. With some luck, and if the American people respond with the kind of energy and initiative they have always shown in the past . . . well, maybe it's time we started thinking about some stand-by tax cuts too. *But you know the great point that they standby tax increase - they cant put it into affect unless they've agreed to our cuts.* But, you know, with regard to the economy I wonder if our political adversaries haven't once again proven that they're our best allies. ~~As you know, some of these folks~~ *They* have spent the last 16 months or so placing all the responsibility for the state

Page 4

of the economy on our shoulders. And with some help from the

media it's been a pretty impressive campaign. They've created quite

an image — we are responsible for the economy;

~~But the doom and gloom brigaders are marching nowhere.~~

Well I assume that we are responsible then for inflation which

~~After~~ 2 years of back-to-back double-digit inflation, ~~we've done~~ been

got here has now been reduced

~~brought inflation down~~ to 3.9 percent in 1982 ~~-- and 4.1 percent~~

(IT RAN AT ONLY 1.1%)

For the last 3 months of that year. In 1982, real wages

increased for the first time in 3 years. Interest rates have

dropped dramatically with the prime rate shrinking by nearly

50 percent. And in December the index of leading indicators was

a full 6.3 percent above last March's low point and has risen in

8 of the last 9 months. Last month housing starts were up

95 percent and building permits 88 percent over last year at this

time. New home sales are up 75 percent since April and

inventories of unsold homes are at the lowest levels in more than

a decade. Auto production this quarter is scheduled to increase

by 22 percent and General Motors alone is putting 21,400 workers

back on the job. Last month's sharp decline in the unemployment

rate was the most heartening sign of all. It would have taken a 5 B

bill to reduce unemployment by the same amount.

~~So fellow conservatives, maybe our liberal friends have~~

Its time to ~~so~~ admit our guilt,   OUR LIBERAL (

~~done us another favor. Maybe it's~~ time we admitted that ~~they~~

have been (all the time)   they should go right on

~~were~~ right ~~just this once~~ and ~~maybe we should be encouraging them~~

~~to go right on~~ telling the American people ~~what they've been~~

~~saying all along.~~ that the state of the economy is precisely the

fault of that wicked creature ~~named~~ Kemp/Roth and its

havoc-wreaking twin ~~called~~ Reaganomics.

Let's admit

~~Yes, I do think~~ we've turned the corner on the economy. And

we're

~~I'm~~ especially proud of one thing. When ~~this Administration~~ hit
                                                        we

heavy weather we didn't panic; we didn't go for fast bromides and

Page 5

quick fixes, the huge tax increases or wage and price controls
recommended by so many. And ~~I think~~ our stubbornness, if you
want to call it that, will quite literally pay off for every
American in the years ahead.

So let me pledge to you tonight: Carefully, we have set out
on the road to recovery. We will not be deterred. We will not
be turned back. ~~Once again I would say~~, I reject the policies of
the past, the policies of tax and tax, spend and spend, elect and
elect. The lesson of these failed policies is clear: I've said this before You can't
drink yourself sober or spend yourself rich; you can't prime the
pump without pumping the prime — like to 21½% in 1980.

And a word is in order here on the most historic of all the
legislative reforms we have achieved in the last 2 years, that of
tax indexing. You can understand the terror THAT ~~such a provision~~
strikes in the heart of those whose principal constituency is Big
Government. Bracket creep is ~~Government's~~ hidden incentive to inflate the
currency & bring on inflation. Indexing will end those ~~and those~~ huge hidden subsidies for bigger and bigger
Government. ~~are now suddenly going to end~~. In the future, if the
advocates of Big Government want money ~~to pay~~ for their social
engineering schemes, they've got to go to the people and say we right out
and want more money from your weekly paycheck — we're raising taxes.

So all the professional Washingtonians, FROM ~~the~~ bureaucrats, TO ~~the~~
lobbyists, TO the special interest types are frightened -- plain
scared -- and they're working overtime to take this one back. I
think I speak for all conservatives when I say: Tax indexing is
non-negotiable -- it's a fight we'll take to the people and it's
a fight we'll win going away.

Page 6

But I think you can see how even this debate shows things
changing for the better. It highlights the essential differences
between two philosophies now contending for power in American
political life. One is the philosophy of the past -- a
philosophy that has as its constituents an ill-assorted mix of
elitists and special interest groups who see Government as the
principal vehicle of social change, who believe that the only
thing we have to fear is the people, ~~that they~~ who must be watched
and regulated and superintended from Washington.

On the other hand ~~there is~~ our political philosophy -- ~~a philosophy that~~ is at the heart of a new political consensus that
emerged in America at the start of this decade; one that I
believe will dominate American politics for many decades. The
economic disasters brought about by too much Government were the
catalysts for this consensus. During the seventies the American
people began to see misdirected, overgrown government as the
source of many of our social problems -- not the solution.

This new consensus has a view of Government that is
essentially that of our Founding Fathers -- that Government is
the servant, not the master, that it was meant to maintain order,
to protect our Nation's safety -- but otherwise in the words of
that noted political philosopher, Professor Jimmy Durante, "Don't
put no constrictions on da people. Leave 'em ta heck alone."

~~And because~~ The overriding goal during the past 2 years has
been to give Government back to the American people, to make it
responsive again to their wishes and desires, ~~we've wanted~~ to do
more than bring about a healthy economy or a growing GNP. We've
TRULY ~~also~~ brought about a quiet revolution in American Government.

Page 7

For too many years, bureaucratic self-interest and political maneuvering held sway over efficiency and honesty in government; Federal dollars were treated as the property of bureaucrats, not taxpayers; those in the Federal establishment who pointed to the misuse of those dollars were looked upon as malcontents or troublemakers.

This Administration has broken with ~~the Washington~~ what was a kind of buddy system. ~~And that is why~~ There have been dramatic turnabouts in some of the MORE ~~most~~ scandal-ridden and wasteful Federal agencies and programs. ONLY A few years ago the General Services Administration was racked by indictments and report after report of inefficiency and waste. Today at GSA, Jerry Carmen has not only put the whistleblowers back in charge -- he's promoted them and given them new responsibilities. Today GSA work-in-progress time is down from 30 days to 7 ~~days~~ even while the agency has sustained budget cuts of 20 percent, office space reductions of 20 percent and the attrition of 7,000 employees.

At the Government Printing Office under Dan Sawyer losses of millions of dollars have suddenly been ended as the workforce was cut through attrition and a hiring freeze, and overtime pay was cut by $6 million in 1 year alone. The Government publication program, which ran a cumulative loss of $20 million over a 3-year period registered a $4.1 million profit last year.

It has been said of this Administration by some that it has turned a blind eye to waste and fraud at the Pentagon while over zealously concentrating on the social programs. Well, at the Pentagon under Cap Weinberger's leadership and our superb service secretaries Jack Marsh, John Lehman and Verne Orr, we have

Page 8

identified more than a billion dollars in savings on waste and
fraud and, over the next 5 years, multi-year procurement and
other acquisition initiatives will save us almost $15 billion.

These are only three examples of what we are attempting to
do to make Government more efficient. The list goes on: We have
wielded our inspectors general as a strike force accounting for
nearly $17 billion in savings in 18 months. With Peter Grace's
help, we've called on top management experts from the private
sector to suggest modern management techniques for every aspect
of government operations. And with an exciting new project
called Reform 88 we're going to streamline and reorganize the
processes that control the money, information, personnel and
property of the Federal bureaucracy, including the maze of 350
different payroll systems and 1,750 personnel offices.

There is more, much more, from cutting down wasteful travel
practices to reducing paperwork, from aggressively pursuing the
$40 billion in bad debts owed the Federal Government to
preventing publication of more than 70 million copies of wasteful
or unnecessary government publications.

But, you know, making Government responsive again to the
people involves more than eliminating waste, fraud and
inefficiency. During the decades ~~of liberal dominance, while~~ when
Government was intruding into areas where it is neither competent
nor needed, it was also ignoring its legitimate and
constitutional duties such as preserving the domestic peace and
providing for the common defense.

I'll talk about defense in a moment but on the matter of
domestic order a few things need to be said. First of all, it is

Page 9

abundantly clear that much of our crime problem was provoked by a
~~Liberal~~ social philosophy that saw man as primarily a creature of
his material environment. The same liberal philosophy that saw
an era of prosperity and virtue ushered in by changing man's
environment through massive Federal spending schemes also viewed
criminals as the unfortunate products of poor socio-economic
conditions or an underprivileged upbringing. Society, not the
individual, they said, was at fault for criminal wrongdoing. <u>We</u>
were to blame.

Today ~~this~~ new political consensus utterly rejects this
point of view; the American people demand that Government
exercise its legitimate and constitutional duty to punish career
criminals -- those who consciously choose to make their living by
preying on the innocent.

We conservatives have been warning about the crime problem
for many years, about that permissive social philosophy that did
so much to foster it, about a legal system that seemed to
specialize in letting hardened criminals go free. And now we
have the means, the power to do something. Let's get to work.

~~For example,~~ Drug pusher after drug pusher, mobster after
mobster, has escaped justice by taking advantage of our flawed
bail and parole system. *(To avoid punishment)* ~~And~~ Criminals who have committed
atrocious acts have cynically utilized the technicalities of the
exclusionary rule, a miscarriage of justice unique to our legal
system, ~~to avoid punishment~~. Indeed, one National Institute of
Justice study showed that of accused drug felons in the State of
California alone in 1981, nearly 30 percent were *sent back out on* ~~returned to~~ the
streets because of perceived problems with the exclusionary rule.
*The exclusionary ~~is not~~ rule is not law — it's what is called case law
the result of a judicial decision. If a law enforcement officer obtains
evidence as the result of a violation of the laws regarding search &
seizure that evidence can not be introduced in . Trial once it it knows the*

Page 10 *guilt of the accused. This is hardly punishment, of the officer for his violation of legal procedures and it's only effect is to ~~free~~ free someone patently guilty of a crime.*

This Administration has proposed vital reforms of our bail
and parole systems, (the exclusionary rule) and criminal forfeiture
and sentencing statutes. Those reforms were passed by the Senate
95 to 1 last year. ~~But~~ They never got out of committee in the
House of Representatives. The American people want these reforms
and they want them now. I'm asking tonight ~~then~~ that you
mobilize all the powerful resources of this political movement to
get these measures passed by the Congress.

On another front, all of you know how vitally important it
is for us to reverse the decline in American education -- to take
responsibility for the education of our children out of the hands
of the bureaucrats and put it back in the hands of parents and
teachers. That's why the Congress must stop dithering -- we need
those tuition tax credits. We need a voucher system for the
parents of disadvantaged children, we need Education Savings
Accounts, a sort of IRA for college, and, finally -- don't think
for a moment I've given up -- we need to eliminate that
unnecessary and politically engendered Department of Education.

There are other steps we are taking to restore Government to
its rightful duties, to restore the political consensus upon
which this Nation was founded. ~~For example, it is true~~ that Our
Founding Fathers prohibited a Federal establishment of religion,
but there is no evidence that they intended to set up a wall of
separation between the state and religious belief itself.

The evidence of this is all around us: in the Declaration
of Independence alone, there are no fewer than four mentions of a
Supreme Being. "In God We Trust" is engraved on our coinage, the
Supreme Court opens its proceedings with a religious invocation

Page 11

and the Congress opens each day with prayer from its chaplains.
~~I just think~~ The schoolchildren of the United States are entitled
to the same privileges as Supreme Court Justices and Congressmen.
~~And I ask you to~~ Join me in persuading the Congress to accede to
the overwhelming desire of the American people for a
constitutional amendment permitting prayer in schools.

Finally on our domestic agenda, there is a subject that
weighs heavily on all of us, the tragedy of abortion on demand.
This is a grave moral evil and one that requires the fullest
discussion on the floors of the House and Senate.

As we saw in the last century with the issue of slavery, any
attempt by the Congress to stifle or compromise away discussion
of important moral issues only further inflames emotions on both
sides and leads ultimately to even more social disruption and
disunity.

So, tonight, I would ask that the Congress discuss the issue
of abortion openly and freely on the floors of the House and
Senate. Let those who believe the practice of abortion to be a
moral evil join us in ~~making~~ TAKING this case to our fellow Americans.
And let us do so rationally, calmly, and with an honest regard
for our fellow Americans. Speaking for myself, I believe that
once the implications of abortion on demand are fully aired and
understood by the American people, they will resolutely seek its
abolition. *(I know there are many who sincerely believe limiting abortion the right to abortion violates the freedom of choice of the individual. But if the unborn child is a living entity then 2 individuals, each with*
~~And while we're on the subject of our domestic agenda,~~
~~something very important needs to be said here. Much of the~~
~~credit for our success in getting conservative issues before the~~
~~Congress goes to one very brave, very dynamic Senator -- a man of~~
the right to life, liberty & the pursuit of happiness are involved. Unless & until someone can prove the unborn is not alive (and all medical evidence indicates it is) then we must concede the benefit of the doubt

Page 12

honor and conscience and character. He isn't loved by the
Potomac backbiters but he's a favorite with me and with you
and -- as I am quite sure next year's election will show -- with
the people of North Carolina. Jesse Helms is a great Senator and
a great American. Tonight we all salute him.

But whether it's cutting spending and taxing, shrinking the
size of the deficit, ending overregulation, inefficiency, fraud
and waste in government, cracking down on career criminals,
revitalizing American education, pressing for prayer and abortion
legislation -- I think you can see that the agenda we have put
before America these past 2 years has been a conservative one.
Oh, and two other matters that I think you'd be interested in:
first, as part of our federalism effort, next week we will be
sending to the Congress our proposal for four megagrants that
will return vital perogatives to the States where they belong;
and, second, the Office of Management and Budget will press ahead
with new regulations prohibiting the use of Federal tax dollars
for purposes of political advocacy.

And these important domestic initiatives have been
complemented by the conservative ideas we have brought to the
pursuit of foreign policy. In the struggle now going on for the
world, we have not been afraid to characterize our adversaries
for what they are. We have focused world attention on forced
labor on the Soviet pipeline and Soviet repression in Poland and
all the other nations that make up what is called the "fourth
world" -- those living under totalitarian rule and who long for
freedom. We have publicized the evidence of chemical warfare
and other atrocities by the Soviets and their clients in Cambodia
(which we are now supposed to call Kampuchea)

Page 13

and Afghanistan. We have pointed out that ~~the Soviets~~ <ins>TOTALITARIAN POWERS</ins> hold a
radically different view of morality and human dignity than do
we. ~~We have said that we can seek no final accommodation with
the evils of totalitarianism but~~ <ins>WE</ins> must develop a forward strategy
for freedom, one based on our hope that someday representative
government will be enjoyed by all the peoples and nations of the
Earth.

~~And~~ <ins>We</ins> have been striving to give the world the facts about
the international arms race. Ever since our nearly total
demobilization after World War II, we in the West have been
playing catch-up. Yes, there has been an international arms
race. <ins>(as some of the declared Dem. Candidates for the Presidency tell us.)</ins> ~~But let's tell the truth:~~ there's only been one side
<ins>But let them also us —</ins> doing the racing.

Those of you in the front line of the conservative movement
can be of special assistance in furthering our strategy for
freedom, our fight against totalitarianism.

First of all, there is no more important foreign policy
initiative in this Administration -- and none that frightens our
adversaries more -- than our attempts through our international
radios to build constituencies for peace in nations dominated by
totalitarian, militaristic regimes. We've proposed to the
Congress modest but vitally important expenditures for the Voice
of America, Radio Free Europe/Radio Liberty and Radio Marti.
These proposals stalled last year -- but with your help we can
get them through the Congress this year. Believe me, nothing
could mean more to the Poles, Lithuanians, Cubans and all the
millions of others living in the Fourth World.

Page 14

Secondly, we must continue to revitalize and strengthen our
armed forces. Cap Weinberger has been waging a heroic battle on
this front. I'm asking you the conservative leaders here tonight to
make support for our defense build-up one of your top priorities.

But beside progress in furthering all of these items on the
conservative agenda, something else is occurring -- something
that someday we conservatives may be very proud happened under
our leadership.

Even with all our recent economic hardships, I believe a
feeling of optimism is just now entering the American
consciousness, a belief that the days of division and discord are
behind us and that an era of national unity and renewal is upon
us.

A vivid reminder of how our Nation has learned and grown and
transcended the tragedies of the past was given to us here in
Washington only a few months ago.

Last November, on the mall between the Lincoln Memorial and
the Washington Monument, a new memorial was dedicated -- one of
dark, low-lying walls inscribed with the names of those who lost
their lives in the Vietnam conflict. Soon there will be added a
sculpture of three infantrymen representing different racial and
ethnic backgrounds.

During the dedication ceremonies, the rolls of the dead were
read for 3 days in a candlelight ceremony at the National
Cathedral. And those veterans of Vietnam who were never welcomed
home with speeches and bands -- but who were undefeated in battle
and were heroes as surely as any who have ever fought in a noble
cause -- staged their own parade on Constitution Avenue.

Page 15

As America watched them -- some in wheelchairs, all of them
proud -- there was a feeling that as a Nation we were coming
together again and that we had -- at long last -- brought the
boys home.

"A lot of healing . . . went on," said Jan Scruggs, the
wounded combat veteran who helped organize support for the
memorial.

And then there was this newspaper account that appeared
after the ceremonies. I would like to read it to you:

"Yesterday, crowds returned to the memorial. Among them was
Herbie Petit, a machinist and former marine from New Orleans.
'Last night,' he said, standing near the wall, 'I went out to
dinner with some other ex-marines. There was also a group of
college students in the restaurant. We started talking to each
other and before we left they stood up and cheered.'
'The whole week,' Petit said, his eyes red, 'it was worth it
just for that.'"

It has been worth it. We Americans have learned again to
listen to each other and to trust each other. We have learned
that Government owes the people an explanation and needs their
support for its actions at home and abroad. And we have
learned -- and I pray this time for good -- that we must never
again send our young men to fight and die in conflicts that our
leaders are not prepared to win.

Yet the most valuable lesson of all -- the preciousness of
human freedom -- has been relearned not just by Americans but by
all the people of the world. It is "the stark lesson" that
Truongs Nhu Tang, one of the founders of the National Liberation
Front, a former Viet Cong minister and vice-minister of the
postwar government in Vietnam, spoke of recently when he
explained why he fled Vietnam for freedom.

Page 16

"No previous regime in my country," he wrote about the concentration camps and boat people of Vietnam, "brought such numbers of people to such desperation. Not the military dictators, not the colonialists, not even the the ancient Chinese overlords. It is a lesson that my compatriots and I learned through witnessing and through suffering in our own lives the fate of our countrymen. It is a lesson that must eventually move the conscience of the world." *This man learned the value of freedom only after helping to destroy it.*

~~This is~~ The task that has fallen to us as Americans ~~is~~ to

move the conscience of the world, to keep alive the hope and

dream of freedom. For if we fail or falter, there will be no

place for the world's oppressed to flee to. This is not a role

we sought -- we preach no manifest destiny -- but like the

Americans who brought a new Nation into the world 200 years ago,

history has asked much of us in our time. Much we have already

given. Much more we must we prepared to give.

This is not a task we shrink from. It is a task we welcome.

For with the privilege of living in this kindly pleasant greening

land called America, this land of generous spirit and great

ideals, there is also a destiny and a duty, a duty to preserve

and hold in sacred trust mankind's age-old aspirations of peace

and freedom and a better life for generations to come.

Appendix 6

Our Noble Vision:
An Opportunity Society
for All

1984

THE SECRETARY OF THE TREASURY
WASHINGTON 20220

March 1, 1984

1984 FEB 30 PM 12: 25

MEMORANDUM FOR THE HONORABLE BEN ELLIOTT
              DEPUTY ASSISTANT TO THE PRESIDENT
              AND DIRECTOR OF SPEECHWRITING
              THE WHITE HOUSE

Subject: Conservative Political Action Conference Dinner
         Address

This is an excellent speech. I do have a few comments.

Page 5. You may wish to refer to the dollar as "strong"
rather than to the over- or under-valuation question, although
I agree that the dollar is valued correctly by the market, all
things considered. Even if certain price computations on a
narrower perspective showed no differentials in international
costs of production, there would always be those who want a
"weaker" dollar and higher inflation.

I have stated in hearings that the dollar is strong for
several reasons, including our greatly improved inflation
performance, stronger real growth, and improved after-tax rates
of return on investment in plant and equipment in the U.S.
These surely are part of what is meant by "the remarkable
performance of our economy." You may wish to list some of the
causes to show the multiplicity of factors which affect exchange
rates.

The dollar could decline somewhat relative to other nations'
currencies should they follow our lead in reducing inflation and
restoring growth. However, in that event, I would be prepared
to attribute this to renewed strength abroad, which would be
admirable, rather than to backsliding in the U.S., which would
be undesirable.

I agree that we should not talk the dollar down. Markets
eventually shrug off loose talk and follow the fundamentals.
In the meantime, however, there is temporary fear in the markets
that a policy change has been signalled, particularly if a
person in authority has made the observation. In the short run,
markets are needlessly and unfairly disrupted, and large sums
are won and lost for no valid reason. Such random shocks weaken
the market, which is a valuable resource for stability. We do
not want to thin the market by scaring participants away.

Our export performance has been unusually good for this
stage of the cycle, due in part to productivity gains and
diminished unit labor costs assisted by the tax and regulatory

- 2 -

relief portions of the President's program. You may wish to
mention those factors. Your export figures include services.
I have long felt that services -- such as financial services --
have been underrated; I am pleased to see this point made.

A capital inflow was expected when the President's program
was first proposed. The reduction in tax and regulatory burdens
was a deliberate effort to raise the reward to plant and equipment in the U.S. Consequently, more U.S. capital has remained
at home as you have pointed out on page 6.

The fear of foreign capital is overdone. I am pleased to
see your reassurances on that point. As long as an investment
is in economically sound, productive assets in a growing economy,
the additional output due to the additional capital will earn
more than enough to repay the investor, whether foreign or
domestic. Your historical example illustrates that fact.

I realize that developed nations are usually capital
exporters, but only when their domestic rates of return have
fallen due to a relative glut of capital compared to the situation abroad, and only after differential risks, regulations and
tax burdens are taken into account. We have rather suddenly and
forcefully -- and deliberately -- improved our investment climate,
and may well attract funds for a period, as we did for many years
in the past. We are certainly under no obligation to try to
create a worse investment climate than in foreign nations to repel
capital in order to equalize world capital endowments. In fact,
a growing U.S. economy, by being a better customer, raises investment prospects and income levels abroad, as in your "engine for
worldwide recovery" metaphor.

Page 9. There are two points concerning tax simplification
and fairness which you may wish to mention, if space allows. We
are aiming at a broader tax base, which may produce higher revenues, but for the right reasons. First, the tax base and tax
revenues may expand through faster economic growth prompted by
lower tax rates and a simpler tax code. Second, revenues may be
enhanced if the use of tax shelters and the underground economy
are discouraged, both through the carrot of lower tax rates and
the stick of closing loopholes. Thus, although the Treasury tax
simplification study is aimed at a revenue neutral proposal,
in the static sense, it could well produce higher revenues due
to faster growth and greater economic efficiency.

Donald T. Regan

cc: Richard G. Darman
     Assistant to the President

Appendix 7

Forward for Freedom

1986

P resident Reagan's speech drafting and White House staffing
memos reveal how Reagan was reflecting on the theme of
CPAC in 1986: the future of conservatism.

THE WHITE HOUSE

WASHINGTON

JANUARY 21, 1986

MEMORANDUM TO BEN ELLIOTT

FROM: CECI COLE MCINTURFF

SUBJECT: PRESIDENT'S REMARKS TO CPAC RECEPTION JAN. 30

The President has addressed 11 of the 13 conferences ever held by the Conservative Political Action Committee (CPAC).

This year's, called CPAC 86, will the largest ever. It is principally sponsored by the American Conservative Union and the Young Americans for Freedom, in conjunction with the weekly Human Events and the magazine National Review.

The theme this year is "toward a conservative agenda for the '90s." Speakers are being asked to focus on where conservatives should be going as opposed to simply reflecting on where conservatives have been.

The President will be awarded the first annual Ashbrook Award, being presented jointly by ACU and the Ashbrook Center in Ohio (named for former Rep. John Ashbrook (R-Ohio)). Either F. Clifton White or Bill Rusher will actually present the award to the President.

Worth noting is the entertainment: Jakov Smirnoff, a Russian emigre and comedian, will perform. Smirnoff was quoted in Time magazine as saying that having come to America, the only unrealized part of his dream is the desire to perform before the President.

Also, the dinner the President addresses is in honor of Jonas Savimbi. The President may want to refer to this.

There are several other points worth incorporating into the President's remarks:

-- Stress the historical significance of ACU and YAF to the conservative movement. Both organizations were founded when it was less fashionable to pursue consistently conservative goals, and the rightward movement in our national agenda has been greatly contributed to by the activities of these groups.

-- Review the accomplishments of the Reagan Administration generally.

-- Thank these two groups and all others represented at the dinner for members' assistance not only to the conservative cause, but to the President personally.

-- Pitch the importance of the budget by making the following
points:
    *On the conservative agenda that the President initiated with
his election, the major obstacle still to be overcome is
reduction of the federal deficit.
    *The President's budget takes advantage of an historic
opportunity: Gramm-Rudman.
    *The President's budget meets Gramm-Rudman's $144M deficit
level, and does so without hurting programs for the poor and
laying open conservatives to the charge of unfairness, does so
while providing for 3% growth in defense spending, and does so
without raising taxes.
    *Any opposing the President's budget reductions is saying just
this: they want to raise taxes.

I hope this is helpful.

The President has seen 1/30

(Dolan)
January 29, 1986
12:30 p.m.

PRESIDENTIAL REMARKS: CONSERVATIVE POLITICAL ACTION
                        CONFERENCE DINNER
                        THURSDAY, JANUARY 30, 1986

I am delighted to be here tonight and I want to extend my
heartfelt thanks to the American Conservative Union along with
Human Events, National Review and Young Americans for Freedom for
putting on this conference and for extending this invitation.

Tonight my thoughts cannot help but drift back to another
conservative audience of more than 20 years ago and a
presidential campaign that the pundits and opinionmakers said
then was the death knell for our movement. But just as the
opinion leaders had been stunned by Barry Goldwater's nomination,
so too they would be shocked by the resiliency of his cause and
the political drama to unfold around it: the rise of the New
Right and the religious revival of the mid-70's, and ~~the nearly
successful challenge for the Republican nomination in 1976~~, and
the final, triumphant march to Washington in 1980 by
conservatives.

And, you know, that last event really did come as a shock of
seismic proportions to this city; I can remember reading about a
poll taken at a Washington National Press Club luncheon in
January of 1980, on the eve of the primary season. Those in
attendance were asked who would be the next President of the
United States. Jimmy Carter got a large number of votes; so did
Teddy Kennedy; ~~and so did~~ ~~fellow Republicans who~~
But there was one candidate on the (?) (Reagan, who
~~were running that year for President. Forgive me for this, but,~~
~~you know, one candidate~~ got so few votes from the wisemen of

Page 2

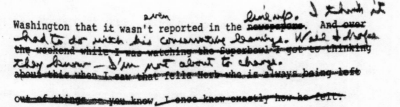

Washington that it wasn't reported in the ~~newspapers~~ line up. ~~And over had to do with his conservative leanings. Well I hope the weekend while I was watching the Superbowl I got to thinking~~ they know — I'm not about to change. ~~about this when I saw that fella Herb who is always being left out of things — you know. I once knew exactly how he felt.~~

But while official Washington always underestimated our cause, some of the shrewder journalists did over the years sense something astir in America. Theodore White, asked openly just after Barry Goldwater's campaign: "Was it only the dying echo of a past long gone, or was it the harbinger of an age to come?"

And you know, to be here tonight and be part of this conference -- the largest in your history; to look at your program for the next 2 days and all the important people and discussions; to stand here now with the Presidential seal on this podium ~~and the cameras whirring~~, to feel the energy, the almost festive air of this audience -- I think you've provided an answer to Teddy White's question about the fate of our movement, the state of our cause. Fellow conservatives, it took us more than 20 years -- but who can deny it -- we're rockin; and we're rollin.

Now I know a few liberal observers will try to downplay all this -- but don't you think they're going to sound a bit like Yogi Berra on that famous occasion when he said of a restaurant: "It's so crowded nobody goes there anymore." And, as for those liberals who finally are catching onto the idea that there is a conservative movement; ~~ladies and gentlemen, do~~ they remind you ~~as much as they remind me~~ -- of the cowboy who was out ~~walking~~ hiking in the desert one day and came across the Grand Canyon; "WOW" he ~~the cowboy~~ said, "something sure happened here."

Page 3

Well, something has happened in America; in 5 short years we
have seen the kind of political change rarely seen in a
generation. On nearly every issue -- Federal spending, tax cuts,
deregulation, the fight against career criminals and for tough
judges, military readiness, resistance to Soviet expansionism and
the need for candor about the struggle between freedom and
totalitarianism -- the old taboos and superstitions of liberalism
have collapsed and been all but blown away, to be replaced by a
robust and enlightened conservatism, a conservatism that brings
with it economic prosperity, personal opportunity and a shining
hope that someday all the peoples of the world -- from
Afghanistan to Nicaragua to Poland and, yes, to Angola -- will
know the blessings of liberty and live in the light of freedom.

Those in this room know how often we were told the odds of
accomplishing even a small part of this were all against us. I
remember my own first visit up to the Hill after the 1980
election when issues like the tax cuts came up. And, you know, I
can remember meeting MET a congressman there -- a kind of big fella
as I recall, lots of white hair, from the Boston area, I think --
maybe you know him -- he smiled very indulgently and told me not
to expect too much because I was, to use his words, "in the big
leagues now."

But, you know, as a conservative, I had an advantage. Back
in the hard years, the lean years, when we were forming our
political PACs, sending out our fundraising letters and working
for candidate after candidate in campaign after campaign, all of
us learned something vital, something important about our
country, something became an article of faith, a faith that

Page 4

sustained us through all the setbacks and the heartache. You
see, we knew then what we know now: that the real big leaguers
aren't here in Washington at all but out there in the
heartland -- out in the real America, where folks go to work
everyday and church every week, where they raise their families
and help their neighbors, where they build America and increase
her bounty and pass on to each succeeding generation her goodness
and her splendor. And we knew something else too: that the
folks out there in real America pretty much see things our way
and that all we ever have to do to get them involved is: be
brave enough to trust them with the truth and bold enough to ask
them for their help.

And it's here we find the explanation for the successes of
the last 5 years, the reason why on issue after issue the
liberals in this town have lost and are still losing; they've
forgotten who's in charge, who the big leaguers really are.
Reminds me of a favorite little story of mine about a career
naval officer who finally got his four stripes, became a captain
and took over command of a giant battleship. And one night he
was out steaming around the Atlantic when he was called from his
quarters to the bridge and told about a signal light in the
distance. The captain told the signalman, "Signal them to bear
starboard." Back came the signal from ahead saying, "You bear
starboard." Well, as I say, this captain was very aware he was
commander of a battleship, the biggest thing afloat, the pride of
the fleet. And he said, "Signal that light again to 'Bear
starboard now.'" And once again, back came the answer, "Bear
starboard yourself." So, the captain, determined to give his

Page 5

~~unknown~~ counterpart a lesson in sea-going humility, ~~endored~~ ^as he said^ "Signal
again and tell them 'Bear starboard, I am a battleship.'" And
back came the signal, "Bear starboard yourself, I am a
lighthouse."

^Well^ ~~Yes~~, the American people have turned out to be just what the
forefathers thought they would be when they made them the final
arbiter of political power; a lighthouse to the ship of state --
a source of good judgement and common sense signalling a course
to starboard. But I come here tonight not just to celebrate
these successes of our past but also to strike a serious, even
somber note -- to remind each of you not only of how far we have
come together but how tragic it would be if we suddenly cast
aside -- in a moment of dreadful folly -- all our hopes for a
safe America and a freer world. My fellow conservatives, I want
to speak to you tonight about our movement and -- a great danger
that lies ahead.

Now some of you may think I am reacting here to claims that
1985 was a disappointing or, at best, mediocre year for
conservatives. In fact, I want to take sharp issue with this and
suggest to you that those claims themselves are evidence of the
broader problem I'm talking about: the danger of growing soft
with victory, of losing perspective when things go our way too
often, of failing to appreciate success when it occurs or seeing
danger when it looms.

First, let's talk about 1985 and three legislative victories
whose strategic significance were both enormous and largely
overlooked. Now, some of you who go back with me to that
campaign in 1964 can remember how easily the liberals dismissed

Page 6

(us ~~were told~~ toward bring prosperity)

our warnings then about the dangers of deficit spending; others
of you know how passionately the liberals believed in the use of
high and punitive tax rates to redistribute income; and, finally,
all of us can remember how liberals found in the post-Vietnam
syndrome a form of religious exercise, a kind of spiritual
ecstasy, however much that syndrome paralyzed American foreign
policy and jeopardized freedom.

Now, let me ask you: if someone had come up to you even as
late as a few years ago and told you that by 1985 all of these
cherished liberal doctrines -- a belief in deficit spending, the
politics of envy via high tax rates, and the refusal to help
those resisting communist dictatorship -- would be formally and
publicly rejected in a single 12-month period by the liberal
Democrats themselves -- wouldn't you have thought that person
prone to acute shortages of oxygen in the cerebral hemispheres?
But consider 1985: we saw a de facto balanced budget amendment
passed by both Houses of the Congress; we saw a House of
Representatives under liberal leadership agree to cut the top
marginal tax rate to the 35 to 38 percent range; and we even saw
that same House not only approve funds for an insurgency against
a communist government but spontaneously repeal that symbol of
liberal isolationism, the Clark amendment.

So, friends and neighbors, salute Halley's Comet, salute
(Im to old fashioned to call it Uranus,)
that spaceshot to Uranus; just remember politics in 1985 was ~~the~~ 2 also
celestial phenomenon ~~of the decade~~ -- Steven Spielberg all the
way.

Actually, the remarkable year of 1985 at home was a
reflection of a broader, even brighter strategic picture. In

Page 7

Europe and Asia, statism and socialism are dying and the free
market is growing. And all across the world the march of
democracy continues. Yet, even as I think the tide of history is
all but irreversibly turned our way and this strategic picture
will continue to improve, we must guard at all costs against an
unnecessary but costly tactical defeat ahead; I am talking, of
course, about the elections in November.

Now this isn't going to happen; as long as we conservatives
will shoulder the burden of our recent successes; if we'll
realize how much is at stake this November, forget for the moment
the flowers and the sunshine and summon once again those deep
reserves of will and stamina that won for us our first victories.

And bear in mind: this will require a supreme effort; our
job is going to be even tougher this year. The very years of
prosperity and peace that conservative programs have given
America may in a strange way actually help those who fought the
hardest against them. Good times, after all, tend to favor
incumbents and fortify the status quo.

Yet, you and I know how unacceptable that status quo is, how
much -- on everything from Right to Life, prayer in the public
schools, enterprise zones, aid to anti-communist insurgents --
still waits to be done.

So we must go to the record, get the facts to the American
people. The Speaker of the House has already indicated a tax
increase is the solution to our problems and recently another
important member of the House leadership echoed his words. Not
much has changed on Federal spending either. Sure, the liberals
are angry about Gramm-Rudman, but they aren't looking

Page 8

realistically at our bloated expenditures, only talking nonsense
about shutting down the F.B.I. and the I.R.S. -- though I do
admit that in mentioning that last point they may be tempting me
beyond my strength. And as for defense -- let me assure you the
liberals haven't changed a bit -- they are still looking at
America's defense budget with lust in their hearts. *a lust to*
strip it bare & use the funds for more of their social experiments.
         Yes, this year we have to work even harder at summoning the
vigor to tell the American people the truth and the vigor to ask
their help; to remind them that what they do this November will
decide whether the days of high taxes and higher spending, the
days of economic stagnation and skyrocketing inflation, the days
of national malaise and international humiliation, the days of
"Blame America First" and "inordinate fear of communism," will
all come roaring back at us once again. More than that, we must
tell the American people that the progress we made thus far is
not enough; that it will never be enough until the conservative
agenda is enacted and that means enterprise zones, prayer in the
public schools and protection of the unborn. And that's why, my
fellow conservatives we have to stop limiting ourselves to
talking about holding onto our strength in the Senate and start
talking about conservative control of the House of
Representatives *which has been in the hands of our opponents for*
virtually half a century.
         ~~And it goes even beyond these issues.~~ Never forget that for
Those nearly 50 years the liberals had it all their own way in this
city, and that the loss of such great power is rarely accompanied
with graceful acquiescence.
         Well, the liberals are feeling pretty sorry for themselves
and that's why they're anxious about this election; they know

Page 9

that unless they deliver a telling blow this year to
conservativism, the 1988 Conservative Political Action Conference
will see every major presidential candidate from both parties
demanding a chance to appear here and claim the mantle of
conservativism. So, this year is breakpoint; and the liberals
are pulling out all the stops. And, you know, I think it's going
to be worthwhile reminding the American people of how desperate
the liberals are; how so much of their strength in the House of
Representatives -- as many as 18 or 23 seats -- is due to
gerrymandering on a scale unprecedented in modern history. And
this is not to mention the outrageous episode in which a
legitimately elected member of the Congress and the people of
Indiana's 8th district were disenfranchised in the House of
Representatives.

But there's another issue that I also believe vividly
illustrates how seriously out of touch the liberals are with the
American people. We sometimes forget that no one is more
realistic about the nature of the threat to our freedom than the
American people themselves. In fact, their intuitive realism is
why that Bear in the woods ad some of you can remember from
1984's Presidential campaign was so successful. Yes, the
American people want an Administration that pursues every path to
peace; but they also want an Administration that is realistic
about Soviet expansionism, committed to resisting it and
determined to advance the cause of freedom around the world.

Now, we know what happens when an administration that has
illusions about the Soviets takes over. First there are the
illusions, then the surprise and anger when the Soviets do

Page 10

something like invade Afghanistan. Any way you look at it, it
heightens tension and the prospects for conflict. In fact, the
liberal conduct of foreign policy reminds me a little of a story
~~about~~ a game Notre Dame played against Army in 1946. When Notre
Dame player Bob Livingstone missed a tackle, his teammate Johnny
Lujack screamed, "Livingstone, [you, so and so, you, such and
such]." And just then Coach Frank Leahy said, "Another sacrilege
like that, Jonathon Lujack, and you will be disassociated from
our fine Catholic university." ~~But, then~~ Well, on the very next play,
Livingstone missed another tackle and Coach Leahy turned to his
bench and said: "Lads, Jonathon Lujack was right about Robert
Livingstone."

And that's why it's important to go to the record; I
remember a little booklet that came out a few years back;
although it was by the Republican Study Committee and titled
"What's The Matter With Democratic Foreign Policy," it was really
about a shrinking group of foreign policy liberals here in
Washington. And I just think if we were able to get some of
those choice quotations on issues like Vietnam, Grenada and
Central America before the American people and they were able to
see what the Washington liberals really believe about foreign
policy -- the naivete and confusion of mind -- I believe we would
shock the American people into repudiating these views once and
for all.

And let me interject here two points that I think can be
important this year. First, the question of defense spending.
During the last few weeks, there have been a number of columns,
editorials or speeches calling for a slash in the military

Page 11

budget: and quoting President Eisenhower as justification.

President Eisenhower did warn about large concentrations of power

like the military industrial complex but what's being left out is

the context of that quote. In his farewell address to the *AMERICAN PEOPLE*

YES HE DID WARN US ABOUT THE DANGER OF AN ALL POWERFUL MR. INDUSTRIAL COMPLEX

~~American people, President Eisenhower~~ *BUT HE ALSO* reminded us America must

always be vigilant because, "We face a hostile ideology -- global

in scope, atheistic in character, ruthless in purpose, and

insidious in method." *The pundits haven't been quoting that part Chairperd*

~~And a second point~~. I know ~~that~~ there's been a great deal

of talk in the media recently about the situation in Southwest

Africa and especially Angola. And I also know you will be having

a special guest here tomorrow evening as I did this morning in

the Oval Office. Well, let me just say now it would be

inappropriate for me as President to get too specific tonight.

But I do want to make a comment here on some recent history and

let you draw your own conclusions.

Last September, at the Lomba River in southern Angola, when

a force of Unita rebels met an overwhelmingly superior force of

government troops directly supported by the Soviet bloc, the

Unita forces defeated the government troops and drove them and

their communist allies from the field. In the history of

revolutionary struggles, of movements for true "national

liberation," there is often a victory like this, that electrifies

the world and brings great sympathy and assistance from other

nations to those struggling for freedom. Past American

Presidents, past American Congresses and always of course the

American people have offered help to others fighting in the

freedom cause we began. So, tonight each of us joins in saluting

Page 11

budget: and quoting President Eisenhower as justification.
President Eisenhower did warn about large concentrations of power
like the military industrial complex but what's being left out is
the context of that quote. In his farewell address to the *American people*
YES HE DID WARN US ABOUT THE DANGER OF AN ALL POWERFUL MIL. INDUSTRIAL COMPLEX
~~American people, President Eisenhower~~ reminded us America must
BUT HE ALSO always be vigilant because, "We face a hostile ideology -- global
in scope, atheistic in character, ruthless in purpose, and
insidious in method." *The pundits haven't been quoting that part of his point*

~~And a second point.~~ I know ~~that~~ there's been a great deal
of talk in the media recently about the situation in Southwest
Africa and especially Angola. And I also know you will be having
a special guest here tomorrow evening as I did this morning in
the Oval Office. Well, let me just say now it would be
inappropriate for me as President to get too specific tonight.
But I do want to make a comment here on some recent history and
let you draw your own conclusions.

Last September, at the Lomba River in southern Angola, when
a force of Unita rebels met an overwhelmingly superior force of
government troops directly supported by the Soviet bloc, the
Unita forces defeated the government troops and drove them and
their communist allies from the field. In the history of
revolutionary struggles, of movements for true "national
liberation," there is often a victory like this, that electrifies
the world and brings great sympathy and assistance from other
nations to those struggling for freedom. Past American
Presidents, past American Congresses and always of course the
American people have offered help to others fighting in the
freedom cause we began. So, tonight each of us joins in saluting

Page 12

the heroes of the Lomba River -- and their leader, the hope of
Angola, Jonas Savimbi.

So, you see, like the Panama Canal in 1976, foreign policy
issues like defense spending and aid to the freedom fighters may
prove the sleeper issues of the year.

So let me urge you all to return to your organizations and
communities, and to tell your volunteers and your contributors
that the President said that they are needed now as never before,
that the crucial hour is approaching, that the choice before the
American people this year is of overwhelming importance: whether
to hand the government back to the liberals or move forward with
the conservative agenda into the 1990s.

My fellow conservatives, let's get the message out loud and
clear. The Washington liberals and the San Francisco Democrats
aren't extinct. They're just in hiding, waiting for another try,
their main chance. Let us make it clear to the American people,
they must choose this year between those who are enemies of Big
Government and the friends of the freedom fighters and, on the
other hand, those who are advocates of Federal power and a
foreign policy of illusion. So let the choice be clear. Will it
be "Blame America First?" Or will it be "On to Democracy" and
"Forward for Freedom?"

And freedom is the issue. The stakes are that high. You
know, recently Nancy and I saw together a moving new film, the
story of Eleni, a woman at the end of World War II caught in the
Greek civil war, a mother who, because she smuggled her children
out to safety, eventually to America, was tried, tortured and
shot by the Greek communists.

Page 13

It is also the story of her son, Nicholas Gage, who grew up
to become an investigative reporter with the New York Times and
who, when he returned to Greece, secretly vowed to take vengeance
on the man who had sent his mother to her death. But at the
dramatic end of the story, Nick Gage finds he cannot extract the
vengeance he has promised himself. To do so, Mr. Gage writes,
would have relieved the pain that had filled him for so many
years but it would also have broken the one bridge still
connecting him to his mother and the part of him most like her.
As he tells it: "...her final cry, before the bullets of the
firing squad tore into her, was not a curse on her killers but an
invocation of what she died for, a declaration of love: 'My
children!'"

How that cry has echoed across the centuries, a cry for all
the children of the world, a hope that all of them may someday
live in peace and freedom. And how many times have I heard it in
the Oval Office while trying to comfort those who have lost a son
in the service of our nation and the cause of freedom.

"He didn't want to die," the wife of Major Nicholson said
at Fort Belvoir last year about her husband, "and we didn't want
to lose him, but he would gladly lay down his life again for
America."

So we owe something to them, you and I. To those who have
gone before -- Major Nicholson, Eleni, the heroes at the Lomba
River; and to the living as well -- to Andre Sakharov, Lech
Walesa, Adolfo Calero and Jonas Savimbi -- their hopes reside in
us, as do ours in them.

Some twenty years ago I told you, my fellow conservatives,

Page 14

that "You and I have a rendezvous with destiny." And tonight
that rendezvous is upon us; our destiny is now; our cause is
still, as it was then, the cause of human freedom.

Let us be proud that we serve together; and brave in our
resolve to push on now towards that final victory so long sought
by the heroes of our past and present, and now so near at hand.

EXECUTIVE OFFICE OF THE PRESIDENT
OFFICE OF MANAGEMENT AND BUDGET
WASHINGTON D.C. 20503

OFFICE OF
THE DIRECTOR

1/27/86

Ben --

Busy day!

Attached is an interpretation of the Battle
of Freeman's Farm that differs somewhat from
the one in the speech. It is the work of
Thomas Rinehart, Al Keel's military aid.

You may want to call him directly to clear
this up -- but probably want to be very careful to make sure we've got all our facts
straight on this one!

Jeff

C: Dave Chew

Page 12, <u>Second paragraph of President's Remarks</u>: Conservative Political
Action Conf. Dinner.

<u>with 6,000 troops</u>

Burgoyne crossed the Hudson on 19 September 1777 and marched south of Saratoga, where his advance was blocked by Gates with 7,000 troops. Burgoyne attacked the American high ground at Freeman's Farm that dominated the left flank of the American position. The attack ended in a very limited and costly success. Depleted in strength and short of supplies, Burgoyne made one final effort (Battle of Bemis Heights on 7 October 1777) to dislodge the Americans. However, his maneuver was disrupted by American counteraction and he withdrew to Saratoga where, surrounded by constantly increasing American troops, he was forced to capitulate. (From <u>The West Point Atlas of American Wars</u>, Volume I.) It is therefore inappropriate to suggest that the Americans won the battle of Freeman's farm or to draw a parallel to the Unita rebels battle at the Lambo River where Unita forces routed a numerically superior opponent.

Appendix 8

A Future That Works

1987

EW

46222155
PR007-02   he President has seen   2/20

RR

THE WHITE HOUSE
WASHINGTON

FEBRUARY 18, 1987

TELEPHONE CALL TO
CONSERVATIVE POLITICAL ACTION COMMITTEE CONFERENCE
THURSDAY, FEBRUARY 19, 1987
8:40 p.m.

FROM: MITCHELL E. DANIELS, JR. *Mitch D.*

I.   PURPOSE

To welcome attendees to the 14th annual CPAC
conference, and preview your comments before the group
which are scheduled to be delivered at lunch on
Friday.

II.   BACKGROUND

This conference, sponsored by the American Conservative
Union and Young Americans for Freedom, in conjunction
with Human Events and National Review, is the major
annual gathering of conservative activists.

James A. Lennon, Second Vice Chairman of American
Conservative Union will M.C. the program and will
introduce your phone call to the audience.

III. PARTICIPANTS

Approximately 2,000 activists from across the nation
will be assembled at dinner to hear your brief remarks
via telephone.

IV.   PRESS PLAN

Some press will be covering the dinner, and will hear
your remarks, although the major press coverage will
result from your remarks in person to the group at
Friday's lunch.

Attachment: Talking Points   *Call made*

SUGGESTED TALKING POINTS FOR TELEPHONE CALL TO CPAC
-- Thank you Jim, and good evening to all my good friends and
loyal conservatives gathered there at dinner this evening.
I know you are about to hear from the Attorney General, and I
thank you, Ed, for filling in for me tonight.

-- I look forward to being there personally tomorrow, joining you
for the largest of C-PAC's 14 conferences, involving 50 groups
representing some three million Americans.

-- I'll spend time tomorrow outlining goals for the future. But
for tonight, let me deliver to you my deep and lasting thanks for
what you believe, and for what you have done in the name of those
beliefs.

-- Well, we'll talk more tomorrow. For now, enjoy the assembled
stars of Broadway, and the talents of my friend, Yakov Smirnov,
who I know you all will join me in congratulating on acquiring
his U.S. citizenship this year.

--Till tomorrow then. God bless you all, and goodnight.

THE WHITE HOUSE

WASHINGTON

February 17, 1987

MEMORANDUM FOR DONALD T. REGAN

THROUGH: WILLIAM HENKEL

FROM: JAMES L. HOOLEY

SUBJECT: DROP-BY 14TH ANNUAL CONSERVATIVE POLITICAL ACTION
                CONFERENCE LUNCHEON ON FRIDAY, FEBRUARY 20, 1987

Attached is a summary schedule and an attachment for the
President.

EVENT CONCEPT

On Friday, February 20, 1987, the President will drop-by the
14th annual Conservative Political Action Conference (CPAC '87)
luncheon at the Washington Hilton Hotel.

Upon arrival the President will proceed on-stage and make remarks to
approximately 600 conservative activists at the conclusion of their
luncheon.

Following his remarks, the President will depart the Washington
Hilton Hotel en route the White House arriving at approximately
1:35 p.m.

You should be aware that the original invitation from CPAC to the
President included a VIP reception and dinner on Thursday night with
a "Broadway Review " in his honor, and most CPAC attendees are under
the impression that this program stands. We are working with Mitch
Daniels to insure that CPAC officials inform dinner guests that the
President will not be attending, which they had not intended to do.

It should also be noted that CPAC will be lobbying heavily for
additional time in order to accommodate their "absolute need" for a
photo reception (80 people). We will continue to work with Mitch
Daniels and Fred Ryan to find an acceptable solution.

Memorandum for Donald T. Regan   **PAGE 2**

<u>RECOMMENDED PRESS COVERAGE</u>

1. Arrival/Departure at the Washington Hilton Hotel - OFFICIAL
    PHOTOGRAPHER ONLY

             Approve _____   **Disapprove** _____

2. Remarks - OPEN PRESS COVERAGE

             Approve _____   **Disapprove** _____

cc: P. Buchanan
      M. Daniels
      D. Thomas
      D. Chew
      J. Courtemanche
      T. Dawson
      F. Ryan
      T. Dolan
      J. Kuhn
      M. Weinberg

                                              02/17/87 1:00 p.m.

Appendix 9

On the Frontier of
Freedom

1988

(Dolan)
February 8, 1988
6:00 p.m.

PRESIDENTIAL REMARKS: CONSERVATIVE POLITICAL ACTION
                        CONFERENCE DINNER

It's great to be here tonight and I'm delighted to see so
many old friends. Now let's get right to it. About the
interview. You know the one about the Soviets not wanting to
dominate the world anymore. You think it's as hard on you; what
about me? You know what it's like at ~~this point in my career~~ to [my age]
he getting fan mail from ~~Jane Fonda?~~ [Dr. Spock?] Or have Daniel Berrigan and
Teddy Kennedy invite you to come along as they chain themselves
to the gate of an MX missile factory?

Anyway, all I can say is what Louis Satchmo Armstrong said
shortly after he signed an exclusive contract, the company heard
the unmistakable sound of Satchmo's horn on another label. They
called him for a meeting, they presented the evidence. And old
Stachmo showed himself the master of comedic reconciliation. He
said: "I didn't do it -- and I'll never do it again." [I'll get ¹/₂]
to this [xote] [little later but]
~~And then there's~~ the I.N.F. treaty. How do you think I felt
when Gorbachev called a week and a half ago and asked if our
first on-site inspectors could be the Denver Broncos secondary?
And then along came the contra vote -- I felt so terrible I
almost called Dan Reeves and John Elway to tell them what a rough
week I had. [and the missed] [~~He change~~ there for,]

But let's all congratulate the Washington Redskins. Believe
me, after the contra vote, ~~it's great~~ [a victory for peace and] it's great to know there's some people
in Washington who ~~know how~~ to play to win. And, believe
me, I'll ~~the~~ get back to ~~this~~ [the] ~~little~~
~~later too.~~

the contra vote a little
later too,

- 2 -

Refers I do though,

~~By the way,~~ something odd happened just before I got here tonight that I think you should know about. I got a message from Dave Keane reminding me that this was the eve of Lincoln's birthday *and* ^ suggesting I go upstairs and check on the ghost in Lincoln's bedroom. I did, *At* what do you know? ~~There~~ was Stan Evans ~~covered~~ *bundled* *s tet* ~~in~~ a sheet saying: "Listen to Jesse Helms, listen to Jesse Helms."

Actually, I do want to thank you ~~tonight~~ for that warm welcome. But I hope tonight isn't going to be like what happened to that fella I knew back in my *movie* ~~Hollywood~~ days. We had an actor there who was only in Hollywood long enough to get the money to go to Italy, because he aspired to an operatic career. And then he was asked to sing in "Pagliacci," the very spiritual fountainhead of opera. And he did an aria, and he received such thunderous and sustained applause that he had to repeat the aria as an encore. And again the same sustained, thunderous applause, and again he sang "Vesti la Giuba." And this went on until finally he motioned for quiet, and he tried to tell them how full his heart was for this reception. "But, " he said, "I have sung 'Vesti la Giuba' now nine times. My voice is gone, I cannot do it again." And a voice from the balcony said, "You'll do it until you get it right." *get it right taylot and let's*

But let's *start* were we should start. A couple of weeks ago, I talked about the state of our Union; tonight I'd like to talk about the state of our movement -- and forgive me if in many ways I think the two are synonymous. *plenty of* ~~Many~~ questions have been asked about the conservative movement *during the past year* by

- 3 -

some people who were surprised to find out back in 1980 there was such
a conservative movement capable of running a victorious
national campaign based as unabashed appeal to the American people for
conservative ideas and principles.

You know there's a story from Jeff Greenfield the real
campaign which I occasionally recall and it might do all of us
well to remember this year. Back in February of 1980 -- and the
primaries were already underway -- the question was asked at a
Washington Press Club luncheon who would be the next President of
the United States. And do you know that there was a whole list
of candidates -- seven or eight of them, from Mr. Carter to
Mr. Ted Kennedy who got sizable blocks of votes -- but only one candidate
couldn't get enough votes to get mentioned in the newspaper
accounts. I think you can guess who that was but let me add
quickly that I don't mention that poll tonight because it's
underestimated yours truly; because that's important to remember
I mention we conservative have been
in Washington for a while and we occasionally need to remind ourselves what
brought us here in the first place; a solid, unshakable all—
encompassing skepticism about the prevailing Washington wisdom.
The American politicians answer to UFO sightings;

Right now, some of the Potomac seers and soothsayers are
saying conservative are tired, or that we don't have a candidate
don't know what to do with ourselves this year. I even hear
some of those candidates in the other party talking about how
its going to be to win the Presidency this year for their liberal
agenda. In fact, I've got a quote too for them
Well, I've got a reminder for them. It's a quote from
Napoeleon. The morning of Waterloo. At breakfast with his
generals. He said, "I tell you Wellington is a bad general, the

called

- 4 -

English are bad soldiers; we will settle the matter by
lunchtime."

My fellow conservatives, I think that's exactly what this
next year is about. Settling the matter by lunch time. Letting
the liberals in Washington discover once again the lesson they
refuse to learn. That the only real friends of the conservative
movement aren't the denizens of power who have entrenched
themselves in the capital for 50 years; the only real friends of
the conservative movement are an entity who get heard from in a
big way every 4 years: who are going to be heard from this year.
I'm talking about the people.

who, if the case is put before them, will vote for limited government, family values and tough foreign policy every single time. I'm talking about the American people

THE WHITE HOUSE

WASHINGTON

February 9, 1988

MEMORANDUM FOR TONY DOLAN

FROM: FRANK J. DONATELLI

SUBJECT: CPAC SPEECH

I recommend that the President acknowledge Soviet defectors Alex
and Irina Ushakov at the CPAC dinner on Thursday, February 11.
This is the first Presidential event for this young, attractive
couple. They are a part of the summit success story and
personify the conservative principles of democratic idealism and
individual commitment. The following details are background
information on them:

* Since her release from the Soviet Union, the Ushakovs have
appeared on several network TV interview programs.

* Irina was released by the Soviet Union shortly after the
Summit, on Christmas Day, 1987.

* Prior to the Summit, Secretary Shultz personally met with
Irina in the Soviet Union.

* Since arriving in the U.S., doctors here have given her the
good news that her breast tumors are benign.

* Alex defected in 1984 after writing anti-Soviet literature.
He has continued his writing in the U.S.

For any additional information, Alex can be reached at his office
at the State Department (235-2450) or at their home (379-9015).
For NSC concurrance, Fritz Ermarth (5112) is familiar with their
case.

TONY

THE WHITE HOUSE

WASHINGTON

February 3, 1988

MEMORANDUM FOR TONY DOLAN
              DEPUTY ASSISTANT TO THE PRESIDENT
              AND DIRECTOR OF SPEECHWRITING

THROUGH: FRANK J. DONATELLI
              ASSISTANT TO THE PRESIDENT FOR POLITICAL
              AND INTERGOVERNMENTAL AFFAIRS

FROM: REBECCA S. MCMAHAN
              ASSOCIATE DIRECTOR, OFFICE OF POLITICAL AFFAIRS

SUBJECT: CONSERVATIVE POLITICAL ACTION CONFERENCE
              FEBRUARY 11, 1988

On Thursday, February 11 the President and First Lady will attend
the dinner of the 15th Annual Conservative Political Action
Conference (CPAC) at the Omni Shoreham. The President's remarks
should be twenty minutes in length and will be open to the press.
Although you are familiar with this event, below I have listed
background information and some suggested points for inclusion.
Please contact me at x7983 if you have any questions.

Background on Conservative Political Action Conference

*This is the 15th Annual Conservative Political Action
Conference. The President has attended this function every year
it has been held except 1976 and 1980, when he had campaign
scheduling conflicts.

*The conference is for three days -- February 11, 12 and 13. It
consists of issue seminars by renowned conservatives. Two
Republican Presidential candidates will address CPAC this year --
Jack Kemp and Pat Robertson.

*Approximately 1200 people are expected to attend CPAC this year.

*Those who will be present at the head table with the President
and First Lady include: David Keene, Chairman, American
Conservative Union (ACU); Thomas Winter, Vice Chairman, ACU;
James Linen, IV, Second Vice Chairman, ACU; Yakov Smirnoff,
Entertainer; Sergio Picchio, Chairman, Young Americans for
Freedom (YAF); Dr. Robert Grant, invocation; Dr. Fredrick
Chien, Representative, Taiwan Coordination Council for North
American Affairs; Arnaud De Borchgrave, Editor-in-Chief,
Washington Times; F. Clifton White, Director, John M. Ashbrook
Center for Public Affairs; and possibly William Rusher,
Publisher, National Review. The President should mention that he
sees "so many of my old friends here and in the audience."

CPAC/Page Two

*Prior to the dinner, the President will attend a private
reception with a photo opportunity for approximately 80 major
donors. He will then go into the dinner and his remarks will
follow the meal.

Suggested Issues to Address

*The President should thank this group for their many, many years
of loyal support. It is the people in this room who were with
him from the beginning of his political career. They have
supported him through thick and thin, and for that he is
grateful.

*This is the opportunity to make the conservative case for this
Administration. List the accomplishments: lower inflation,
a better economy, increased military strength and optimism about
the future. We have not accomplished everything, nor could we.
But we have come a very great distance.

*However, there is still more to be done. The President has no
intention of being a "lame duck". This final year of his
Presidency will be an important one, both electorally and
policy-wise. Among his goals and issues for this year will be
support for the Freedom Fighters, adoption of SDI and a push for
further spending restraints for the federal government.

*Depending on the outcome of the Contra vote, this issue should
be mentioned. Conservative leaders were extremely helpful in
mobilizing support for continued aid.

*This dinner could possibly be a good forum for the President to
point out the positive factors of the INF treaty. It would have
to be dealt with carefully, though, due to partial opposition
within the audience.

*The President will actively campaign this year for our Party's
nominee and our Senate and House candidates. We need to elect
conservatives to continue the programs we began.

*The President can comfortably support whoever our nominee is and
he would ask them to unite behind him when he is selected.

THE WHITE HOUSE

WASHINGTON   2/9/88

MEMORANDUM TO TONY DOLAN
FROM: REBECCA G. RANGE *RR*
COMMENTS ON CPAC SPEECH

We need to hit a couple of issues if
possible:
    Crime and Pornography Bills
    Pro-Life Bill
    More on SDI
    Grove City Bill
This draft deals with what has been done, but
not with what we still want to do and with
what the conservatives can help us.

I suggest the following on Grove City
(perhaps to be added on P. 10):

I would like to put to an end, for once and
for all, one of the liberals most sought
after goals--the so-called Civil Rights
Restoration Act of 1987. This one measure
breaks new ground in assuring the
government's intrusion into virtually every
aspect of American life: from the operation
of Mom and Pop businesses and the exercise of
fundamental religious rights to private
efforts to help the poor help themselves.
In the name of civil rights, the liberals
have paved the way for an unprecedented
regulation of American business and the
centralization of programs for the needy and
disadvantaged. I want the liberals to know
that the so-called Civil Rights Restoration
Act will be met at the White House door with
a veto--a sustainable veto.

THE WHITE HOUSE

WASHINGTON

from Gary Bauer's
office & for
CPAC
speech

Five themes for CPAC speech

1. Contra Aid: The Democrats, if they have their way,
will turn Central America into another Vietnam. They
are bleeding the freedom fighters slowly to death.
This policy of incremental surrender is precisely the
one that another Democratic administration consolidated
in Vietnam. Avoiding it is the true "lesson of Vietnam."
We will work with Congress to ensure that the freedom
fighters get the support they need for a transition to
democracy in Nicaragua.

2. Strategic Defense: If a single missile were launched
today from the Soviet Union, or another hostile power,
against a major American city, we would be totally
helpless. Millions of citizens would be wantonly
destroyed. This is bad enough, but to demand that the
situation stay this way--to resist avenues out of
this defenselessness--that is insanity. I pledge to
stick with strategic defense, insurance policy against
nuclear attack. When it is ready, it will be deployed.

3. Protectionism: I notice that, shy of taking on the
Soviet Union, some in the Democratic party want to
stand tough against Taiwan and South Korea. Not exactly
my definition of a profile in courage. What's bad
about protectionism is not just that it hurts consumers
and raises prices. Protectionism costs jobs. It puts
more people out of work than it employs. Not in
recent memory has an idea so universally rejected by
economists been taken up with such enthusiasm by a
major politician party. If I may borrow a phrase from
Vice President Bush, it's voodoo economics.

4. Abortion: We are entering a new phase of the abortion
debate. I predict that it is a historic moment. The
propagandists for abortion keep citing polls, but
emotionally, philosophically, morally they are on the
defensive. The message is coming home pretty clear to
the American people that the crushed body of a fetus
is not exactly a symbol of the triumph of civil
liberties. Rather, it suggests that something is deeply
wrong. We are taking steps to correct that. Here
mention Title X regulations, Human Life Bill.

5. Family: I've been amused by recent reports that
Democrats are rediscovering the family. After deriding
and abusing the family and calling for alternative
arrangements, they are now returning to profamily
rhetoric. That's good. But let's make sure that
their policies are in tune with their rhetoric. Early
indications are not good. Cite Grove City interventionism.

Index

U

V